Eugene Odum

Eugene Odum

Ecosystem Ecologist
& Environmentalist

BETTY JEAN CRAIGE

The University of Georgia Press   Athens and London

© 2001 by the University of Georgia Press

Athens, Georgia 30602

All rights reserved

Designed by Kathi Dailey Morgan

Set in 10 on 15 Electra by G & S Typesetters, Inc.

Printed and bound by McNaughton & Gunn

The paper in this book meets the guidelines for permanence
and durability of the Committee on Production Guidelines
for Book Longevity of the Council on Library Resources.

Printed in the United States of America

05 04 03 02 01 C 5 4 3 2 1

Library of Congress Cataloging-in-Publication Data

Craige, Betty Jean.

   Eugene Odum : ecosystem ecologist and environmentalist / Betty
Jean Craige.

     p. cm.

   Includes bibliographical references (p.) and index.

   ISBN 0-8203-2281-4 (alk. paper)

   1. Odum, Eugene Pleasants, 1913–   2. Ecologists — United States —
Biography.   3. Environmentalists — United States — Biography.
I. Title.

QH31.027 C73 2001

577′.092 — dc21

[B]   00-056826

British Library Cataloging-in-Publication Data available

Contents

Preface

Gene and Martha Odum became close friends of mine in the 1980s, when our common interests in art and holistic ways of thinking brought us together. They invited me, with my dogs, to their home on Fripp Island, where I spent many enjoyable and educational weekends over the years. During this period I learned that on their trips to the coast Martha was taping interviews she conducted in the car with Gene about their life together and his achievements in ecology.

Martha died of cancer in 1995, but before her death I spoke with her about my desire to write Gene's biography. Although I am not a scientist, I felt that my friendship with Gene would enable me to portray to interested readers in the present, and to ecological historians in the future, the personality of a man whom I considered a visionary environmentalist. Martha was enthusiastic about my idea, and she gave me copies of her audiotapes as well as a complete set of her Christmas letters to use in reconstructing Gene's life chronologically. Gene supplied me with everything I asked for, including articles and books he had published, articles and books other ecologists had published, unpublished materials, and correspondence with his parents and his siblings. And he spent many hours telling me about his science, his relationships with family members, his motivations, and his vision of the future. Much of what I have written in this book about Gene's character, habits, and attitudes I cannot document, for I have acquired my understanding of him through time spent with him.

I must express my deepest gratitude to the many friends who read critically parts or all of my manuscript: first, to geneticist John Avise, ecologist Frank Golley, botanists Ann Stoneburner and Robert Wyatt, and novelist Phil Williams for reading the whole book; and to Judy Meyer, Patty Gowaty, Jim and Karen Porter, and Alex Rosenberg for reading chapters in their early stages. I thank Robert McIntosh and Frank Egerton for their extraordinarily useful reader reports for the University of Georgia Press. For stimulating conversations that taught me much about ecosystem ecology I thank Wyatt Anderson, Janet Westpheling, and Philip Youngman. I also thank H. T. Odum and Mary Frances Schinhan, Gene's siblings, for their helpfulness regarding family history; Valerie and Bob Greenberg for their hospitality in Rensselaerville, where I visited the Edmund Niles Huyck Preserve; Richard L. Wyman, executive director of the Huyck Preserve, for providing information about Gene's employment there in 1939; and Ramón Margalef, whom I visited in Barcelona, and Edward O. Wilson, whom I interviewed in Cambridge, for explaining aspects of Gene's role in the development of ecology.

Although I began the project by interviewing Gene's friends and colleagues, I ended up by focusing more on Gene's published papers, which provide a clear record of his intellectual journey through ecosystem ecology into environmental activism. His obsessions — such as his advocacy of holism — are as evident in his essays as in his actions. Nonetheless, I am grateful to all the people who talked with me about Gene and gave me insight into his way of thinking. So, thank you, I. Lehr Brisbin, Jack Burke, Marion and Wilbur Duncan, Whit Gibbons, Gene Likens, Joe Pechmann, Nat Frazer, Larry Pomeroy, Shelton Reed, Homer Sharpe, Mike Smith, Deborah Stinner, and Carolyn Lee Thomas.

I thank Frank Charles Winstead for permission to include his excellent photograph of Eugene Odum.

For various other kinds of assistance in putting the book together I thank Lloyd Winstead, Julie Dingus, and Stacy Smith.

Finally, I thank Barbara Ras, senior editor of the University of Georgia Press, and Karen Orchard, director of the University of Georgia Press, for their invitation to submit the manuscript to the University of Georgia Press and for their excellent guidance.

Introduction

In July 1969, when astronauts Neil Armstrong and Buzz Aldrin landed on the moon and sent back photographs of the earth rising above the moon's surface, Americans were given a new and unique view of the planet that is our home. We could see oceans, deserts, and clouds in those photographs, but no political boundaries and no people. From the perspective of the moon, human beings were indistinguishable components of the indivisible biosphere.

Even the environmental degradation that Rachel Carson had made a subject of media attention seven years earlier with her book *Silent Spring* did not appear in those awesomely beautiful

pictures. But the sight of the blue planet spinning in space alerted its inhabitants to its vulnerability and reminded us of our dependence on its stability.
We recognized that humans were now capable of altering the biosphere to
such an extent—by pollution of air and water, by nuclear war, by habitat
disruption, and by soil damage—as to render it inhospitable to our existence.
To learn more about the changes under way in our global ecosystem, and to
forestall some of them, Americans turned to ecology.

The media, publicizing our "ravaged environment" in illustrated stories
about the nation's smoggy, noisy cities and contaminated rivers and lakes,
announced a dramatic shift in American social and scientific priorities. *Time*
magazine predicted that pollution would "soon replace the Viet Nam war as
the nation's major issue of protest" and called 1969 "the year of ecology." In
an article introducing the leading ecologists of the day, whom the magazine
designated "the new Jeremiahs," *Time* associated ecology with environmentalism because of ecology's assumption "that all nature is interconnected
and that any intervention has far-reaching effects." *Newsweek*, in early 1970,
heralded the dawn of "the Age of Ecology," in which ecologists would teach
society about the "web of life."[1] On 22 April 1970, Americans celebrated the
first Earth Day.

The following year, sales peaked on Eugene Pleasants Odum's *Fundamentals of Ecology*.[2] Odum, who had been identified by both *Time* and *Newsweek*
as one of the country's leading ecologists, had brought the word *ecosystem*
into common parlance by making it the organizing concept in his textbook.
The ecosystem, Odum had written in its first edition, published in 1953, is a
system composed of biotic communities and their abiotic environment interacting with each other. A lake can be regarded as an ecosystem; so can a
marshland; and so can the earth. A "mature" ecosystem, characterized by
high species diversity and relationships of interdependence among its component organisms, approaches stability, or homeostasis, and represents nature's "balance." To understand nature in terms of ecosystems is therefore to
see its diverse "parts" as interdependent. *Fundamentals of Ecology*, which
begins "top-down," with a discussion of the whole ecosystem rather than its
parts, made the ecosystem concept central to ecology and in so doing profoundly influenced the environmentalist movement.

The extraordinary sales of *Fundamentals* signaled the extent of the environmental revolution that took place in the 1970s, when colleges and universities around the world instituted ecology courses and degree programs and the public became familiar with arguments advocating the need to preserve ecosystems. The textbook was ultimately translated into twelve languages, and Gene Odum was hailed as "the father of modern ecology."

The Ecosystem Model

The ecosystem was a concept invented in 1935 whose time in the public spotlight had come in the 1970s. It was scientifically appealing to ecologists, who sought ways to understand the function of organisms in relation to each other and to the land. It was politically appealing to environmental activists, who sought justification for their arguments against pollution, because it showed that human society and nonhuman nature make up a single interactive system in which pollution of any part potentially affects the whole. It was philosophically appealing to intellectuals, who saw a relationship between the Vietnam War, racism, capitalism, and environmental destruction, because it was a theory of connectivity. And it was ethically appealing to many anti-authoritarian thinkers who, after rejecting religion in favor of science, liked the idea that cooperation among organisms is as important to their survival as competition.

Gene Odum encouraged students to see the social implications of ecosystem science. According to an ecology student who heard Odum speak at Yale in 1975 on cooperation, mutualism, and interdependence in nature, he imparted the message that if humans acknowledge their interdependence with the other components of an ecosystem, then they must also acknowledge the necessity to preserve the health of that system.[3] Odum's focus on the whole brought interconnectivity—and hence social responsibility—to the fore, said Karen Porter, who later became a colleague of Odum's in the Institute of Ecology at the University of Georgia. "Gene was a proselytizer of holism, and his message of interconnectivity inspired a generation of ecologists."

The holistic vision of nature represented by the ecosystem concept constituted a radical departure from mainstream Western thought. For more than two thousand years, cultural expression of all kinds had embodied an atomistic and dualistic model of reality. According to that model, spirit—whether in the form of God, the soul, the self, or the mind—is separable from a material world, which is composed of discrete entities that interact mechanically. The tendency to understand phenomena in terms of discrete entities can be traced back to the principle, propounded first by Leucippus and Democritus in the fifth century B.C., that nature is composed of particles, or atoms. It remains evident in the individualism that has shaped Western economics, politics, philosophy, and religion. The tendency to dichotomize everything—into oppositions of spirit and matter, soul and body, self and world, and culture and nature—can be traced back to the metaphysics of Plato, who differentiated the static realm of Ideas from the dynamic one of their appearance in nature.

Western science grew out of this conceptual predisposition. The perceived separability of the mind from the material world made objectivity seem a theoretical possibility, and the presumed divisibility of that world into parts made investigation of the parts seem an appropriate approach to knowledge. In 1637, philosopher René Descartes enunciated in *Discourse on Method* a means of obtaining knowledge that is now called "reductionism": dividing the object of investigation into parts and proceeding from the simplest to the most complex. The Cartesian method of studying the parts before the whole, which presupposed the whole being equal to the sum of its parts, made specialization in the parts the means by which society advanced in its understanding of nature. In the Cartesian paradigm, the compilation of information acquired by specialists in nature's parts resulted in knowledge of the whole. The method produced the "bottom-up" approach to the study of nature that ordered biology and ecology textbooks prior to *Fundamentals of Ecology*.

The culture/nature dualism inclined the public to think of "nature" as simply a site for the development of "culture"; it also made "nature" appear to be a repository of "natural resources" available for human use, and land to be potential property. The dualism of "civilized" and "primitive," a correlative of the culture/nature dualism, sanctioned Westerners' conquest of the earth's "uncivilized" inhabitants and expansion over the earth's "uncivilized" regions, which they undertook sometimes in the name of Christianity and sometimes in the pursuit of the wealth that "civilization" required. The externalization of nature in the culture/nature dualism thus turned nonhuman nature into a threat to culture, making the "subduing" of nonhuman nature appear both appropriate and necessary. That philosophy rendered theoretically unnoticeable the interdependence of humans and other organisms of the earth.

This was the model that ecology had challenged from its Darwinian beginnings. In 1859 Charles Darwin showed in *On the Origin of Species* that species interact with one another and evolve by natural selection. And in his concluding portrayal of nature as a "tangled bank" of plants, birds, insects, and worms, he marveled that "these elaborately constructed forms, so different from each other, and dependent upon each other in so complex a manner, have all been produced by laws acting around us."[4] Ten years later, German biologist Ernst Heinrich Haeckel, who had coined the word *Oecologie* in 1866, described the new discipline as the study of that tangled bank:

> By ecology we mean the body of knowledge concerning the economy of nature — the investigation of the total relations of the animal both to its inorganic and its organic environment; including above all, its friendly and inimical relations with those animals and plants with which it comes directly and indirectly into contact — in a word, ecology is the study of all those complex interrelations referred to by Darwin as the conditions of the struggle for existence. This science of ecology, often inaccurately referred to as "biology" in a narrow sense, has thus far formed the principal component of what is commonly referred to as "Natural History."[5]

Although Darwin and Haeckel opened the way for scientists to consider organic and inorganic nature as interrelated, ecology remained focused on organic nature until 1935, when British ecologist Sir Arthur Tansley named and defined *ecosystem* in an article published in *Ecology* titled "The Use and Abuse of Vegetational Concepts and Terms." Tansley advanced the argument that the basic units of nature are systems, or "ecosystems," "in which plants and animals are components, though not the only components."[6] The ecosystem, that is, includes the abiotic environment of the organisms as well.

The ecosystem concept enabled the development of a new kind of science that focused on nature as a set of systems, each of which could be studied as a "whole." Gene Odum and his younger brother, Howard Thomas Odum, who contributed to *Fundamentals of Ecology*,[7] created nonreductionist methods to study the systems by treating them as energy circuits and material flows. Unlike Tansley, who had expressed reservations about the philosophy of "holism" as expounded in 1926 by Jan Christiaan Smuts, the Odums proceeded on the assumption that the whole has properties of its own that are undetectable through examination of the constituent parts alone.[8]

Gene Odum is identified with one statement more than any other: "The ecosystem is greater than the sum of its parts." Those words are inscribed on the bronze bust of him that adorns the entrance to the Ecology Building at the University of Georgia.

Resistance to the Ecosystem Concept

In 1995, Alston Chase published a scathing denunciation of ecosystem environmentalism motivated by ecosystem science in a book titled *In a Dark Wood: The Fight over Forests and the Rising Tyranny of Ecology*. In it he called the ecosystem concept, which he said the Odum brothers had helped to install as the cornerstone of modern ecology, "a sledgehammer of an idea with which to change the world." And he sounded the alarm against the "growing cadre of political philosophers [who are] transforming the doctrine into political theory."[9]

In a Dark Wood identifies the ecosystem concept as the foundation for the late twentieth-century environmentalist agenda. According to Chase, the ecosystem concept gave rise to the political ideology of "biocentrism," which he characterized as a "misanthropic ethic of nature": "If everything is dependent on everything else, . . . then all living things are of equal worth, and the health of the whole — the ecosystem — takes precedence over the needs and interests of individuals."[10] The two assumptions that Chase said radical environmentalists derive from the theory of interconnectivity — that "all living things are of equal worth" and that "the health of the whole . . . takes precedence over the needs and interests of individuals" — he associated with the

Endangered Species Act, the resistance to the logging of old-growth forests, and ecotage.[11] He cited the creed of the radical environmentalist group Earth First!—that humans have no divine right to subdue the earth or to take dominion over other species—as an example of the pernicious ramifications of ecosystem ecology.[12]

Every science has its enemies. Copernican physics aroused the ire of the Catholic Church for several centuries, until the accumulation of information about the universe antiquated any claim that the universe was geocentric. Darwinian biology, by discrediting the doctrine that humankind was specially created by God, antagonized—and continues to antagonize—believers in the biblical account of the origin of species. In the 1980s and 1990s defenders of the faith in divine creation organized a nationwide political campaign to introduce "creation science" into the public schools to combat the teaching of evolution in classes of biology. Ecology, with its ecocentric view of nature, might be expected to have the creationist movement as its primary enemy as well, but ecology has actually found its strongest opposition elsewhere, in the political sphere. Because in an ecosystem the constituent parts are interdependent and subordinate to the whole, ecosystem ecology offers a philosophical challenge to individualism and a political challenge to capitalism and free enterprise. The political opponents of the holistic model implicit in the ecosystem concept are thus ideological individualists such as Chase who fear that the acknowledgment of interconnectedness and the concern with the natural environment will bring about legal constraints on individuals'—and corporations'—freedom of action. In the dualist model in which nature and culture are opposites and therefore competitors for resources, to attend to the needs of nature is to neglect the needs of culture.

Ecosystem ecology breaks down the perceived barrier between science and politics. The inclusion of *Homo sapiens* in the ecosystem forces ecologists to consider human influences on the natural environment. And the information acquired by ecologists about the impact of human civilization on the earth and the potential for destruction of human life-support systems stimulates political disagreement over solutions to environmental problems. The disagreement inevitably reflects a tension between attention to the individual and attention to the whole, between promotion of the individual good and promotion of the public good.[13] Since ecosystem ecologists concern themselves with the whole, they often meet resistance to their ideas from advocates for individual rights.

Capitalism grew out of both individualism and the culture/nature dualism. The Western model of culture supports the ownership of natural resources by individuals or corporations and justifies the right of cities, states, and nations to seek wealth, expansion, and technological improvement. Such activities are deemed an exercise of freedom. Moreover, in the atomistic model of nature, the extraction of resources does not appear to be exploitation, because theoretically it is not disruptive of a whole. On the other hand, the depiction of nature as an ecosystem vulnerable to disruption presents such exploitation as dangerous to the well-being of humans, who are part of the system, and thus jeopardizes public support for capitalists engaged in such behavior. Actions once applauded for the increased wealth they produced are now condemned for the dangers they pose to the whole. The once unquestioned notion of individual freedom of land use is now under fire by environmentalists, whose efforts to preserve ecosystems are politically threatening to capitalists. The very concept of the ecosystem undermines traditional capitalist values.

The ecosystem concept really did "change the world." It provided a perspective that complemented reductionism in biology and led to the development of methods to analyze large-scale systems. It allowed ecologists to assess more concretely than before the impact of human civilization on nonhuman nature. It became an instrument to curb the actions of capitalists. It begat a discipline capable of investigating large-scale socioenvironmental problems. And it became a vision of interconnectedness that today motivates global environmentalism and influences the politics of nations.

Chase's "growing cadre of environmental philosophers" are exploring the political implications of the ecosystem concept as well as the implications of other theories of nature. In an age when globalization is turning the world into an interdependent global system of nations and is dramatically increasing nations' cultural and racial heterogeneity, the ecosystem concept provides a way to interpret shifting geopolitical relationships. The concept's association of interdependence with cooperation makes the establishment of more harmonious political relationships among culturally and racially unlike peoples appear historically inevitable. To those for whom international and intercultural cooperation signifies the advent of world governance and an end to national autonomies, and to those afraid that the concern for the whole means restriction of the individual's freedom of action, the ecosystem concept is indeed dangerous.

Eugene Odum, Environmentalist

In April 1969 Eugene Odum published in *Science* a paper that provoked heated debate over one of ecology's most basic questions: how biotic communities change over time. Since the beginning of the twentieth century, ecologists had made "succession" studies central to their discipline, believing that determining how species replace each other in areas undisturbed by technology would enable them to understand the way living nature works.[14] In that paper, titled "The Strategy of Ecosystem Development," Odum replaced the word *succession* with the word *development* and argued that the interaction of organisms with one another and with their physical environment brings about the orderly evolution of ecosystems over time toward a state of equilibrium. Although he was not the first to conceive of succession as orderly development, Odum was the first to claim that all ecosystems— terrestrial and marine—have the same development "strategy." He employed a formula for determining when an ecosystem is in its growth stages, producing more than it needs to maintain itself, and when it is in equilibrium, with production balancing maintenance costs. He was later to apply that formula—the ratio of energy production to energy expended on maintenance—to cities and other human institutions. Odum's scientific hypothesis was bold, and the plan for environmentalist action that he extrapolated from the science was equally bold. Repeating the observation he had made in *Fundamentals of Ecology* that "the landscape is not just a supply depot but is also the *oikos*—the home—in which we must live,"[15] he proposed the creation of landscape zones, or compartments, to restrict the spread of human activity and ensure the preservation of the green space necessary for the health of the planetary ecosystem. Humankind would thereby live in harmony with the processes of nature. "An understanding of ecological succession," Odum noted in a subtitle, "provides a basis for resolving man's conflict with nature."

Although it attracted broader notice than most of his other scientific papers achieved, "The Strategy of Ecosystem Development" was typical of Odum's essays. He often converted what he learned about the function of nature into lessons for society and futuristic proposals for societal change. Odum assumed that the public could understand ecological principles if ecologists explained them well. And he believed, with perhaps unwarranted optimism, that knowledge of those principles would incline the public to behave in ways more protective of our "home." His colleague Judy Meyer observed that the use of ecology to inspire alternative patterns of human activity is part of Odum's legacy to the discipline.[16]

Throughout his life Odum extended ecosystem ecology to society, turning ecological principles into an environmental ethic. He never acknowledged disciplinary boundaries, such as the distinction many scientists see between basic science and applied science, or between ecology and environmentalism, because he inherited from his father and his grandfather an imperative to use his learning to make a better world. In his ideal intellectual order, scientists, social scientists, and humanists would work together to understand and solve problems, just as in his ideal community academic intellectuals, economists, politicians, journalists, and citizens with different interests would all communicate with each other to make a more harmonious society. Odum viewed the many parts of a system as interdependent, convinced that if a society is to function effectively, the many individuals who compose it must cooperate.

Because he considered his students and his readers to be not just scientists-in-the-making but "decision makers," Odum inserted into many of his articles and all of his textbooks suggestions for improving the health of the natural environment.[17] *Fundamentals of Ecology* ends with a chapter titled "Applications: Human Society," which warns against overpopulation and calls for birth control around the world.[18] The epilogue to *Basic Ecology* proposes a "holoeconomics . . . that will include cultural and environmental values along with monetary ones."[19] *Ecology and Our Endangered Life-Support Systems* includes commentaries on the importance of recycling; the dangers of overpopulation; the interdependence of the city and the countryside; the preferability of natural, genetically engineered pesticides to chemical pesticides; the environmental utility of tax and zoning policies; and the habits of humans. His short *Ecological Vignettes: Ecological Approaches to Dealing with Human Predicaments*, which he wrote in his eighties for the general public, employs a set of aphorisms to show "what we learn from ecology about" growth, energy, organization, change, behavior, and diversity. *Ecological Vignettes* concludes:

> We must begin to devote more of our human wealth, energy, and engineering skills to servicing and repairing our "big house," the biosphere, which provides not only a place to live and enjoy but also all of our life-support needs. In a very real sense, humanity is a parasite on the biosphere, since as a non-green consumer organism we depend among other things on green plants for food and oxygen and on microorganisms to recycle nutrients. As we learn from studying parasite-host relations in nature, a prudent parasite that has only one host does not kill off that host, since that will result in its extinction. The prudent parasite moderates its demands on the host, and in many cases actually does things to help its host prosper. . . . In ecological language this is *co-evolution for co-existence.*[20]

In the course of his career Odum won almost all the major honors and awards for achievement in ecology: the presidency of the Ecological Society of America; election to the National Academy of Sciences; election to the American Academy of Arts and Sciences; the Eminent Ecologist Award of the Ecological Society of America; the Prix de l'Institut de la Vie, which he shared with his brother, H. T.; the John and Alice Tyler Award; and the Crafoord Prize for Ecology from the Royal Swedish Academy of Science, which he shared with H. T. He also won numerous awards for his environmental activism, among them the Georgia Wildlife Federation's Conservationist-of-the-Year Award, the Gold Seal Award of the National Council of the State Garden Clubs, the U.S. Department of the Interior's Conservation Service Award, the Georgia Ornithological Society's Earle R. Greene Memorial

Award, the Chevron Conservation Award, the Silver Trout Award from "Trout Unlimited of Georgia," the Theodore Roosevelt Distinguished Service Award, and the Georgia Conservancy's Distinguished Conservationist Award. At the University of Georgia, he was instrumental in the founding of the Savannah River Ecology Laboratory, the Institute of Ecology, and the Marine Institute on Sapelo Island; he received the University of Georgia Alumni Society's Faculty Service Award and was named Alumni Foundation Distinguished Professor of Zoology and Fuller E. Callaway Professor of Ecology. He received honorary doctorates from Hofstra University (1980); Ferum College (1986); the University of North Carolina, Asheville (1990); la Universidad del Valle, Guatemala (1996); Ohio State University (1999); and la Universidad de San Francisco, Quito, Ecuador (1999). *Eugene Odum: Ecosystem Ecologist and Environmentalist* is a portrait of the man who built out of the ecosystem concept a science for the investigation of large systems, explained the ecosystem concept to millions of students, employed it as a model of societal behavior, and through his long life used it as the foundation for his campaign to promote environmental health. It is also an account of the relationship of ecosystem ecology to environmentalism. Its theme is Eugene Odum's effort to influence human behavior, through science, toward "more cooperation and less confrontation, both within the human population and between the human population and nature."[21]

1 *Chapel Hill*

On 8 December 1995, at the age of eighty-two, Eugene Odum drove the seventy-five miles from his home in Athens to the Ritz Carlton Hotel in northeast Atlanta to attend a luncheon sponsored by the *Atlanta Journal/Constitution*. Jim Auchmutey, managing editor of what was to be the newspaper's *Olympic Atlanta* magazine, had invited Odum to join a group of journalists and prominent southerners to help the newspaper select ninety-six individuals who would be "defining the South in years to come." [1] On the list of guests Odum was described as the author of *Fundamentals of Ecology*, "a seminal textbook in the field."

Auchmutey asked the gathering to try to predict which individuals presently active in such fields as environmental preservation, agriculture, education, government, business, the arts, science, medicine, law, and human rights would have a powerful influence on the region in the future. Because the environment was first on the agenda, Odum was the first to speak. Odum opened the discussion by genially challenging the premise of the meeting. "Is it worthwhile these days to single out individuals as instruments of change?" he asked. "Is it worthwhile to talk about the South as a distinct region anymore?" [2]

Despite his reservations regarding the purpose of the meeting, Odum had completed his assignment. He presented a typed list of thirteen people that included nine ecologists who had shaped public opinion in ways beneficial to the natural environment.[3] Among them was Odum's younger brother, Howard Thomas Odum, a professor of environmental engineering at the University of Florida in Gainesville and the proponent of a controversial new energy economics. Odum then argued that in a large and complex society, individuals have much less influence and power than organizations or groups of interacting individuals. Rather than look for heroes to solve our problems, as most people tend to do, he said, the *Atlanta Journal/Constitution* should develop a list of *groups* that would define the South in the future. His candidates were the Nature Conservancy, the Wildlife Federation, state pollution prevention teams, "green" corporations, and social welfare organizations.

Underpinning all of Gene Odum's ideas about the world is a holism he inherited from his sociologist father, Howard Washington Odum. In his youth Gene had turned toward science in order to escape his well-known father's influence. But Gene brought to his study of nature a habit of thought and a manner of argument that were almost indistinguishable from his father's. The ecosystem concept Gene employed in his research and taught to the thousands of students who bought his textbook served him as a model for social interaction in which interdependence necessitates cooperation and thereby contributes to stability. Not until long after he had used the holistic principle to analyze social systems did he realize that it was the same principle that had motivated his father's work. The priority Gene gave to groups over individuals as agents of social change reflected his father's tendency to attribute human behavior to social structures; and the priority he gave to the ecosystem over the ecosystem's individual components reflected his father's advice to look at "the big picture."

Howard Washington Odum

Howard Washington Odum saw society as a system of interdependent parts in which the improvement of one part, such as the rural areas of the South, required attention to the problems of the other parts. "Progress in society," he said, "is clearly the end in view, the attainment of which inevitably boosts progress in all divisions thereof."[4] Howard Odum wrote two dissertations on African American life in the South and obtained Ph.D.s in both psychology and sociology. He passed on to his sons a compulsion for work, which Gene's wife, Martha, called "the Odum drive." It involved a faith in social progress, a commitment to social reform, a propensity to see phenomena as interrelated, and a passion for explaining things.[5]

Howard Odum was born in 1884 in Bethlehem, Georgia, not far from Athens. His great-grandfather Elisha Odum, who came to Bethlehem from South Carolina; his grandfather John Wesley Odum, who fought in the Civil War; and his father, William Pleasants Odum, were all small farmers with little formal education. Elisha and John could neither read nor write, and William had to drop out of school during the fourth grade to help his father on the farm after the war. William valued education highly, however, and in 1897 he and his wife, Mary Ann Thomas Odum, whose slaveholding family had lost all their wealth and power in the fall of the Confederacy, moved their family from Bethlehem to Covington, Georgia, so that their five children could attend Emory College in nearby Oxford. According to Gene Odum, it was Mary Ann who determined that education would give her offspring the social standing her family had lost. Howard's struggle at Emory to compete successfully against students with better academic preparation influenced his later campaign to improve schools in the rural South.

Howard Odum graduated from Emory College in 1904 with an A.B. in classics, taught briefly in Toccopola, Mississippi, and then earned an M.A. in classics in 1906 from the University of Mississippi. At "Ole Miss" Odum became acquainted with a professor of psychology and education named Thomas Pearce Bailey, from whom he acquired an enthusiasm for the "scientific" study of race and a conviction that social science was a tool for social service. He had already embraced his family's Methodist belief in the importance of service to others.[6] Under the influence of Bailey, who was a scholar of race relations, Odum began to amass material on African American culture, recognizing that social progress in the South would not occur without greater understanding of African Americans. He took his collection of African American folk songs with him to Clark University in Massachusetts, where Bailey had arranged a graduate fellowship with the distinguished psychologist G. Stanley Hall, Bailey's mentor and dissertation director. There Odum met Anna Louise Kranz, an M.A. student of Hall's from Hendersonville, Tennessee, whom he subsequently married.[7]

At Clark University Odum wrote a dissertation on "Negro Folk-Song and Character" for his Ph.D. in psychology in 1909. He then went to Columbia University, where he wrote another dissertation based on his previous research in Mississippi and obtained his Ph.D. in sociology in 1910. In the second dissertation, which Columbia published under the title *Social and Mental Traits of the Negro: Research into the Conditions of the Negro Race in Southern Towns*, Odum expressed the assumption that "the races have different abilities and potentialities. Those who would assist the Negro should remember this and not exact too much of him, either in demanding his results or offering him the completed ideals of the whites." Odum changed his views on becoming acquainted with the results of experiments conducted during World War I that contradicted his assertions, and in 1936 he refused to allow *Social and Mental Traits* to be reprinted.[8]

In 1912 Howard accepted an offer from the University of Georgia to teach "Educational Sociology and Rural Education" in the College of Education. Considering sociology a practical discipline, Howard introduced courses that dealt with race, mob psychology, labor, women's rights, and prison reform; urged the university to take responsibility for improving rural education in Georgia; served on the Athens Board of Education; and became director of the College of Education's summer school for teacher training.[9]

Convinced that "the groundwork of an enduring democracy must be based upon an educated and enlightened citizenship and leadership,"[10] Howard Odum did his best to bring about the changes he viewed as necessary for the South. Early in 1919 he accepted an offer to become the first dean of the School of Liberal Arts at Emory University—to supervise its establishment in Atlanta and, he thought, convert it to a major university. He and his wife moved their family, which by then included Gene and his sister, Mary Frances, to Atlanta. He stayed there only a year, however, because his immediate goals—such as increasing the size of the faculty; raising faculty salaries; expanding undergraduate enrollment by one-third; opening the university to women; establishing a graduate school; setting up a school of education, a summer school, an extension service, a "School of Commerce or applied economic and social science, a publicity and promotion agency, and a scholarly 'Journal of Science, Religion and Education'"; and enlarging the physical plant—conflicted with the goals of the conservative chancellor, Bishop Warren Akin Candler, and exceeded the capacity of the school's budget.[11] Moreover, his interest in sociology frightened Bishop Candler, who associated the study of society with communism. From the standpoint of Candler and many other anticommunists, a focus on the whole meant neglect of the individual and therefore constituted a threat to a society founded on individual rights. So in 1920, having received an offer of a professorship in sociology at the University of North Carolina, Howard Odum moved with his family to Chapel Hill.[12]

According to historian Daniel J. Singal, Odum wasted no time settling into his new position. Within a short while he had founded a School of Public Welfare, invited Herbert Hoover to speak at its dedication ceremony, recruited expert faculty for it from all over the country, started raising funds for a social science research institute, planned a series of conferences, and "turn[ed] out an army of eager welfare agents on the unsuspecting backwoods precincts of North Carolina."[13] Moreover, he added to the curriculum a set of courses that disturbed his colleagues for their implicit premise that southern society was defective. The university began offering courses in "Immigration, Community Organization, Poverty and Relief, Educational Sociology, Negro Problems, Problems of the Small Town and Mill Village, Child Welfare, Family Casework, and Field Training."[14] In 1922 Odum launched the bimonthly *Journal of Social Forces*, which he declared would be a medium for self-criticism in the South.[15] And in 1924 he created his Institute for Research in Social Science and with his associates initiated investigative studies of farm tenancy, the living conditions of blacks, and labor relations in the textile industry.[16]

It was in *Social Forces*, whose stated purpose was to make "democracy effective in the unequal places," that Howard laid out his notion of democracy. If all the constituents are not healthy participants in the system, he said, the system is itself unhealthy; and equality of opportunity is not enough to ensure that all the constituents of the society function well.[17] He believed that democracy must be understood not only as a guarantee of political opportunity and equality but also as a mandate for justice and social progress. "It seems necessary," he wrote, "to define a comprehensive democracy and to work out a social organization through which such an adequate democracy may be made effective in the unequal places and to the unequal folk, at the same time that it tends to reduce constantly the ratio of inequality."[18]

In his widely read *Southern Regions of the United States* Odum developed the concept of "regionalism," the liberal alternative to agrarianism and "sectionalism," and assembled a mass of information regarding the causes of the South's problems. While arguing that the South was distinct, with its own peculiar strengths and weaknesses, he opposed the chauvinism of the sectionalists and insisted that it was nevertheless part of a whole, the United States.[19]

His obsession with social justice for all led Howard Odum to a lifelong struggle with the question of how black people related to the dominant white culture. Early on he became convinced that amelioration of the living conditions of blacks was a prerequisite to better race relations and to economic progress for all the inhabitants of the South. He came to realize that the South had to abandon segregation altogether. In 1949 he urged southerners "to accelerate the prevailing Southern processes of improving race relations and of increasing and equalizing educational facilities for all people" and "to provide professional and higher graduate instruction for qualified individuals of both races in the same institutions." He proposed the conversion "from segregation to non-segregation in many practicable areas such as transportation and other public services." Addressing standard defenses of southern traditions, he offered a set of reasons for the South to abandon segregation and seek "interracial cooperation."[20] In 1954, the year of his death at the age of seventy, he criticized the South for its failure to eliminate racial discrimination: "There is . . . one major facet of the situation which neither the nation nor the South has been able, or willing, to face in complete frankness, or to approach with adequate facts and statesmanlike strategy. This is the dilemma of discrimination and segregation and the successful integration of the Negro into the total cultural fabric."[21]

Howard Odum's crusade for racial equality provoked controversy on all sides. The Agrarians inveighed against his "progressive liberalism"; his scientific approach to social issues; his efforts to modernize the South socially, economically, and industrially; and his advocacy of federal programs.[22] Religious fundamentalists in North Carolina attacked *Social Forces* as evidence of atheism at Chapel Hill.[23] Textile manufacturers despised Howard for the investigative reports he published on labor relations in North Carolina. Political conservatives condemned him as a socialist.[24] The University of North Carolina's faculty tried to block his attempt to give a woman faculty status in the School of Public Welfare, but he prevailed in making Dr. Katharine Jocher the university's first woman professor.[25]

None of the criticism affected Howard's productivity. During his lifetime he wrote more than two hundred articles as well as twenty-three books—including three novels—all about the South. He became a public intellectual, a man often called on to take professional leadership positions. He served as the assistant director of research for President Herbert Hoover's Research Committee on Social Trends, the president of the American Sociological Society, the chair of the North Carolina Emergency Relief Administration, the chair of the North Carolina Commission on Interracial Cooperation, the president of the Commission on Interracial Cooperation, and the president of the Southern Regional Council, and he was a member of the executive committee of the American Association for the Advancement of Science.[26] He was appointed to a Kenan Professorship at the University of North Carolina and received honorary doctorates from Emory, Harvard, Clark, and the College of the Ozarks. In 1945 the Federal Council of the Churches of Christ in America bestowed on him the Edward L. Bernays Award for "outstanding achievement in Negro-white relations in the United States."[27] In 1953 he won the Oliver Max Gardner Award, an honor given "to that member of the faculty of the Consolidated University of North Carolina, who, during the current scholastic year, has made the greatest contribution to the welfare of the human race." When he died on 8 November 1954, the *Chapel Hill News Leader* said that "no man more than he was responsible for the fact that in the Thirties and Forties the University of Chapel Hill was called and deserved to be called 'the capital of the Southern mind.'"[28]

Howard Odum tried to teach his children that one could accomplish almost anything by working hard and not getting angry. "In the time other people take to get mad at each other or to worry about things, I can write an article," his son Gene often quoted him as saying. The elder Odum would spend nights on end in his easy chair, writing and taking catnaps in his rumpled clothes. Yet he enjoyed the company of his family and his colleagues and claimed that although he had intellectual and political adversaries, he had no personal enemies. Paradoxically, while advocating social reforms that antagonized some people because his work threatened their values and lifestyles, Howard managed to avoid unpleasant confrontations. When arguing with people certain of the truth of their own views, Howard would respond, "That may be true, but let me tell you what else is true." A lover of football, he would advise: "First try going down the middle. If that fails, try an end run. If that fails, pass."

Gene Odum remembered his father as a man of paradoxes. Howard's distaste for personal conflict contrasted with his enthusiasm for debate. And his "common man" posture did not accord with the mansion he built for his family in Chapel Hill, where he had rooms to accommodate not only his three children but also two UNC graduate students and whatever scholars, foundation representatives, or government officials came to visit. Nor did his folksy speech, dress, and manners accord with his stature as a southern intellectual, renowned social scientist, chaired professor, writer, editor, novelist, and breeder of prizewinning Jersey cattle. President of the North Carolina Jersey Cattlemen's Association and winner of the Master Breeders Award of the American Jersey Cattle Club, Howard liked to say, "My bulls are more valuable than my books." [29] He named his cows after his beloved wife and his alma mater — "Anna Louise," "Louise Oxford," "Louise Oxford II," and so on. Some of his North Carolina cattlemen friends never knew of his employment at the university. [30] Howard spent little time on leisure activities, but he never failed to offer his children encouragement, guidance, and love — from their infancy through their adulthood. He urged Gene to write *Fundamentals of Ecology* when Gene was only thirty years old and informed at least one publisher that Gene was working on it. He bought numerous copies of the book for Christmas presents, published a large ad for it in *Social Forces*, and again and again expressed pride in Gene's achievements. [31] When he learned in 1947 that Gene and Martha's second child, Tommy, would be severely retarded and disabled, he wrote them a long letter to share their grief. In it he recalled his own suffering over the childhood deaths of his siblings:

> And I remember well when I learned to whistle, I would always whistle a little louder because I must whistle for the two little fellows that fell by the wayside; and when I grew up, somehow I felt my strength was the strength of three. . . . In crises that are personal and that are beyond our changing, I have always felt that there was a certain strength that can come only from surrender, full and frank, from which then arises virtue, symbolic of both goodness and courage, as well as the capacity for spiritual renewal which is one of Nature's ways of insuring both blessedness and happiness. [32]

Howard taught his sons how to think in terms of the larger system, how to motivate groups of individuals to address problems, how to obtain federal and private grants for university research and service, and how to persist regardless of opposition. He showed them the power of writing. He steeped them in "liberal progressivism" and made them, like himself, crusaders for a better world. And he passed on to them stoic courage in the face of personal hardship.

Anna Louise Kranz Odum

Whereas Gene Odum's father was self-conscious about his rural roots and hungry for education to improve himself, Gene's mother, Anna Louise Kranz Odum, was sophisticated, intelligent, and self-confident. Whereas Howard was obsessed with changing the living conditions of blacks in the South, involved both professionally and personally with the rural poor, attracted to farm life, sloppy in his dress, and generally tolerant of disorder, Anna Louise was fastidious, well groomed, knowledgeable about art and music, attentive to family finances, and concerned with social graces.[33] She was an accomplished pianist. She was also petite and delicate, and she suffered from asthma throughout much of her forty-four years of marriage. According to Gene Odum, her husband "put her on a pedestal," idealizing her obvious virtues and excluding her from his work. Although there was always mutual support, admiration, and love between the two, she was not invited to share Howard's professional preoccupations, nor could she communicate fully to him her own emotional needs.[34]

Anna Louise Kranz was born in 1889 in Hendersonville, Tennessee, where she and her sister Caroline Matilda—Aunt Carrie to Gene, who was devoted to her—grew up in a country house on a farm managed by their father, Eugene Francis Kranz, and tended by black workers. Because her parents considered education to be as important for women as for men, Anna Louise obtained a broad understanding of the liberal arts, first from John Branch's private high school in Hendersonville and the Nashville Conservatory of Music, where she studied piano, and then from Peabody College in Nashville, where she graduated with honors at the age of nineteen. Anna Louise and Carrie both went north for graduate work, Anna Louise to Clark University in Massachusetts and Carrie to Bryn Mawr in Pennsylvania.

Anna Louise met Howard Odum in 1909 when she was completing a master's degree in psychology with G. Stanley Hall, and married him a year later while he was finishing his second Ph.D. at Columbia. A family story has it that when she defended her thesis, Clark University's president, impressed by her brilliance, exclaimed, "Why don't other people know things like you do?"[35] Although she held only one teaching position in her life—at

Morris Harvey College in West Virginia, right before her marriage—Anna was an intellectual leader for her family and friends in Chapel Hill and a charter member of the American Association of University Women. A disappointed writer who had once harbored ambitions to be a novelist, she published only one article, "Some Negro Folk-Songs from Tennessee, Collected and Edited by Anna Kranz Odum," in the *Journal of American Folk-Lore*. But she wrote countless long letters to her family and friends, many of which they kept.

During the summer of 1913, pregnant with her first child, Anna vacationed on Lake Sunapee, New Hampshire, with her husband, mother, father, and sister to escape the summer heat of Athens. On 17 September, after Howard had returned to the University of Georgia to begin the fall term, she gave birth to her first child, whom she named Eugene Pleasants Odum after his two grandfathers: Eugene Kranz and William Pleasants Odum. Forty years later, she wrote to her son of "the great joy this fine, blond, blue-eyed baby boy gave us that Wednesday afternoon, in the small, home-like hospital in Newport, New Hampshire, and has kept on giving us these 40 years." [36]

Anna and Howard spent the early years of their marriage in Athens in a house he built on Milledge Circle on the outskirts of town, not far from the ten acres of land he bought for his Jersey cattle. After the brief experience at Emory University in Atlanta, where Gene went to first grade, Howard and Anna Louise packed up their young family, which by then included an infant daughter, Mary Frances, and drove their Model-T Ford from Atlanta to Chapel Hill, to a house on Rosemary Street that Howard had rented sight unseen. The year was 1920, and Chapel Hill had no paved streets. The glimpse of a rat jumping off the back porch of the family's new house prompted their black hired hand, Charlie Maddox, to say, "Fessor, is this where you brung us to?" Charlie and his family had accompanied the Odums from Athens to Atlanta to Chapel Hill, and were installed on Howard's 150-acre farm in neighboring Carrboro. Four years after moving to Chapel Hill, Howard built his mansion on Briarbridge Lane.

Gene Odum remembered his mother as a beautiful but frail woman who entertained graciously and pleasurably the many sociologists and educators, both white and black, whom Howard invited to lecture or conduct research at his institute. Of German American ancestry and with little of the racial prejudice that her fellow southerners exhibited, Anna Kranz Odum welcomed into their home black guests who would not have found decent accommodations anywhere else in the segregated South. She had maids and cooks to assist her, as well as Charlie, who served as butler at the many formal dinners she hosted for faculty and houseguests. On these occasions her children—Gene, Mary Frances, and young Howard Thomas, who had been born in 1924—ate separately under the supervision of a maid.[37]

Anna helped her older son to overcome his childhood shyness, insisting that he take dancing lessons, tennis lessons, and piano lessons. She wanted her children to be musicians, Gene recalled, and she succeeded with her middle child, Mary Frances, who went on to obtain a bachelor of arts in music from the University of Illinois. She failed with Gene, who spent more time discussing birds than compositions with his piano teacher, Lee Brooks, and decided—as soon as his younger sister surpassed him in skill—that boys should not play the piano. Gene took up the clarinet in order to join his church band.

Anna had Eugene, Mary Frances, and Howard Thomas over an eleven-year period, and she could therefore bestow individualized attention on each. To all of her offspring Anna Kranz Odum passed on a sense of family pride, strong sibling bonds, and the ability to write.

Eugene Pleasants Odum

While he was in grade school, Gene Odum thought he might become a plumber when he grew up so that he could work without having to talk with people. "Whenever my family visited anybody I'd disappear under the house to study their plumbing," he said. "That's probably how I got interested in streams. I used to follow pipes to see where they went and how they were hooked up. I was curious about networks." Gene would get up early in the morning to follow the stream that went through his backyard to Morgan Creek, watching the water flow over the rocks and looking for woodcocks, hooded warblers, and waterthrushes. Having read the Thornton Burgess books about Reddy Fox, Johnny Chuck, and Mistah Mocker, and the Ernest

Thompson Seton books about wild animals and little boys who lived like Indians, Gene knew the woods to be swarming with animal life.

As he grew older Gene became obsessed with birds. In high school, with a typewriter and a mimeograph machine, he started a bird magazine called "The Briarbridge Bird News." Initially by himself, and later with the help of his father's secretary, Gene designed the cover—a red and green watercolor illustration of a female catbird feeding a worm into the wide-open mouth of her offspring—did the lettering, and wrote and typed all the articles.[38] His father, although worried that Gene's fascination with birds was responsible for his low grades in school, proudly showed his son's magazine to Louis Graves, editor of the *Chapel Hill Weekly*, who on 2 August 1929 described it in a story titled "Eugene Odum's Bird Magazine." Graves quoted from an article Gene had written about a catbird's nest:

> The three blue-green eggs hatched the day after we returned [from Winter Park, Florida]. Facts about nesting habits have been repeated many times, but I noticed one thing I have never seen recorded: the silent signal of the catbird. When one adult approaches the nest during incubation, or when the young birds are small, they have a habit of lightly fluttering their wings. This seems to be a signal to the other bird that all is well. When the young grew larger and needed more food this was discontinued, since all time had to be spent in getting food. After some timing I found that the young birds in the nest were fed at the average of every 1 minute and 49 seconds or, roughly, every two minutes.[39]

Gene's friendship with Coit Coker, son of University of North Carolina zoologist Robert E. Coker and nephew of UNC botanist William C. Coker, began when Coit read the piece and asked whether he might contribute to the magazine. The two boys became pals, and when they were not writing articles they were exploring Chapel Hill's streams, following each to its source and to its outlet, making maps and observing birds along the way.

In 1931, after Gene had entered the University of North Carolina, Graves incorporated "The Briarbridge Bird News" into his newspaper as a regular column: "Bird Life in Chapel Hill," by Eugene P. Odum and Coit M. Coker. Gene and Coit alternated writing the weekly essay. In one, Gene offered to annotate Chester A. Reed's guide to land birds east of the Rockies, for owners of the book, with "a brief note above each bird found in Chapel Hill, telling when it is found and how common it is." "This will turn it into an illustrated book of the birds of Chapel Hill," he wrote. He got twelve takers.[40]

"Bird Life in Chapel Hill" presaged Gene's future as an ornithologist, ecologist, teacher, and writer. His interest in bird behavior, "a field that is practically unexplored," he noted in his column in 1931, would influence his later decision to avoid museum ornithology and instead study bird physiology and the relationship of birds' development and behavior to their environment. He learned to distinguish and imitate the calls of all the birds found in Chapel Hill, and his campaign to get Chapel Hill residents to "consider [planting] shrubs that are attractive to the birds as well as ornamental" was the first of countless campaigns to preserve or create environmental conditions hospitable to wildlife. His desire to communicate what he was learning about birds, combined with his optimistic assumption that his readers would share his enthusiasm, turned into a passion for explaining nature not only to students and fellow scientists but to the general public as well. The distinctive style of his writing—conversational, concrete, entertaining, and didactic—would have been recognizable a half-century later to readers of the essays he published on behalf of environmental causes.

Gene spent his junior year in Winter Park, Florida, where his father was a visiting professor at Rollins College. There he learned to drive, took courses in physics that were unavailable in Chapel Hill, and finally overcame his shyness. Returning to Chapel Hill for his senior year, he continued writing "Bird Life in Chapel Hill" and announced that he would be an ornithologist. He graduated with a disappointing grade point average that provoked one of his father's colleagues, A. K. King, to say that he was "not college calibur."

Gene stayed in Chapel Hill during the depression, obtaining his B.A. from the University of North Carolina in 1934 and his M.A. in 1936. He did well in mathematics, genetics, and even in creative writing, but he made a C in his first biology course, which he took with Robert E. Coker. That course influenced his career profoundly, Gene said later. "It required so much dissection of dead frogs, and my hands got so wrinkled up with formaldehyde, that I decided I was more interested in the living world."[41] Gene also believed that the formaldehyde permanently affected his ability to smell. With his love of the outdoors, Gene did better in botany courses, such as the one he took with John Couch, who led the class on plant-collecting trips. During his junior year, when Coker was on leave in France, Gene took a zoology course with Coker's replacement, made an A, and accepted a job as an assistant in the course. Gene remembered that Coker expressed astonishment on his return that a "C student" had obtained the job.

After Gene graduated in 1934, he and Coit bought a used Model-A Ford for $100 and drove to Los Angeles, where Gene's father was teaching a summer course at the University of Southern California. They camped out and cooked their own meals along the way, and proudly reported to Louis Graves, who published excerpts of their letter in the *Chapel Hill Weekly*, that they had each spent a total of $33.44, about $.01 a mile for their three-thousand-mile, twenty-two-day trip to California. From Los Angeles they drove up the coast to Yosemite and Sequoia National Parks, on to San Francisco, then to Crater Lake in Oregon, and back through Rocky Mountain National Park on their return to the East. Their purpose had been to see the country — such scenic spots as El Paso, Juárez (Mexico), Carlsbad Caverns, the Painted Desert, the Petrified Forest, and the Grand Canyon — and to learn about birds, and they were successful in both. Gene wrote to Graves: "We have been getting acquainted with bird men. There is one thing about bird men: no matter how busy they are or how prominent they are, they are always ready to stop and talk about birds. No matter how much like tramps we look, or how big a museum we go into, the ornithologist will always stop and talk to us and give us a long list of other ornithologists in places which we are going for us to look up. It's a great fraternity."[42]

The following summer Gene again traveled to California, but this time with his family. He had obtained an invitation to spend eight weeks at Cal Tech's Kerchkoff Marine Laboratory in Corona Del Mar, where he could learn about marine life from the invertebrate ecologist G. E. MacGinitie. "Everybody there was working on sea urchin eggs," Gene later said of the lab.[43] He and the other ten or twelve students slept on a balcony under the stars.

Gene did his master's thesis with H. V. Wilson, nicknamed "Froggy Wilson" for his interest in laboratory studies of frogs. "Everybody was scared of Wilson," Gene recalled, "so I did a quick master's with him on embryology to get out of there."[44] Gene's thesis research investigated the primordial germ cell theory in relation to toadfish, testing the notion that the germ cells, or gametes, were passed on from one generation to the next and could be traced through the embryo. Gene discovered that the continuity of the germ plasm was not confirmed by the histology of the toadfish. He published his thesis that year under the title "Notes on the History of the Germ Cells in the Toadfish (*Opsanus tau*)."

While completing his M.A., Gene was deciding where to get his Ph.D., and in what field. His father had advised him, as he later advised Mary Frances and H. T., to get some education outside the South. Through Coker, Gene had met an ornithologist from the National Museum named H. C. Oberholtzer, who told him that the future of ornithology lay not in bird taxonomy but in bird physiology and the study of the interaction of birds and their environment. He urged Gene to consider two institutions: Western Reserve University in Ohio, where Charles Kendeigh was studying the physiology of house wrens on the Baldwin Preserve, a major bird-banding station; and the University of Michigan. In March 1936, shortly before getting his degree, Gene borrowed his father's black Ford and drove with two other Chapel Hill students to Cleveland, Ohio, and Ann Arbor, Michigan, for interviews.[45]

The trip was both eventful and successful. Although they lost a wheel while driving through West Virginia, the three southerners put chains on the tires to navigate the snowy roads and managed to get to Columbus with their enthusiasm intact. There they spent the night with Dr. and Mrs. Nice, a physician and an amateur ornithologist whom Gene's mother had met in graduate school. The next day they drove to Cleveland, where the amateur bird-bander Prentiss Baldwin had made reservations for them at the lakefront hotel on his vast estate, Gates Mills.[46]

At the time Gene had hopes of attending the University of Michigan, but he was pleased when Baldwin offered him three years of summer employment in his Baldwin Bird Research Laboratory to supplement a half-time teaching job at Western Reserve. Kendeigh had just accepted a position at the University of Illinois and would therefore be leaving Western Reserve and Gates Mills. Baldwin harbored prejudices against southerners, Gene learned later, but he decided that Gene was smart enough to continue Kendeigh's research because Gene walked fast and talked fast.[47]

Gene failed to get into the University of Michigan because of his undistinguished undergraduate grades and accepted an offer to teach biology during the 1936–37 academic year at Western Reserve, where he could take graduate courses, and work on the Baldwin Preserve in the summers. He later said that he was glad he hadn't gone to Michigan, because he "didn't want to be a museum man — [he] wanted to work with live birds."[48]

Howard Thomas Odum

Gene gave few signs of becoming a good student during his high school and college years, but he gave many signs of becoming a good teacher. His sister, Mary Frances, six years younger, always thought Gene a good communicator, a person able and willing to explain his ideas to others. "Gene was a wonderful big brother," she said. He told her all about birds, and he went slowly enough for her to understand — unlike H. T., "who goes so fast nobody knows what he's talking about." Gene also made her wooden cutouts of different birds and animals, as well as a dollhouse.[49]

According to Mary Frances, "H. T. was the gifted one." UNC psychologists found him extraordinarily original and innovative. H. T. spent much more time talking with his father than did his siblings, and he showed curiosity about everything. Once he got into trouble, she said, when some neighbors spotted him with field glasses near their window. Accustomed to getting up at sunrise and going into the woods to bird-watch, as Gene and Coit had done, he had been mistaken for a peeping tom.[50]

As soon as Howard Thomas could walk and talk, Gene started teaching him about birds. H. T. absorbed his brother's ornithology lessons eagerly. When Gene left Chapel Hill to do graduate work, H. T. wrote him often, describing bird behavior he had witnessed and reporting his experiments on animals. At the age of sixteen H. T. sent Gene a typed and illustrated "Mouse

Story" in which he recounted his accidental capture of a female mouse in a bird-banding trap:

> With the aid of a book, I identified her as the Forest Deer or White-footed mouse: *Peromyscus leucopus novaborancis* [*sic*]. She soon learned to run into the tin box when disturbed (this helped in moving her); and when not disturbed, she would bundle up on top of the box. All eating and gnawing to get out was done at night.
>
> I noticed a peculiar habit of vibrating either of the front paws when she thought she was in danger or when she thought another mouse might be near against the metal or dry leaf in such a manner that the tiny noise could be heard by human ears, perhaps twenty-five feet. She would even answer this vibration if successfully imitated.
>
> Eyesight and hearing seemed equally acute both day or night. Any sharp sound such as that made with the tongue would cause her to jump or at least her ears to do so. This same reaction I noticed in my Guinea pigs.
>
> The mouse began to make a nest of chewed up materials and to wall up the entrance to the tinbox, obscuring vision, because of lowered temperatures—I thought. I gave her some tissue paper to aid her in finding nest material. Because of this it was not until October 9 that I discovered four pink lettle [*sic*] mouselets.[51]

During World War II, after two years as an undergraduate student at the University of North Carolina, H. T. joined the United States States Army Air Force. There he received the training in meteorology that would later incline him to see the atmosphere, the biosphere, the hydrosphere, and the lithosphere as components of a single planetary whole. After returning to Chapel Hill to complete his A.B. degree in zoology in 1947, he went to Yale University to study for his Ph.D. with the famed ecologist G. Evelyn Hutchinson.

In the course of the next several decades, Gene and H. T. developed one of the most unusual sibling relationships in the history of science, one that Gene later described as an intellectual rivalry accompanied by family loyalty and appreciation for the other's work. The rivalry originated, Gene believed, in H. T.'s efforts to distinguish himself professionally from his older brother — efforts not unlike Gene's own attempts to distinguish himself from their famous father. The loyalty was strengthened by confidence in each other's ideas and a shared mission. Their complementary approaches toward nature — Gene thinking like a physiologist and H. T. like a physical scientist and engineer — and their common conceptual model, the holistic model their father had bequeathed to them, made them an effective team in their crusade to establish the ecosystem as the basic unit of ecology.[52] Histories of the discipline that included the Odums' contributions started appearing in the 1980s with Robert McIntosh's *Background of Ecology: Concept and Theory*. A reviewer of the 1992 book *An Entangled Bank: The Origins of Ecosystem Ecology* labeled Joel Hagen's account of ecology "A Tale of Two Brothers."[53] Not all the accounts were complimentary. Alston Chase's *In a Dark Wood* expresses less admiration for the Odum brothers, blaming them, along with their distinguished predecessors A. G. Tansley and G. Evelyn Hutchinson, for developing a model of nature that made the individual human being a "subordinate member of an indivisible organic community of interdependent parts."[54]

Martha Ann Huff Odum

Gene Odum met Martha Ann Huff through his sister, Mary Frances. In the fall of 1935 Mary Frances had entered the University of Illinois, encouraged by her father, who had been invited to spend that year in the university's Sociology Department. She roomed with Martha in the Delta Gamma sorority house, and in the summer of 1938 she brought Martha to Chapel Hill for a few weeks. Although she could not introduce Martha to her older brother on that visit, because Gene had gone to Gates Mills, Ohio, to finish the research for his dissertation, she introduced Martha to the rest of the family. "Martha was a hit with everybody," Gene said, including H. T., who admired her for the knowledge of knots she had acquired while sailing on Wisconsin's lakes.

Martha Ann Huff grew up in the town of Wilmette on Chicago's North Shore, the only child of a successful orthodontist, Ralph Huff, and his wife, Bernice Corliss Huff. Adored by her parents, she had a happy childhood with all the comforts and opportunities available to those of her station in the 1920s. Every summer her family took long, adventurous trips out West, where they often drove on unpaved roads and slept in tents. On those explorations of Utah, Nevada, Wyoming, and the Pacific Northwest, Martha gained a love of wilderness and great open spaces that she would express in her painting the rest of her life. Although he grew weary of dentistry, her father earned a large income from his practice in downtown Chicago, and invested much of it in the stock market. He had just bought himself a seat on the Chicago Board of Trade when the stock market crashed in 1929.

The early 1930s were difficult for all the Huffs. Ralph Huff eventually paid off his debts and restored his family's financial security, but in the meantime Martha learned to live frugally. She attended the University of Illinois rather than Northwestern because it was less expensive, and she majored in design rather than art because commercial art offered a better opportunity to make a living. She later said that she had chosen to go to the state's public university because she wanted to see how people who had not been privileged to grow up on the North Shore lived and thought.

Martha was pretty, fun-loving, and popular. When Gene met her at the University of Illinois in the fall of 1938, she had many suitors. It wasn't until ten days before their graduation, when Martha was to receive her B.A. and Gene his Ph.D., that they started going to movies and dances and playing golf and tennis together. They were both keen competitors at sports. After their engagement — which occurred on their third date — Martha took Gene to Wilmette to meet her parents, who liked him immediately and revealed relief that their daughter was settling down. Martha sent Mary Frances a letter wrapped around two aspirin. "Take these aspirin before reading further," she wrote, and then announced the couple's plans for marriage. This was Gene's only serious love affair, and it would last for fifty-six years.

2 The Ecologist's Early Years

Near the end of his career, Gene Odum described his contribution to ecology as the development of ways to study the interaction of organisms within an ecosystem. "If you want to understand a large-scale system," he said, "you have to start with the function of the organisms in the system. Function before structure."[1] To focus primarily on a natural system's structure, as did his mentor at the University of Illinois, ecologist Victor Shelford, was not to advance beyond description of the system's components, nor to see how the system worked. To focus on the components' functions in relation to one another, as Odum taught more than one generation of ecologists to do through his textbook *Fundamentals of*

Ecology, brought about a reorientation in ecology that inspired an environmentalist movement of global import.

Unwittingly, Eugene Odum applied to nature Howard Washington Odum's holistic model of social interaction. From his sociologist father Gene had inherited the conviction that interdependence necessitates cooperation, an idea he encountered in a different context in Aldo Leopold's 1933 essay "The Land Ethic." He came early to the model of nature as a system, or set of interlocking systems, with interdependent components interacting to create a whole with unique properties.

Graduate Work

Gene Odum spent the 1936–37 academic year, when he was twenty-three years old, at Western Reserve in Cleveland, Ohio, teaching elementary biology courses on a half-time basis and taking a couple of graduate courses in physiology. He was replacing the ornithologist Charles Kendeigh, who had left to take a position at the University of Illinois working with Victor Shelford. In the fall of 1937, Odum followed Kendeigh to the University of Illinois.

The summer of 1937 Odum spent at the Baldwin Bird Research Laboratory in Gates Mills, Ohio, where Prentiss Baldwin, an early pioneer in bird banding, had given him a job banding birds for the Fish and Wildlife Commission. While bird banding did not excite Odum, the prospect of conducting experiments on birds did. It was on the preserve that Odum began research on the heart rates of small birds for the dissertation he was to complete at the University of Illinois in 1939 under Kendeigh's direction.

The impetus for the research came not from Kendeigh but from a manufacturer of piezoelectric crystals, which convert vibrations into electrical charges. In 1937, officials of the Brush Development Company in Cleveland had approached Kendeigh with the idea of testing the crystal in a bird nest to pick up the bird's heartbeat. Kendeigh offered the project to Odum. The possibility of measuring birds' heart rates when the birds were not under stress appealed to Odum because little was known about the metabolism of small birds under natural conditions. Odum recognized immediately that ecologists could employ the device to study the physiological states of animals of all kinds without disturbing them.

During the summer of 1937 Odum used a "piezo cardiograph" machine that a predecessor at the Baldwin Bird Research Laboratory had built in the early 1930s with Brush Company crystals. The machine was cumbersome and unsatisfactory for quantitative work, so Odum redesigned it, incorporating the Brush Company's new pen recorder and creating the "cardio-vibrometer," or "vibrometer."[2]

The cardio-vibrometer, equipped with earphones, enabled Odum both to hear and to record heartbeats. The tiny platform attached to a piezoelectric crystal that Odum placed in the nest communicated the vibrations made by the bird's heartbeat and respiration to an amplifier and an aluminum pen. The pen, receiving the amplified current of electricity, recorded from zero to ninety vibrations per second on a roll of paper being turned by a small motor; the crystal earphones, connected to the amplifier, transmitted the sounds of the bird's movements in the nest to the listener. Odum could thereby determine and distinguish the bird's heart rate and breathing rate.[3] Although he encountered difficulties because the crystal registered all of the bird's movements, Odum made a number of significant observations.

From his study of thirteen species of small birds, Odum deduced that the heart rate is usually inversely related to the bird's size.[4] He discovered that the heart rate of small birds varies from moment to moment in an oscillatory manner, and that the fluctuations are not correlated with events in the breathing cycle. He also noticed a sinus arrhythmia in very low heart rates of some nestling and adult birds. By confining four English sparrows (house sparrows, *Passer domesticus*) and a starling (*Sturnus vulgaris*) in outdoor cages, he learned about the effects of captivity on small birds. He found at the end of three weeks that their heart rate had decreased on average by 19 percent, although their weight had not, and concluded that captivity may permanently affect the circulatory system of birds.[5]

In his dissertation, which he published in *Ecological Monographs* in 1941, Odum explained the significance of his research for ecology: "Although the study of physiology quite logically is concerned at first with the study of the functions of various parts, organs, and systems as separate units, the ultimate aim is an understanding of their function in the organism as a whole. Furthermore, it is the physiology of the whole organism that is of the greatest interest to the ecologist in understanding how organisms are related to and function in their environments."[6] His dissertation research made Odum realize that he did not want to spend his life studying only the parts of the whole; he wanted to study how organisms related to and functioned in their environments.

Odum's interest in the "whole" developed under the influence of Victor Shelford, the animal ecologist in the University of Illinois's Zoology Department, who thought of ecology as the study of biotic communities. Since 1923 Shelford had been writing a book with the plant ecologist Frederic Clements on the concept of the biome; in 1939 it appeared under the title *Bio-Ecology*. The authors defined *biome* as a "plant-animal formation" synonymous with the biotic climax, which is "the final response of communities to climate." They argued that the biome should be regarded as a "complex organism," a "superorganism" that is "more than the sum of its individual parts."[7] Shelford and Clements supported their concept with a statement from Jan Christiaan Smuts's *Holism and Evolution*, which had appeared in 1926: "A whole is a synthesis or unity of parts, so close that it affects the activities and interactions of these parts, impresses on them a special character, and makes them different from what they would have been in a combination devoid of such unity or synthesis. . . . It is a complex of parts, but so close and intimate, so unified that the characters and relations and activities of the parts are affected and changed by the synthesis."[8]

In his classes, Shelford used the invasion of deciduous forest into grasslands as an example of the interactivity of plants and animals; birds and mammals contribute to forest expansion by dropping seeds into the holes small animals make in the prairie sod.[9] Wanting to make sure that his students recognized the roles animals play in the biome, Shelford gave the biotic communities such names as "the spruce-moose biome," which, as Odum recalled, provoked much mirth among the students, who endlessly invented similar names for other areas. For Shelford, ecology was a holistic discipline by necessity; understanding the interactivity of plants and animals in the biome required consideration of the biome as a whole. He taught his students that reductionist biologists, whom he sarcastically called "that Woods Hole establishment," were anti-ecological.[10]

Shelford inculcated in his students a set of ideas about "succession," which for early ecologists constituted the central unifying theory in the investigation of large-scale systems. Succession, according to Clements's definition in his 1916 volume *Plant Succession*, is the sequence of plant communities in which habitat and population interact until a state of equilibrium, the climax formation, is reached.[11] In *Bio-Ecology*, Clements and Shelford outlined the causal relations in succession as follows: The habitat acts on the plant and animal communities, which both react to the habitat and interact—"coact"—with each other, modifying the habitat in the process and producing additional reactions.[12] The dynamic process culminates in the "relatively stable climate and biome."[13] The idea that a state of equilibrium is both possible and natural became deeply rooted in Odum's view of nature.

Shelford thus instilled in Odum four concepts that influenced his thinking thereafter: nature tends toward stability, the whole is "more than the sum of its individual parts," ecology is the study of large-scale systems and the interrelationships therein, and real ecology is not reductionist. Odum would build ecosystem ecology on the basis of these assumptions, and over the next fifty years he would have to defend all of them.

Despite their enthusiasm for holism, Shelford and Clements were criticized for their practice of examining the biotic community independent of its physical environment and for their depiction of the biome as a superorganism. In 1935, while they were still engaged in writing *Bio-Ecology*, the British botanist Sir Arthur Tansley published an article in the journal *Ecology* that named a new approach to the study of nature.

In "The Use and Abuse of Vegetational Concepts and Terms," Tansley challenged the term *biotic community* because it aggregated animals and plants as members of a community without specifying their interrelationships and implicitly separated them from their physical environment. He proposed in its stead the concept of the *ecosystem*. *Ecosystem* signified organization—the result of the components' interaction—and escaped the organicist connotations of *superorganism*. Tansley included in the ecosystem "not only the organism-complex, but also the whole complex of physical factors forming what we call the environment of the biome," thereby defining the ecosystem as a natural system with both organic and inorganic components.[14] Tansley's ecosystem was a more inclusive "whole" than Shelford's biome.

Tansley viewed the ecosystem as a "unit of nature," but not one with boundaries. Like a solar system, a planet, an individual organism, an organic molecule, or an atom, it was a system isolated mentally by scientists for the purposes of study. In reality, ecosystems overlapped, interlocked, and interacted with one another.[15] Tansley denounced the drawing of a line between so-called natural biotic communities and areas under the influence of human activity. "Is man part of 'nature' or not?" he asked.[16]

In distinguishing between biome and ecosystem Tansley was simultaneously reconceptualizing "the natural ecological unit" and revolutionizing its study. Whereas the term *biome*, like *biotic community*, invited description of the structure of its discrete components as a primary approach, *ecosystem* invited examination of the components' functions. Odum had already demonstrated a preference for the analysis of function over description by the time he read Tansley's article at Illinois, and he was excited by Tansley's argument. But under the sway of Shelford, who regarded *ecosystem* as a synonym for *biome*, he did not fully appreciate the significance of Tansley's holism until he began writing *Fundamentals of Ecology* years later.

Although Gene and H. T. Odum developed their ecosystem ecology on the model introduced by Tansley, Gene always said that Shelford was his mentor. Shelford was at his best in the field, where he displayed a vast knowledge of animal and plant life. Believing that ecologists should visit as many biomes as possible during their training, Shelford took his students on extended field trips to the major biomes of North America at every opportunity.[17]

Odum joined Shelford as a teaching assistant on a seven-week excursion to the tundra and the grasslands of western North America in the summer of 1939. He had just received his Ph.D. and had become engaged to Martha

Ann Huff, but he had no summer employment and was thus eager to be the tour's ornithologist at a small salary. Packed into a small bus, the group of twenty undergraduate students, graduate students, and instructors—almost half of them women—traveled north through Manitoba to Hudson Bay, and then west through Saskatchewan and the Canadian Rockies in British Columbia, returning through the Dakotas. A commissary truck led the way to each preselected campsite, where the group either stayed in cabins, as they did at the Itasca State Park field station in northern Minnesota, or set up tents around a campfire. During the day the bus would make frequent stops and Shelford would guide his students across the terrain. When it was time to move on, he would blow first a low-pitched whistle, signaling "We're ready to move," and then, within minutes, a high-pitched one, signaling "All aboard." Anybody who was not in the bus when Shelford was ready to go was left behind, as Odum knew from personal experience. In the evenings, Shelford talked, the students played the guitar and sang, and Odum wrote love letters to Martha.[18]

Before graduating, Odum had applied for a number of academic positions without success. He wanted to live in a college town, having learned that urban universities, such as Western Reserve, were not important to the city's community life. Recalling his year at Western Reserve, Odum said, "In Chapel Hill and Athens, unlike Cleveland, the university is the center of town and the professors live near the university and are the top people. In Cleveland, professors are way down in the pecking order and live in crackerbox houses in the suburbs, and the wealthy people live in the big houses in town. There is no college spirit."[19] He applied to the University of Virginia and Oberlin College, which had advertised jobs for which he was qualified, but was rejected by both. In May, he went to a meeting where William J. ("Wild Bill") Hamilton from Cornell told him that the Edmund Niles Huyck Preserve in Rensselaerville, New York, was looking for a naturalist. Odum sent his resumé to a committee that Hamilton chaired, and by the time he departed on Shelford's trip he had received an offer. On 20 August, driving a new black Chevrolet he had bought for seven hundred dollars, he moved to Rensselaerville.

The Edmund Niles Huyck Preserve and Biological Research Station

The Edmund Niles Huyck Preserve and Biological Research Station adjoins the village of Rensselaerville, twenty-eight miles southwest of Albany. Edmund Niles Huyck, the son of the founder of a felt mill in Rensselaerville, had acquired 470 acres of heavily forested land by the time of his death in 1930, and his family set up the Edmund Niles Huyck Preserve a year later to carry out his goal of preserving the area's natural beauty. The preserve's dual purpose was to save the woods for enjoyment by the people of Rensselaerville and elsewhere and to facilitate the scientific study of nature. Since the land had once been farmed and then abandoned, it was a perfect site for the study of succession. W. J. Hamilton, the chair of the preserve's Scientific Advisory Committee, conducted a biological survey of the area in the summer of 1937 and recommended the establishment of the biological research station. In 1939, the committee selected Eugene P. Odum as the first resident biologist, and Edward C. Raney, who had completed a Ph.D. at Cornell, and Donald R. Griffin, who was finishing a Ph.D. at Harvard, as the first summer research fellows.[20] At the preserve Odum finally shifted his attention from the parts to the whole.

In his annual report for 1939–40, Odum praised the research station for offering field biologists the opportunity to work independent of commercial, economic, and institutional demands. Such freedom was unique, he said, and important to the future of science because biologists knew relatively little about species that had no economic value and even less about "the complicated interrelations of the multitude of organisms living in nature as well as the relations of such forms to economically important species and to man." His own research there would produce a comprehensive vegetation survey with a detailed habitat map of the preserve, a life history of the black-capped chickadee, and a study of the physiological ontogeny of ring-necked pheasant embryos.[21]

For a few weeks after his arrival, Odum lived with Raney and Griffin in a cottage on Lincoln Pond near an old barn the two had converted into a laboratory equipped with a bench, a couple of lab stools, a microscope, a hygrometer, scales, jars, and animal traps.[22] Raney had spent the summer studying green frogs (*Rana clamitans*) and bullfrogs (*Rana catesbeiana*), which he marked, released, and recaptured in order to find out about their life histories; Griffin had begun the research on bat echolocation for which he was to become famous.[23] Griffin had strung piano wires in the barn's loft to try to understand how bats navigated in darkness. Comparing the number of "pings" the bats made when hitting the wires with their senses intact with the number of "pings" they made when their ears were sealed with wax or their mouths glued shut, Griffin learned that bats navigate and avoid obstacles by emitting high-frequency sounds and listening to the echoes.[24]

On 18 November 1939, Gene and Martha were married at Martha's home in Wilmette, Illinois. Gene was twenty-six, tall, blond, and thin, with the aquiline nose characteristic of generations of Odums. Tall, brown-haired Martha was twenty-two; Gene thought she was beautiful. All of Gene's family attended—Mary Frances, H. T., his mother, and his father, who had fun grumbling that the wedding conflicted with the North Carolina–Duke football game.

For Gene and Martha Odum, the year in Rensselaerville with "the natives," as the year-round residents called themselves, was an extended honeymoon. They lived happily in a poorly heated wing of a house owned by a Miss Gathen, with a tiny bedroom and a small window that snow banks would sometimes cover during the winter. Mrs. Edmund Huyck, who was Odum's actual employer and who was very much interested in the scientific research conducted at the preserve, invited them to elegant dinners at her home and introduced them to her many friends. To her great delight, the couple participated fully in the town's social activities, attending an Episcopal church there, going to the square dances, and snowshoeing like natives. Despite the limitations of their kitchen—with its kerosene stove—the Odums entertained their local acquaintances in their apartment. Martha fell into the routine of painting during the day, even when temperatures were low and she had to pour alcohol into her watercolors to prevent their freezing, and at her first show she sold all she had created.

The preserve had a number of visitors that year, including Griffin, the ornithologist George Wallace, the entomologist Frank Miller, the animal behaviorist G. K. Noble, and the evolutionary biologist Ernst Mayr. Fifty-seven years later, in a letter he wrote to Mayr about the candidacy of a scientist nominated for membership in the National Academy of Sciences, Odum reminded the nonagenarian of the spring night they had crawled over wet ground with Noble and Martha to watch salamanders mate.[25]

Odum continued his bird studies at the preserve and also undertook the vegetation survey that allowed him to shift his professional attention from individual organisms to plant-animal systems. He chose the chickadee as the subject for his investigation of a bird's annual life cycle because the bird was nonmigratory and common in the region. As he was to do whenever he became interested in a bird, he learned the chickadee's vocabulary—more than fifteen different calls, each having a different meaning—well enough to distinguish whether a chickadee was warning against a hawk or signaling the presence of a snake. By banding the birds and observing their behavior at feeding stations he had set up throughout the preserve, he detected a pecking order, which he considered probably consequential in mate selection. With the cardio-vibrometer he had brought from Illinois, he recorded the heart rates of the chickadees, other birds, and pheasant embryos. Among other things, he discovered that the ratio of heart rate to breathing rate of birds differs from that of mammals.[26]

More important than his chickadee work for Odum's future as an ecologist, however, was the inventory of the preserve's plants and the habitat map he prepared during that year. The purpose of the project, Odum wrote in his annual report, was to establish a basis for succession studies of the land in the future. Such studies would enable human beings to plan and manage ecosystems: "Only by knowing the nature, extent, and speed of changes as well as factors causing them can man intelligently control his environment in the future."[27] Odum was expressing an assumption common to ecologists of the time—that the value of ecology lay in its applicability to the management of nature.[28]

In 1975, when he returned to the Huyck Preserve to give a paper after an absence of many years, Odum discovered that his prediction of a beech-hemlock climax forest, based on his 1940 observation that 90 percent of the seedlings were either beech or hemlock, had not been realized. He had failed to take into account the actions of the deer, which ate the beech seedlings. This was a lesson in ecosystem dynamics.[29]

Summer brought two new research fellows to the Huyck Preserve: David E. Davis, who had a Ph.D. from Harvard; and William M. Ingram, who had a Ph.D. from Cornell. Davis was interested in territoriality and intraspecies fighting in kingbirds and chipmunks, and Ingram was studying the life history of land snails. Gene and Martha Odum, Bill and Marty Ingram, and Dave Davis all moved into the Lincoln Pond cottage, which had two large rooms and a kitchen downstairs and three bedrooms upstairs. The wives took turns cooking and the husbands did the dishes. Davis, who didn't have a wife, paid for a housekeeper to come once a week. Their dinner conversations became the stuff of family legends, recalled by Martha frequently during their life together as a metaphor for what she called "the Odum drive." The men talked science nonstop and the women listened, pointing, if they needed it, to the salt or pepper or butter. According to Martha, the women won one concession from the men: each was allowed one dinner in which she determined the topic for discussion. Martha chose art, and Marty chose horses. When she had difficulty getting the ice tray back into the freezer one day and discovered a dead bird that Gene had stored in the ice compartment, Martha learned that Gene made use of everything, including their personal refrigerator, for the advancement of science.[30]

On 9 September 1940 the Odums departed the preserve for Athens, Georgia, where Dr. George Boyd, head of biology at the University of Georgia, had appointed Gene an instructor of biology at a salary of eighteen hundred dollars a year. Boyd had learned of Odum's availability for the position from Howard Odum, who at a banquet had told him of his son's scholarly accomplishments and desire to return to the South. Boyd had obtained a foundation grant to expand the department, and he was happy to interview and then hire Gene, to whom he assigned a reduced teaching load the first year.

Following Howard Odum's counsel to arrive in Athens looking "first class," Gene and Martha stayed in the Georgian Hotel at the center of town for a few weeks until they found a place to rent. On his first walk over to the small campus, Gene encountered plant taxonomist Wilbur Duncan, who became a lifelong friend, and whose wife-to-be, Marion Bennett, took Odum's first course, a graduate course in invertebrate zoology. In 1940, Duncan was one of the few scientists at the university seriously engaged in publishing his research.

Because he already owned ten acres of land in Athens—land his father had used for grazing his Jersey cattle twenty years before and had given to him when he graduated from high school—Gene found the prospect of teaching at the University of Georgia attractive. He nevertheless advised Martha not to unpack—and she didn't, for several years.

The 1940s at the University of Georgia

Athens, in Clarke County, was a small town in the early 1940s with a few paved roads and one trolley car. The university's enrollment was a little over three thousand, and the city's population about twenty-one thousand people—two-thirds of them white after the departure of many blacks during the depression. Farms of cotton and corn tended by blacks and owned by whites surrounded the town.[31]

Since few apartments had been constructed there during the depression, Martha and Gene began their life in Athens in the downstairs of an old house that had been converted into a triplex. Their quarters were so small, Martha recalled, that the bathroom also served as the hallway between their bedroom and the kitchen. Their second abode was another makeshift place on Milledge Avenue, and their third was a little house on Milledge Circle, to which they moved when Martha became pregnant with their first child. Born on 1 October 1942, William Eugene Odum was a healthy, happy child who announced at the age of three that he wanted to be an ichthyologist, having learned to fish from his maternal grandfather and to collect specimens from his father.

Because the university permitted air-conditioning only in laboratories that housed live animals—thus inspiring scientists of all kinds to keep mice—Gene, Martha, and young Bill left Athens every summer for cooler places, where Gene conducted research, Martha painted, and Bill fished and trailed after the biologists. Bill eagerly absorbed all that his father could teach him about the natural world and all that his mother could teach him about art.

That decade they spent many summers in Highlands, North Carolina, across the Georgia–North Carolina border.[32]

In 1942, just after he was promoted to assistant professor of zoology, Gene Odum seriously contemplated leaving the university because of Governor Eugene Talmadge's abuse of academic freedom. The segregationist governor of Georgia had packed the university's Board of Regents to obtain the dismissal of the dean of the College of Education for his alleged support of racial integration. Talmadge made his intentions regarding education in Georgia clear: "I'm not going to put up with social equality in this state as long as I'm Governor. They can't slip through no crack and they can't crop up in no funds coming into this state. We don't need no Negroes and white people taught together."[33] Talmadge's firing of Dean Walter Dewey Cocking and a number of other faculty members at state schools whom he suspected of advocating social equality caused the Southern University Conference to expel the University of Georgia from its membership. UGA students protested and burned Talmadge in effigy but could not stop the Southern Association of Colleges and Secondary Schools, in December 1941, from rescinding the accreditation of all the white institutions in the university system of Georgia. Talmadge, who had calculated that his vocal opposition to integration would increase his popularity, lost his bid for reelection in November 1942 primarily because of Georgians' loyalty to the university. The new governor, Ellis Arnall, changed the appointment procedure for regents early in 1943 and instituted other reforms, but by then the university had acquired a national reputation for intellectual backwardness, racism, and lack of academic freedom.[34]

Although in his first year at the University of Georgia he was assigned only the course in invertebrate zoology—to the annoyance of his heavily burdened colleagues—during the war Gene Odum taught basic zoology, human anatomy, physiology, and genetics, as well as ecology. While the parasitologists had all been drafted to fight malaria in the South Pacific, Odum, whose expertise in ecology was not valuable to the armed forces, received a deferment from his draft board to train nurses and pharmacists to assist doctors in the field. His load of three courses and two labs each quarter left little time for research, though his publications in ornithology, many of them based on his summer work, led to his election as a fellow of the American Ornithologists' Union and his promotion to associate professor of zoology.[35] His athletic prowess led to his appointment as coach for the university's tennis team.

It was in this busy period that Odum and his precocious brother, Howard Thomas, eleven years his junior, first became fascinated by the ideas of G. Evelyn Hutchinson, the distinguished Yale ecologist who was studying the mechanics of natural systems with methods developed in the physical sciences. Gene had already realized that the biological sciences alone did not offer adequate conceptual tools or methods to study large-scale natural systems, and he quickly saw the advantage of bringing together the biological and physical sciences.[36] Hutchinson had drawn his attention back to Tansley's concept of an interactive biophysical system, or ecosystem, which, Gene realized, would require a new kind of ecology with a new orientation. Unlike *biome*, which was a biogeographical concept, *ecosystem* described a function: the interaction of biological organisms and their abiotic environment in a system.

Although Tansley had won the credit for naming and defining the ecosystem concept in 1935, several of his contemporaries had also determined that the biological and physical elements of nature together compose systems. In 1933, American wildlife ecologist Aldo Leopold had included both living organisms and their physical environment in his description of land. In "The Land Ethic," first published in 1933 and later revised and expanded for inclusion in *A Sand County Almanac*, Leopold defined *land* as not merely soil but "a fountain of energy flowing through a circuit of soils, plants, and animals." Food chains conduct energy upward, and death and decay return energy to the soil, always with some net loss. In the system Leopold described, individual organisms are simply conduits of energy.[37]

In 1942, Hutchinson's student Raymond Lindeman had published an article titled "The Trophic-Dynamic Aspect of Ecology," which revolutionized the methodology for studying ecosystems.[38] Lindeman rejected as inadequate the biological approaches of his predecessors in ecology and proposed instead that each ecosystem be examined as "a system composed of physical-chemical-biological processes," because energy and materials were continuously exchanged between the organic and inorganic parts.[39] Converting biomass units into energy units, he introduced energetics—that is, the study of energy and its transformations—into ecosystem ecology and thereby shifted the focus from taxonomy to the analysis of energy flow, or function. He also introduced the "black-box" approach to ecosystem study; that is, the consideration of the ecosystem as a whole without attention to the particular organisms interacting within it.

In 1925, nearly a decade before Tansley, Leopold, and Lindeman would publish their work on ecosystems, the American physical chemist Alfred Lotka had argued in *Elements of Physical Biology* that natural systems are constituted by exchanges of matter and energy and can therefore be analyzed according to the laws of thermodynamics. Considering the earth itself as a single interactive system, Lotka saw any separation of biological systems from their physical environment as arbitrary and inappropriate. Although most ecologists did not become acquainted with Lotka's book until its republication in 1956, H. T. Odum read *Elements of Physical Biology* in the late 1940s, while studying with Hutchinson, and alerted Gene to it then.[40]

Tansley, Lotka, Leopold, Hutchinson, and Lindeman presented a model for the understanding of natural phenomena that Odum viewed as more holistic than the one he had embraced in graduate school. Whereas the concept of the biome, like that of the superorganism or the biotic community, perpetuated the dualistic distinction between the living and nonliving elements of a geographical space, the concept of the ecosystem united those elements as equally essential contributors to the functioning of the whole. And whereas the concept of the biotic community elicited the reductionist examination of each of its various species populations, the concept of the ecosystem as an energy circuit required examination of the whole.

Inspired by these new ideas, Odum revamped his ecology course to make the ecosystem central. He started the course with a discussion of the ecosystem as a whole, and then moved to a discussion of its individual components. And he shifted from examination of the structures of biomes to analysis of the function of ecosystems. "If you want to understand a large-scale system, you have to start with the function of the organisms in the system," he would tell his students.[41]

Because all the existing books about nature were "just about the parts," and not about the whole, Odum started jotting down notes for a textbook. There would soon be a demand for the kind of book he would write, he thought, because none of the standard works set forth any principles to explain the functioning of large-scale systems. He could think of *Plant Succession*, by Clements; *Animal Ecology*, by A. S. Pearse; *Animal Ecology*, by Charles Elton; *Bio-Ecology*, by Clements and Shelford, and a couple of books on entomology, but no text that showed how plants, animals, and the elements of their physical environment functioned in relation to one another.

In 1945, the year he was promoted to associate professor, given the University of Georgia's Michael Award for Excellence in Research, and elected a fellow of the American Ornithologists' Union, Odum began to think about staying in Athens. When he had arrived in 1940, the only scientist present with any reputation beyond the campus was George Boyd, who studied malaria. Although Boyd's view of science was narrow, according to Odum, in that he understood science as experimentation with control groups and therefore did not appreciate ecologists' study of large-scale systems, Boyd had a futuristic vision of the University of Georgia as a research institution that appealed to Odum. After his appointment as dean of the Graduate School in 1943, Boyd had petitioned the university's president for funds to buy faculty time for scientific research. With the war over and opportunities for research available once again, Odum could envision a fulfilling career at the University of Georgia.

Certainly his family was beginning to feel settled in Athens. Forced by their landlord to vacate their house on Milledge Circle, for which they had been paying rent of approximately thirty dollars a month, Gene and Martha decided to build on the ten acres of pine woods "Pops" had given Gene on the outskirts of town. They borrowed five thousand dollars from the bank and another several thousand from Martha's father to accumulate, with their own savings, the ten thousand dollars they needed. Because there was no public access to their property, they spent some of the money to purchase fifteen additional acres on which to put a road. Wanting neighbors, they then persuaded Gene's colleague Horace Lund, an entomologist, to buy a few acres nearby.

To save money, Gene and Martha decided to construct their house out of army barracks left over from the war, which they could order from an army surplus dealer. The barracks were delivered in such bad condition, however, that Gene refused to accept the shipment and Martha had to design a frame house out of pine to fit the foundation that had already been poured. The house was not large. It had a living room with a big picture window to let in southern light; a small family room; a small kitchen; a small study for Gene; two bedrooms, one of them downstairs for Bill; and two bathrooms. Over the course of the ensuing years, Martha, who loved big projects, made numerous additions. She remodeled the interior space to make the house passive solar, converted the screened porch into a sunroom with a Jacuzzi tub, added a front room with lots of glass, enlarged Gene's study, and created a studio for herself. With the frugality she had acquired during her adolescence in the depression, she used various shades of white and lavender paint to create an attractive home in which they could watch birds, squirrels, raccoons, possum, rabbits, and deer feed in the woods. Although its interior reflected Martha's taste for modernism, from the outside the house retained the look of a mountain cabin.

The late 1940s were difficult years for Gene and Martha. In 1946, their son Daniel Thomas Odum was born. Because of his severe retardation and physical disability, they were forced to place him in the state hospital in Milledgeville, Georgia, where he spent his forty-one years of life. They gave up their hope of having a third child. Every evening after dinner, Gene took the family car and, leaving Martha home with Bill, returned to his office to work late into the night on his book.

The Writing of *Fundamentals of Ecology*

Odum had actually thought about writing an ecology textbook even before he arrived at the University of Georgia. Having watched his father publish one book after another, he assumed that writing books was what good scholars did, whatever their field of inquiry. So his reading of Tansley, Leopold, Hutchinson, Lindeman, and others was motivated largely by his desire to write a book that would present an ecosystem approach to understanding nature. When he first began work on the project, however, he had qualms about publishing a supposedly comprehensive text in his discipline. After all, he was not yet thirty years old. He asked his father, "What if I don't know enough yet?" "You'll learn as you write," his father responded. "What if I make mistakes?" "You'll correct them in the second edition."[42]

Howard Odum wasted no time informing his acquaintances in the publishing industry that his son had embarked on this ambitious project. After a Macmillan Company editor had sent Gene a letter in January 1944 referring to an inquiry from Howard, Howard wrote his son to apologize: "I hope you don't think that I am trying to rush you and that I have gotten you into the middle of it too soon. It is nice to have those invitations, and it doesn't obligate you at any given time."[43] Gene Odum recalled later that although he was surprised to get the letter from the Macmillan editor before he had written a single chapter, he was not surprised that his father had already been contacting publishers on his behalf. "My father was always involved in our lives, always doing whatever he could for us, professionally and personally," he said.[44]

Gene responded to the Macmillan editor with a description of the book he planned:

> In general I had in mind a sort of introduction to ecology which would be suitable for a college course requiring only the beginning biology courses as a prerequisite; at the same time I want to make it readable enough to be stimulating to amateur naturalists, conservationists and others who should find in ecology a basic discipline. As you know there are good reference books in [the] ecological field and books which deal with plant, animal, or other parts of field, but no book that covers the whole field of ecology in a comprehensive scientific manner. Everyone tells me that there is great need for such a book, and I am sure that there are several ecologists who could do a better job than I, but no one seems to want to tackle it. The only reason I feel willing to try it is [the] fact that I have had a rather broad training in both botany and zoology and have been subjected to several of rather different "schools of thought" in [the] field; for this reason I might be able to present a broader, better organized view of the field which I am convinced should receive more attention in college instruction.[45]

Odum went on to say that "after the war there will be a great revival of interest in ecology and in applied fields which spring from it such as conservation, forestry, and wildlife managements, etc. With all [the] distruction [*sic*] now going on, it will be practically essential for us to give more thought to our shrinking environment in more ways than one!"[46]

The end of the war brought an influx of students to the university. Enrollment during the 1946–47 academic year swelled to 6,643, of whom more than 4,000 were veterans.[47] The Department of Biology moved from Le-Conte Hall to Baldwin Hall, where the scientists converted the large classrooms into laboratories and received approval from the Board of Regents to offer a doctorate in zoology. To accommodate the students applying to its graduate program, the department hired additional faculty and adopted a new curriculum. At one of the many department meetings that took place in the fall of 1946, Odum enthusiastically proposed that his ecology course be required of all biology majors. To his dismay, he was soundly rebuffed by his colleagues, who laughed at the notion and expressed the common view that ecology was a subordinate branch of biology and less important than "basic disciplines" such as physiology and morphology.[48] Odum recalled later: "My colleagues of those days confused ecology with natural history and voiced the opinion that no new ideas or principles were likely to be revealed in an ecology course that had not already been covered in courses in taxonomy, evolution, physiology, and other subjects considered to be more basic."[49]

Fundamentals of Ecology was born, Odum was fond of saying in later years, at the moment the department spurned his proposal. Odum stormed out of the meeting in anger. Afterward, several of his colleagues, recognizing that their mockery of ecology had hurt his feelings, stopped by his office to apologize. "We actually don't know much about ecology," they said. "Why is ecology important? Does ecology have any principles?" "Of course ecology has principles," Odum replied, only to realize that no principles had yet been formulated. At home that night he began writing down a set of principles for ecology, which he then used to order his book.[50]

From the time he had left Chapel Hill, when he was twenty-three and H. T. was twelve, Gene Odum had kept up a frequent correspondence with his brother. Gene counseled H. T., whom he called Tom at the time, on bird-watching, sent him detailed accounts of his work at Western Reserve University and at the University of Illinois, and in return received detailed accounts of H. T.'s work at the University of North Carolina and Yale. They enjoyed a remarkably close personal and intellectual relationship. The letters in which H. T. described his experiences at Yale included not only extensive reports of his courses, his research, and his sometimes difficult relationship with Hutchinson, but also course notes, term papers, and examination questions. H. T. was taking his Ph.D. preliminary examination in four fields: the geochemistry of the ocean, the geochemical migrations of the alkaline earth, the biology and biochemistry of skeletons, and the uptake of ions by organisms. From these letters and from their numerous conversations, Gene began to see the usefulness of biogeochemistry to the development of the new ecosystem ecology. So in 1949, when H. T. was in his third and last year at Yale, Gene invited him to co-author *Fundamentals of Ecology*.[51]

H. T. wrote back: "Your offer about the ecology text was most generous. Certainly after all the time and energy you have put into my education, you should get some return. However by now you have accumulated years of preparation so that my contribution would in no way match. How about a couple of chapters rather than co author. Then after I have done a little more work I can really contribute to cooperative ventures. Needless to say this is one of the big reasons for wishing to come south to cooperate on southern ecology."[52]

Fundamentals of Ecology, by Eugene P. Odum, was published by W. B. Saunders in 1953. Despite expressing early interest, Macmillan had turned down the project, as had several other publishers, having concluded from a survey of ecology courses in American universities that there would be no demand for a text of its kind. Odum knew that he was departing from the standard model for the teaching of ecology, but he was confident that his book filled a niche. He stated in the book's preface that its organization was "without precedent in previous books on ecology" because it began with "the basic principles — that is, the general truths and concepts which apply widely and are not restricted to any particular segment of the subject."[53]

Fundamentals of Ecology approached nature, as Odum liked to say, "from the top down, ecosystem first," and for decades it was the only text that did so.[54] It was revolutionary in two respects: "(i) principles were presented in a whole-to-part progression with consideration of the ecosystem level as the first rather than the last chapter, and (ii) energy was selected as the common denominator for integrating biotic and physical components into functional wholes."[55] By his arrangement of chapters and his orientation toward the ecosystem, Odum rejected the traditional reductionist methodology of Western science in favor of a more holistic methodology. Consequently, the book had a powerful ideological influence on the many readers of its three editions. It taught several generations of students to focus on the whole — and in so doing blurred the line between ecology and environmentalism. Humans are part of the whole, he pointed out in "Human Ecology," the book's concluding chapter.

The arrangement of chapters also made *Fundamentals of Ecology* extremely useful in the classroom.[56] The three sections — "Basic Ecological Principles and Concepts," "The Habitat Approach," and "Applied Ecology" — allowed a variety of pedagogical experiments. The instructor could begin with part 1, the theory, and use part 2, oriented toward field and laboratory work, for reference; or begin with part 2 and use part 1 for reference. Or the class could go through both parts simultaneously and conclude with discussions stimulated by part 3.[57] Whichever plan the instructor chose, he or she would be teaching students how the "whole" functioned.

H. T. Odum, according to Gene Odum's preface to the first edition, "read and criticized all of the manuscript and . . . contributed much to the material in Chapters 4 to 7."[58] Although Gene thanked H. T. in the preface, he did not note their collaboration on the title page, to H. T.'s distress. The title page of the second edition, published in 1959, bore the words "Eugene P. Odum" in large type and "In collaboration with Howard T. Odum" in smaller type. Gene wrote in the preface to this edition: "In the preparation of both editions I have been especially fortunate to have the close collaboration of my brother, Howard Thomas Odum, Director of the Institute of Marine Science, University of Texas. Especially important has been his coauthorship of the chapter on energy relations, a field in which he is making important and highly original contributions. His contributions to all of the manuscript have helped insure a broad coverage of ideas and literature." The third edition, published in 1971, carried Eugene P. Odum's name alone, because by that time H. T. was publishing his own books and had lost interest in revising *Fundamentals*.[59] H. T. shared in the royalties of the first two editions.

The Holistic Vision of *Fundamentals of Ecology*

In *Fundamentals of Ecology* Odum enunciated a theory of nature that would become the basis of ecosystem ecology and would govern all aspects of his professional and personal lives. It rested on the assumption, which Odum took from Clements's notion of ecological succession, that undisturbed natural systems tend toward stability. Stability is, in fact, a predominant characteristic of the ecosystem according to Odum's definition: "Any entity or natural unit that includes living and nonliving parts interacting to produce a stable system in which the exchange of materials between the living and nonliving parts follows circular paths is an ecological system or ecosystem."[60] Ecological succession is "directional," in that change continues until the community of organisms can modify its habitat no further: "The orderly process of changes which we define as ecological succession results from the interaction of the organisms themselves which produces conditions favorable for a new set of organisms until the final state is reached."[61] "The final or stable community . . . is self-perpetuating and in equilibrium with the physical habitat."[62] Odum described this order as a "dynamic balance of nature."[63]

Odum's concept of stability—of the "dynamic balance of nature"—was intrinsically bound up with two other concepts: that of the interdependence of organisms in an ecosystem and that of the *whole*. Although interspecies competition had been widely noticed since Darwin's time, "cooperation" in nature, in which species benefit from their interaction, had been underestimated in its effect. Listing some of the ways in which two populations can interact, Odum called attention to commensalism, in which one population benefits; protocooperation, in which both populations benefit; and mutualism, in which both populations benefit and become interdependent, as examples of interspecies cooperation.[64] Such relationships of interdependence, he believed, help to stabilize a system.[65]

Odum rejected Clements's metaphor of the superorganism for the biotic community but retained the Clementsian conviction that communities and populations are "real entities," "group units [that] have *characteristics additional to the characteristics of the individuals composing them.* The forest is more than a collection of trees. The whole is not simply a sum of the parts."[66] Odum was applying the theory of Smuts, which he had learned from Shelford and Clements, that "both the individual functions of the parts (cells, organs, etc.) and their composition or correlation in the complex are affected and altered by the synthesis which is the whole. Not only does the synthesis of the parts influence and indeed constitute the whole; the whole in its turn impresses its character on each individual part, which feels its influence in the most real and intimate manner."[67] Because interaction among organisms affects the organisms' functions, the ecosystem has properties not predictable by analysis of its components in isolation.

Evident in Odum's vision of nature is a deep faith in an "orderly" universe with "self-design" capability. He argued that "diverse organisms usually live together in an orderly manner, not just haphazardly strewn over the earth as independent beings," for which reason he considered *synecology*, the study of groups of organisms associated together as a unit, to be central to modern ecology.[68] "As the community goes," he said, "so goes the organism."[69] Communities change in an orderly way, in ecological succession, in their progress toward an energy-balanced climax state.[70]

It was this picture of nature, whereby undisturbed ecosystems undergo orderly change in their achievement of a "dynamic balance," that made ecosystem ecology a foundation for environmentalism. Odum himself moved freely throughout *Fundamentals of Ecology* between scientific description of nature and advocacy for conservation, declaring that "the principle of the ecosystem . . . is the basic and most important principle underlying conservation."[71] He was optimistic about the power of the discipline to make a better world: "Thus, if understanding of ecological systems and moral responsibility among mankind can keep pace with man's power to effect changes, the present day concept of 'unlimited exploitation of resources' will give way to 'unlimited ingenuity in perpetuating a cyclic abundance of resources.'"[72]

Odum noted that the recognition of interdependence in ecosystem ecology required attention to the impact of human civilization on nonhuman nature. If ecosystems tend toward order and stability, on which the continuance of the human species depends, then human beings must take care not to disturb their surroundings excessively. Knowledge of ecological principles enables human beings to adjust their behavior appropriately. Since humans interact with the other organisms and with the abiotic habitat of ecosystems, ecology should expand its field of inquiry into "human ecology," Odum proclaimed. He concluded his textbook with a discussion of the population ecology of humans: "Populations of men, like other populations, are a part of larger units," he wrote; "i.e., biotic communities and ecosystems."[73] "Careful study and cooperation with natural cycles rather than wholesale 'tamperings' beyond our ability to comprehend would seem to be the sensible road to take if we are to avoid detours (perhaps permanent!) in the achievement of true dominance and the complete orderliness of man and his environment."[74]

Odum derived his vision of nature from Clements's theory of the climax formation, or superorganism; Shelford's concept of the biome; Smuts's articulation of the characteristics of the whole; Tansley's ecosystem concept; Leopold's definition of land; Lotka's theories of energy transfer; and Lindeman's energetics. However, he and H. T. had inherited their predisposition toward holism from Howard Washington Odum, who had devoted his life to promoting social harmony among the diverse inhabitants of the South. Historian Donald Worster attributed the Odum brothers' ecosystem ideology directly to the famous sociologist:

> Like him, they believed in achieving a holistic outlook on the world, not being trapped in overspecialization; and like him they wanted to see harmony flourish everywhere — harmony in the old divisive South, harmony in the nation, harmony between nations, harmony between humans and nature — instead of bitter, competitive struggle everywhere. Ecology appealed to the boys because it seemed

to be a science that dealt with harmony, a harmony found in nature, offering a model for a more organic, cooperative human community.[75]

Gene Odum encountered in Leopold's "land ethic" a connection between interdependence and cooperation not unlike that of his father's social vision. Leopold had extrapolated from his theory of natural order an ideal social order predicated on interdependence. Asserting that human beings in the course of history had expanded their communities to include all those with whom they had formed relationships of interdependence, Leopold argued that the recognition of interdependence brought about cooperation. Cooperation took the form of ethics, which Leopold defined as limitations on the individual's freedom of action in the struggle for existence that are established by the community for the benefit of the community as a whole. Once humans acknowledged their dependence on soils, waters, plants, and animals, Leopold predicted, they would enlarge their ethical community to encompass the "land."[76] Odum's environmentalism grew directly out of this creed: interdependence leads necessarily to cooperation.

Odum's argument in *Fundamentals of Ecology* that mature ecosystems achieve a state of equilibrium influenced environmentalists in the 1970s, who used the ecosystem concept as a theoretical basis for assessing human disturbance of natural processes. His inclusion of human beings in ecosystems turned ecosystem ecologists into environmentalists — that is, advocates of policies and social behaviors protective of the natural environment — erasing the line traditional to Western thought between science and politics.

Fundamentals of Ecology approached the earth as a set of interlocking ecosystems whose stability is a function of the interdependence of their component parts. With this understanding of nature, Odum was destined to advocate cooperation and attention to the whole in his politics. Odum never flagged in his advocacy of cooperation. But he achieved his great successes as a scientist, creator of institutions, and protector of the environment by being, his friends and colleagues said, "fiercely competitive"; he was a leader rather than a collaborator.[77]

3 *The Atomic Age*

The first edition of *Fundamentals of Ecology* sold nine thousand copies, a respectable number considering that few American colleges and universities even offered courses in ecology during the 1950s. Having been promised a second edition by its publisher, W. B. Saunders, and remembering his father's advice that a second edition would give him the opportunity to correct any mistakes he had made in the first, Eugene Odum began work on the revision as soon as the 1953 "red book" appeared in print. The successor "green book" did well immediately, selling more than five thousand copies in 1959, the year of its release. Not until the late 1960s, however, when the environmentalist movement was in full flower, did *Fundamentals of Ecology* make Odum famous. Between 1969 and 1971, annual sales of the textbook went from approximately sixty-two hundred to almost forty-two thousand, and Odum's picture appeared in stories on the environment in *Time, Life,* and *Newsweek.*[1] As a result of the textbook's popularity — in English and in translation into twelve other languages — *ecosystem* became the watchword of environmentalism.[2]

The preface to the second edition of *Fundamentals of Ecology,* by Eugene P. Odum in collaboration with Howard T. Odum, showed clearly the Odums' assumption that ecology would enable human beings to make a better world. "Fortunately," Gene Odum wrote, "biologists and the public alike are beginning to realize that ecological research of the most basic nature is vital to the solution of mankind's environmental problems."[3] The Odums' motivation to put ecology in the service of environmentalism came not only from the predisposition toward social responsibility they had inherited from their sociologist father and their Methodist grandfather but also from the development of atomic energy, which they recognized would generate hazardous radioactive wastes. An understanding of earth's ecosystems was urgently needed:

> Since the supply of fossil fuels is rapidly being depleted, civilization must look to atomic energy and sun energy to an increasing extent. It is generally conceded that environmental contamination, with its concurrent dangers of genetic damage, stands as the most important limiting factor in the large scale use of atomic energy in the immediate future. Even more important is the upsurge of the world's human population and its skyrocketing demands for water, food and living space. Both increasing human populations and increasing radioactivity (not to mention other forms of environmental pollution) pose difficult problems in which ecological considerations are paramount.[4]

Odum's preoccupation with the dangers environmental pollution and overpopulation posed to human civilization appeared again and again in his books and essays in the form of environmentalist advice inserted into explanations of natural phenomena. In his life as well, Odum recognized no sharp division between scientific research and its application to what he called "real world problems." For him and for H. T., ecology brought together not only biology, geology, chemistry, and physics but also the natural sciences and sociology, economics, and public policy.

The 1950s were busy years for Gene Odum. He established a research station at the Savannah River Atomic Energy Plant, conducted with H. T. a landmark study of a coral reef community on Eniwetok Atoll, attended the 1955 Geneva Conference on the Peaceful Uses of Atomic Energy as a delegate for peace, applied for and received a 1957–58 National Science Foundation Senior Postdoctoral Fellowship to study "radiation ecology," added a chapter on radiation ecology to *Fundamentals*, and began thinking of founding an institute of ecology on the campus of the University of Georgia. Odum's legacy at the university is largely in the institutions he created or helped to create: the Savannah River Ecology Laboratory near Aiken, South Carolina; the Institute of Radiation Ecology, which became the Institute of Ecology at the University of Georgia; and the Marine Institute on Sapelo Island, Georgia.

The Savannah River Ecology Laboratory

Early in 1951, the Atomic Energy Commission (AEC) announced the establishment of a plant on a 250,000-acre tract on the Savannah River outside Augusta near Aiken to produce plutonium for nuclear weapons.[5] The AEC's Division of Biology and Medicine invited proposals from the University of South Carolina and the University of Georgia for grants to provide "preinstallation" environmental inventories of the area before the construction began. Gene Odum, taught by his father to take advantage of federal support for research, saw this invitation as his chance to develop a large-scale, long-term investigation of succession in a restricted area.

On 12 April, Odum and his colleagues submitted a very ambitious proposal titled "An Ecological Study of the Savannah River AEC Installation Area," which would cost $150,000 for the first year and would put six teams into the field. It would be not merely a "survey" of the plants and animals, Odum wrote, but an "ecological study of interrelationships, indicators, population dynamics, and rate of change." The ecologists would not only give special attention to the aquatic vegetation, aquatic invertebrates, fishes, and amphibians that would be most affected by the by-products of the radio-active materials produced by the nuclear plant, but would also investigate the "total ecological complex . . . since no one can predict what problems may arise in the future." Odum would be the field director for the project.[6] On 26 April, two weeks after sending it to the Division of Biology and Medi-cine, Odum was informed that the proposal had been rejected.[7]

The Division of Biology and Medicine then invited officials of the University of Georgia and the University of South Carolina to meet at the Savan-nah River Plant site on 6 June. The president of the University of South Carolina and several of its biologists represented the University of South Carolina; and George Boyd, dean of the Graduate School and director of research, and Odum, then an associate professor of zoology, represented the University of Georgia. Walter D. Claus, chief of the Biophysics Branch of the Division of Biology and Medicine at the AEC, presided. At the meeting Claus announced that the AEC was prepared to grant $10,000 each to the University of South Carolina and the University of Georgia if they would produce an inventory of terrestrial flora and fauna.

After Claus left, the two teams divided their responsibilities: South Caro-lina would make a botanical survey and a checklist of cold-blooded ver-tebrates, and Georgia would make a checklist of invertebrates, especially arthropods, and warm-blooded vertebrates. Odum saw the imminent aban-donment of the Aiken farmlands to the forces of nature as a "golden oppor-tunity" to study old-field succession. He decided that his team would do "functional" rather than taxonomic ecology, and would address the ecosys-tem as a whole rather than separating terrestrial from aquatic research. Both groups planned to experiment with radionuclide tracers and to investigate the effects of radiation.[8]

When Odum reported the results of the meeting to his colleagues at the University of Georgia, many of those who had signed on to the origi-nal $150,000 proposal dropped out. Odum could hardly blame them, for a $10,000 grant would require them to scale down their plans considerably. He himself, however, was imagining numerous projects that could be ac-complished with a good strategy. That good strategy—which turned out to be extraordinarily good—was to bring graduate students, instead of faculty, to do the fieldwork at the Savannah River Plant (SRP) and thereby simultaneously save money and enhance the university's new Ph.D. program in the biological sciences.[9]

On 14 June 1951, Odum sent to the Atomic Energy Commission "A Proposal for an Ecological Study of Land-Use, Succession, and Indicator Invertebrate and Warm-Blooded Vertebrate Populations of the Savannah River Operations Area." The proposal called for researchers to produce an ecological map of the area that would give land-use history and successional relations; to study the populations of warm-blooded vertebrates with a census of "indicator species"—that is, those animals that would be most likely to respond to a major change in their environment; and to study the relation of arthropod populations to plant succession. Odum's aim was to initiate long-term ecological research while accomplishing the immediate objectives of the AEC. The budget of $11,934, which allotted the university $884 for overhead, included $6,600 for annual salaries for three graduate student research assistants at $2,200 each; $1,750 for a pickup truck; $1,700 for field expenses; and $1,000 for field equipment and supplies. The University of Georgia would pay Odum's salary and the salary of the assistant director, entomologist Joseph J. Paul; provide support for an additional two senior researchers; furnish secretarial assistance; and make available a reference collection and library. The five-person field team would be aided by other faculty on campus when their expertise was needed.[10] On 20 June, the Atomic Energy Commission approved the proposal, and on 23 June, according to his account, Odum logged his first full day in the field.[11]

During the summer of 1951, Odum recruited three graduate students from other universities to work at the Savannah River Plant: William H. Cross from Florida State University; Edward J. Kuenzler from the University of Florida, whom H. T. Odum had recommended; and Leslie B. Davenport Jr. from the College of Charleston.[12] By enrolling Cross and Davenport in Ph.D. programs at the university and Kuenzler in an M.S. program, Odum simultaneously built into his SRP project a link with the university's graduate school, increased the number of graduate students in the biological sciences, made the SRP a training ground for ecologists, and made the University of Georgia a center for ecological research. The Savannah River Plant would attract graduate students in ecology for the university, and the university's reputation in biology would be enhanced by the research done at the site. Because Odum had his students publish their research in refereed journals, their work, and by extension the University of Georgia, received national attention.[13] His strategy of using grant money for research assistantships proved to be brilliant, for it not only enabled him to have an operation of significant size, but also justified the university's continued involvement with the Atomic Energy Commission.[14]

That first year, Odum set up headquarters in an uncompleted mill house on the Beulah Pond dam at the northwest corner of the reservation, which he rented for twenty dollars a month. There he and his young colleagues installed a refrigerator, a couple of tables, and some bunks and set up a laboratory with microscopes, Burlese funnels, other laboratory equipment, and field gear. They used a sheet-metal trash burner as a stove for cooking—and for warmth during the winter. Beulah Pond, a small artificial lake, yielded fresh fish and frog legs for the dining table.[15]

The United States government was still in the process of moving six thousand residents and their belongings off the tract, and it had not yet purchased the land owned by Hunter M. Henry, an Augusta resident whose barn and two-bedroom cottage overlooked Beulah Pond. Henry was happy to have the University of Georgia researchers use his barn and later his cottage. When the government completed land acquisitions in 1954 and destroyed the barn and the cottage, the ecologists sorrowfully moved their headquarters into a duplex in Jackson, South Carolina, which they used for sleeping even after the AEC granted them laboratory space on the SRP reservation in 1955. By that time, the AEC had increased the University of Georgia's grant sufficiently to allow Odum to hire a fourth graduate research assistant and the site's first full-time resident ecologist, Robert A. Norris, an ornithologist and naturalist.[16] Odum designated the facility the Laboratory of Radiation Ecology.

At the outset, Odum recalled later, the SRP researchers were "beginning to think holistically, but were, in practice, acting as reductionists," dividing up the work into specific tasks that could be carried out by small groups working independently. Neither he nor his teammates "had any conception as to how the parts were supposed to fit together." Nevertheless, in January 1952, when

Odum had to brief Karl Herde, the AEC's coordinator of environmental research, Odum was able to synthesize their goals in the long-range study of succession as an exploration of the functioning of the ecosystem. "Since energy is the common denominator for all components of an ecosystem (and for man and nature as a whole)," he told Herde, the researchers "proposed to use energy flow through biological food chains as a means of linking plants and animals."[17]

The instrument that would enable Gene Odum and his colleagues to follow the energy flow through the ecosystem was the radioactive isotope. In the middle of the decade, as questions arose regarding the movements and impacts of radioactive materials in ecosystems, ecosystem ecologists attempted to apply their understanding of food webs and biogeochemical circulation to movements of radioactive pollutants. They also used radioactive tracers to delineate food webs and to measure rates of chemical transfers and transformations. The work they did with the aid of government grants had consequences for ecology far beyond the information that was of use to the AEC, however. The ecologists at the Savannah River Plant began using radionuclide tracers to track the movements of materials through trophic levels and determine turnover rates in ecosystems. Although they were not the first to experiment with the technology, the SRP ecologists were at the forefront of ecosystem tracer studies because of their access to a plentiful supply of radioactive isotopes.[18]

The radionuclide tracers enabled ecologists both to track and to quantify the movement of materials and energy through an ecosystem. By injecting radionuclides into the stems of plants, they could follow nutrients from the plants into the animals that fed on them, and then into the animals that fed on those animals. They even discovered that ants feeding on a plant protected that plant from other insects. Thus, by determining who ate whom in the food chains, the scientists were able to develop food web maps. They also gained considerable knowledge about the relationship between the metabolism of different organisms and their rate of excretion by employing radionuclide tracers in bioelimination studies. They tagged organisms with the radionuclide tracer, put the organisms back out in the wild, and after an appropriate interval located them and measured the remaining level of radioactivity. The most active organisms eliminated the most. Finally, they determined the time required for energy to move through a food chain by measuring the time necessary for radioactive carbon to move from the plant to the end of the food chain.

Thus, by using radioactive tracers the "radioecologists" could address fundamental questions regarding any ecosystem: What are the pathways of energy flow? What is the rate of energy flow? What is the residence time for elements to remain within a particular compartment? And what is the turnover rate for their moving from one compartment to the next? Radionuclides allowed ecologists to conduct an "ecological study of interrelationships, indicators, population dynamics, and rate of change" at the Savannah River Plant after all, as Gene Odum had proposed initially to the AEC.[19] The new subdivision of ecosystem ecology created at the Savannah River Plant came to be known as "radioecology."

Odum credited radioactive tracers with propelling the shift from the focus on structure to the focus on function that for him characterized modern ecology. "Just as the microscope extended our powers of observation of biological structure, so tracers have extended our powers of observation of function," he wrote in 1962.[20] For Odum, modern ecology *was* ecosystem ecology, the study of the whole.

It was during the course of his research on old-field succession at the Savannah River Plant that Odum espoused the theory of emergent properties, which he was to lay out in 1977 in a paper published in *Science*. "An important consequence of hierarchal organization," he said, "is that as components, or subsets, are combined to produce larger functional wholes, new properties emerge that were not present or not evident at the next level below."[21] Having long been familiar with that notion through his reading of Smuts's book *Holism and Evolution*, Odum turned the controversial hypothesis into an argument for the holistic study of ecosystems in the service of "solutions to most of the long-range problems of society."[22]

During the 1950s, while he was the principal investigator on the project, Odum spent much time at the Savannah River Plant. Because the SRP was a production site for plutonium, researchers there had to acquire "Q-Clearance," for which they underwent an FBI check, and neither wives nor foreign students could get it. On many weekends during the academic year, Gene left Martha and Bill alone in Athens while he did fieldwork. After Gene had established a research laboratory on Sapelo Island in 1954, he left them on Sapelo. The island proved a desirable home base, for Gene could commute along back roads between there and the SRP, and Bill and Martha loved spending time at the seashore.[23]

The Laboratory of Radiation Ecology acquired increasing importance during the late 1950s as a place for radioecologists to study the effects of radioactive contaminants in the natural environment and to use radioactive tracers to learn about the food chain. By 1960 Odum had persuaded the AEC to make the University of Georgia's laboratory a permanent institution at the Savannah River Plant, and a year later the group took over two barracks that had formerly been used by security personnel. Between 1962 and 1967, under the direction of Frank B. Golley, its first resident director, the Laboratory of Radiation Ecology was designated the Savannah River Ecology Laboratory (or SREL). Golley promptly hired ecologist Richard Wiegert, a secretary, and a technician. In 1964 the laboratory's budget increased to $170,000 and the staff grew to twenty scientists.[24]

In creating the SREL, Eugene Odum was putting into practice what he had learned from his father, who "was always running up to New York to get money from foundations."[25] Just as Howard W. Odum had taken full advantage of external grants to build up the sociology program at the University of North Carolina, Gene took advantage of the grant from the Atomic Energy Commission to build up ecology at the University of Georgia. He had been educated to realize that the actual size of the initial grant was less important than the relationship the receipt of the grant brought about. At a time when relatively few scientists were obtaining external support for their research, Gene Odum understood the dynamics of the grant-getting process.

The University of Georgia Marine Institute on Sapelo Island

On 11 August 1948, Odum was bird-watching on Sapelo Island, off the coast of Georgia, with Donald C. Scott, a colleague at the University of Georgia, and James Jenkins, an employee of the Georgia Game and Fish

Commission who was contemplating graduate work in the university's Department of Biology. Jenkins, having met the island's caretaker from an earlier trip, had obtained permission for them to search for a Mexican pheasant called the chachalaca (*Ortalis vetula*), which had been introduced to the island as a game bird in 1923. They spotted two of them. While exploring the island in the caretaker's jeep, they encountered Sapelo's owner, Richard J. Reynolds Jr. The tobacco heir was delighted to meet the naturalists, and he asked the men to examine an unusual fish that had washed ashore. He joined them in the jeep for a ride on the beach and then invited them to his oceanside cottage for lunch.[26]

The lunch was enjoyed by all. Reynolds brought out fine Scotch and engaged his visitors in a long conversation about possible uses for the island, asking whether "professors" might want to spend time there studying the vegetation and conducting experiments on the land. He had already made plans to transform the elegant "Big House," which Reynolds's pregnant wife, a coterie of medical personnel, and other guests were presently occupying, into the Sapeloe Plantation Inn resort. And in hopes of fostering research in agriculture, he had converted the island's wetlands to a cattle pasture and had expanded the animal husbandry operation.[27]

Reynolds had purchased Sapelo Island from Howard Coffin in 1933 to use primarily for vacations. Unlike his grandfather, who had made the fortune in tobacco, and his father, who had increased the family's wealth, R. J. Reynolds Jr. had done nothing more than spend it. Now he was ready to do something worthwhile for society with the land that had once been Sapelo Plantation. That August afternoon, Odum, Scott, and Jenkins tried to persuade Reynolds to set up a marine station to study the marshes and estuaries, but although Reynolds obviously enjoyed his visit with the professors, he did not share their enthusiasm for marine research. He was more inclined to pursue agriculture and forestry.[28]

Four years later, after the Sapeloe Plantation Inn had failed, Reynolds decided to set up a foundation to support a research facility in biology, agriculture, or forestry and invited President O. C. Aderhold of the University of Georgia to bring a delegation of scientists to Sapelo Island to discuss the matter. Aderhold took Odum, the deans of agriculture and forestry, and an administrative associate to meet with Reynolds, tour the island, and assess its potential for research in their respective areas of responsibility. Afterward, in October 1952, Aderhold asked the four for their views on the usefulness of the island to the university. Only Odum offered a positive response. The others said that the university already had enough research sites for agriculture and forestry elsewhere in the state.[29]

As he was to do so often, Odum seized the opportunity to extend ecological investigation to areas in the state remote from the Athens campus. He saw in Sapelo Island a research station perfect for studying the salt marshes separating the barrier islands from the mainland. On receiving an invitation to send a proposal to Reynolds's Sapelo Agriculture and Forestry Foundation, Odum submitted with Don Scott a plan for a biological research laboratory that would integrate aquatic research, which was their primary interest, with terrestrial research, Reynolds's interest. The proposed annual budget of $50,000 would support a resident staff member at an $8,000 yearly salary and three graduate students at $2,000 each. Reynolds liked the proposal and in the summer of 1953 signed a contract with President Aderhold and George H. Boyd, the dean of the Graduate School, to establish the University of Georgia Marine Biological Laboratory. The initial grant was for $25,000.

Reynolds turned over to the university the whole south end of the island, including the cattle trough, the barn, and the apartments. By the end of August Odum had identified the new resident director of the Sapelo Laboratory: Robert A. Ragotzkie, a hydrologist who had just received his Ph.D. from the University of Wisconsin.[31]

The Sapelo research staff grew rapidly. By 1956 it included Ragotzkie; Lawrence R. Pomeroy, an invertebrate zoologist; and John Teal, an ecosystem ecologist, all of whom had been given the title of assistant professor of biology at the University of Georgia. They lived in the apartments and worked in the barn, which had been converted into a laboratory with offices in the former cow stalls. The cattle trough was transformed into a running seawater system. The staff used a tugboat, the *Kit Jones*, which Reynolds had bequeathed them, to bring equipment back and forth from the mainland. The limited electricity, which a diesel generator provided, poor heating and air-conditioning in the apartments and the lab, and ubiquitous rats made conditions less than ideal, but the scientists were satisfied with the work they were able to accomplish.[32]

Odum had no administrative role in the development of what became, in 1959, the University of Georgia Marine Institute. Ragotzkie reported directly to Boyd, who had designated himself the principal investigator of the Reynolds grant. Odum did, however, send many graduate students to Sapelo to conduct their thesis and dissertation research, and he visited frequently and for extended periods in the summers, bringing along Martha, who painted, and Bill, who fished, while he studied the marshlands. Over the many years in which Gene maintained a research connection with the Marine Institute, Martha produced hundreds of watercolors, which made her famous as a chronicler of the island.[33]

The insight Odum gained from his first encounter with Sapelo's salt-marsh estuary profoundly influenced his environmentalist philosophy. He recalled his introduction to the estuary decades later:

We moved up tidal creeks in small outboard motorboats on ebbing tides. As the water rushed by and the boats sank lower, we found ourselves in deep canyons of golden mud banks (the color, as we were to learn later, due to immense populations of diatoms and other algae), topped by six-foot high stands of marsh grass looking for all the world like a well-fertilized stand of sugar cane. Samples of the outrushing water revealed a heavy load of suspended matter which most people would call mud, but which on closer inspection, proved to contain large amounts of organic detritus (particulate organic matter rich in vitamins and calories). The notion came to us, in those early days, that we were in the arteries of a remarkable energy-absorbing natural system whose heart was the pumping action of the tides. The entire tideland complex of barrier islands, marshes, creeks, and river mouths was a single operational unit linked together by the tide. If we were right, each part of the system would have to be dependent for its life-sustaining energy not only on the direct rays of the sun, but also on the energy of the tides. Could it be, we asked, that organisms in this environment have not only evolved to become adapted to the stresses of this energetic environment, but have learned (through natural selection) how to convert some of the tidal energy to useful metabolism for their own advantage? Does nature routinely exploit tidal power as men have dreamed of doing for centuries? In the past biologists who studied estuarine and seashore organisms had been preoccupied with how such life adapts to the obvious stresses; that some of the stresses might be converted to subsidies was, and still is, something of a new theory. This germ of an idea, subsequently developed by twenty years of team research on Sapelo, will, we hope, provide the basis for man to design with, rather than against, nature on this remarkable sea coast.[34]

Odum was quick to recognize in 1954 that designing *with* such forces rather than against them would serve human beings well in the long term, for he had just been writing about cooperation in nature in his textbook. The analogy of the ecosystem to the circulatory system of an organism came naturally to him. He had often explained his shift from the study of individual organisms — his dissertation on the heart rates of birds — to the study of ecosystems as an expansion of his interest in physiology. He had gone from a focus on the function of a bird's circulatory system to a focus on the function of an ecosystem's circulatory system. The common denominator was his interest in how systems worked.

Eniwetok

"All in all there is no better way to become impressed with the functional operation of a community than to put on a face mask and explore a coral reef," Gene Odum wrote in the 1959 edition of *Fundamentals of Ecology*.[35] That is just what he and H. T. did for six weeks in the summer of 1954, when they traveled to the Japtan Reef in the Eniwetok Atoll of the South Pacific, where the United States government had been testing atomic weapons.[36]

Eniwetok had been a United States marine base and a nuclear test site since World War II. Increasing concern over the effects of nuclear fallout and radiation on living organisms led the AEC, which had already established an association with Gene Odum through the Savannah River Plant, to contract with Gene and the University of Georgia for a detailed ecological study of the atoll. Gene asked H. T. to join him on the project because H. T., then an assistant professor of biology at the University of Florida, had been developing techniques to study energy flow in an ecosystem.[37] The graduate work he had done with G. Evelyn Hutchinson at Yale on the biogeochemistry of the ocean also made H. T. a valuable partner for the project. They could use H. T.'s techniques to test a controversial idea: that the live coral polyps and the green algae growing on them formed a symbiotic animal-plant relationship.

Gene and H. T. recognized that the one-way flow of water across an inter-island coral reef would enable them to determine the reef's metabolic activity. All they needed to do was sample the water before and after it went through the reef and record the differences. They selected for their experiments the relatively undisturbed Japtan Reef, situated between two uninhabited islands a short helicopter ride away from the military base.

For their investigation of the reef Gene and H. T. outfitted a small raft with empty wooden ammunition boxes to hold their face masks, snorkels, life preservers, a portable battery-powered colorimeter for measuring phosphorus levels in the water, a battery-powered lantern for alerting the marine helicopter of their location when it came to pick them up at night, an underwater flashlight for nighttime snorkeling, notepads and pencils, and the sandwiches and soft drinks the cooks at the base had prepared for them. They would anchor the raft in waist-deep water and spend up to six hours wading, sometimes at high tide and other times at low tide, taking measurements and examining the coral. Although they wore shirts and hats, their faces got very sunburned, and because of the strong currents their calves got very muscular. They wore high-topped tennis shoes and gloves to protect themselves from the sharp coral.

Their measurements showed that the water alone was too poor in nutrients—with too little plankton—to support the rapid growth of the coral, thus demonstrating the dependence of the coral polyps on the photosynthesis of the algae that bored into the coral's calcium skeleton. The coral head in turn recycled nutrients to the algae. Their detection of much higher levels of radioactivity in the algae on the dead reef surfaces than in the algae on the live coral led the Odums to deduce that the living polyps not only supported the algae nutritionally but also protected them from radioactivity and other environmental dangers.[38] In such "mutualistic" relationships, as defined in *Fundamentals of Ecology*, the "growth and survival of both populations is benefited and neither can survive under natural conditions without the other."[39]

Zoologists had long been interested in coral because of the difficulty of classifying it. In one of his later textbooks Gene would describe it as follows:

> Coral is a plant-animal "superorganism," since algae, called zooanthellae, grow
> in the tissues of the animal polyp. The animal component gets its "vegetables"
> from the algae growing in its belly, and obtains its "meat" by extending its ten-
> tacles at night to fish for zooplankton in the water flowing past its limestone
> house—which the colony builds by depositing calcium carbonate from raw mate-
> rial that is plentiful in the ocean. The plant component of this partnership gets
> protection and nitrogen and other nutrients from the animal component.[40]

The Odums had shown that symbiosis maintained the relationship between the coral and the algae in equilibrium. But it was not simply the explanation of that relationship that made their Eniwetok study important to ecologists; it was the scientific method by which Gene and H. T. proved that relationship. For an ecosystem to achieve a "steady state" its gross production (P) must be approximately equal to its consumption, or respiration (R). That is, the rate of photosynthesis, or oxygen production, must be approximately equal to the rate of respiration, the energy the system expends on maintenance. Gross production is the total amount of energy that is converted from sunlight into food or other organic materials. When P equals R, the system is in equilibrium. Gene and H. T. applied a "diurnal flow" method, which H. T. had developed a couple of years earlier, informed by a technique two scientists working in the Marshall Islands had invented at the end of the 1940s to derive an ecosystem's energy budget. By measuring dissolved gases in the water at night, in the absence of photosynthesis, and during the day, in its presence, they were able to generate an energy balance sheet.[41] Gene and H. T. discovered that the coral reef community was actually producing slightly more than it consumed, about 4 percent; that the coral and algae were symbiotic; and that the ecosystem was functioning "not far from a steady state balance of growth and decay." In their conclusion they cited

S. J. Holmes's stability principle: "as an open system, the construction of self regulating interactions has led by selective process to the survival of the stable."[42]

The Odums had proven that the coral reef was operating "not far from a steady state balance of growth and decay" by employing a functional approach to the ecosystem rather than the structural approach characteristic of most ecological studies of biological communities. If they had focused on the coral reef's structure, they would have had to acquire knowledge of the multitudinous species in the biological community before concluding that it had achieved a steady state. The brothers actually had little such knowledge, being so unfamiliar with coral that they could identify few of the species they were encountering. Their work opened up the possibility of recognizing a steady state and evaluating stages of succession in an ecosystem without having to develop an encyclopedic catalog of the ecosystem's components. They showed that the metabolism of the whole can be understood without comprehensive information about the metabolism of its constituent organisms.[43]

In the jargon of ecologists, Gene and H. T. had "black-boxed" the coral reef. Gene later explained the method's advantages to both scientific investigation and environmental management:

> In this approach, one first delimits an area, a system, or a problem of interest, as a sort of "black box." Then the energy and other inputs and outputs are examined, and the major functional processes of the system as a whole are assessed. Following the parsimonious principle, one then examines such operationally significant components or groups of components (populations and physical factors) as are determined by observing, by modeling, or by perturbing, the system (as a means of identifying operationally important components). In this approach, one goes into great detail in the study of components, but only as far as may be necessary to understand or manage the system as a whole.[44]

The Odums published their findings in *Ecological Monographs* in July 1955 in a paper titled "Trophic Structure and Productivity of a Windward Coral Reef Community on Eniwetok Atoll." The article won the Mercer Award from the Ecological Society of America in 1956, and came to be considered a "landmark in ecological research." It was important to the discipline of ecology for the understanding it provided of a stable, self-regulating ecosystem, and important to the Odums as confirmation of their belief in the "balance of nature."[45] Controversial for challenging the prevailing opinion about coral, the article sparked intense discussion at a 1956 Scripps Institute of Oceanography international conference. Gene was sent free airline tickets to La Jolla, California, to engage in debate with experts in marine biology skeptical of his findings. Gene was not at all taken aback by the skepticism he encountered there: "I have never been disturbed if my theories were not proven right," he said many times. "I wanted to stimulate work. In this case our theory was proven right." The article was stimulating indeed. It inspired numerous other studies of mutualism and influenced ecosystem ecology for the next several decades.

The Eniwetok article substantially advanced the ecological reorientation then under way, which shifted the attention of ecologists from organisms to, in Aldo Leopold's words, the "fountain of energy flowing through a circuit of soils, plants, and animals." Initiated by Leopold and Lindeman, the reorientation actually represented a revolution in the history of Western thought. Darwin had undermined, but not overthrown, the atomistic, mechanistic, and dualistic model of nature implicit in Western science and philosophy since the seventeenth century. In that model, originating in Greek antiquity, nature ultimately consisted of atoms interacting mechanically with each other to form a world that humans, possessed of a mind separable from material nature, could observe and describe impartially.[46] With the theory of evolution by natural selection Darwin undermined the spirit/matter dualism and its corresponding man/nature dualism when he depicted nature as a dynamic system of which human beings are an integral part, having evolved like all other organisms according to nature's laws. But it was Leopold, with his argument that food chains are conduits of energy, and Lindeman, with his black-box method for studying an ecosystem's energy flow, who presented a nonatomistic model of nature in which the component organisms are but vessels through which energy passes. The Odums used this nonatomistic model as the foundation for ecosystem ecology.

Although the Odums were not themselves aware of the metaphysical implications of their focus on energy flow through ecosystems rather than on populations within them, philosopher J. Baird Callicott, thirty years later, recognized that focus as a reversal of traditional conceptual priorities. Callicott saw ecosystem ecology as moving in the same direction as physics, in which "energy seems to be a more fundamental and primitive reality than are material objects or discrete entities." For ecosystem ecologists, Callicott said, "ecological interactions, primarily and especially trophic relationships, constitute a macrocosmic network or pattern through which solar energy, fixed by photosynthesis, is transferred from organism to organism until it is dissipated. Organisms are moments in this network, knots in this web of life."[47] Whereas in the atomistic view of nature entities determined the nature of relationships, in physics and in ecosystem ecology relationships determine the nature of the entities. More concretely, "ecosystemic wholes are logically prior to their component species because the nature of the part is determined by its relationship to the whole. That is, more simply and concretely expressed, a species has the particular characteristics that it has because those characteristics result from its adaptation to a niche in an *ecosystem*."[48]

Thus ecosystem ecology, as the Odums defined it, abandoned both the philosophical assumptions that governed Western science and the reductionist methodology that grew out of them. That methodology the Odums considered appropriate to the study of mechanical interactions but not to the study of complex biological systems. Just as Gene Odum had employed a whole-before-the-parts approach in *Fundamentals of Ecology*, Gene and H. T. looked first at the coral reef as a complex whole and *then* at its parts. When they looked at the whole from a functional perspective, they saw emergent properties, properties not predictable from reductionist analysis of the individual components of the system.

"We theorized," Gene wrote later, "that the observed high rate of primary production for the reef as a whole was an emergent property resulting from symbiotic linkages that maintain efficient energy exchange and nutrient recycling between plant and animal components."[49] In his 1983 textbook *Basic Ecology*, Gene described the productivity and diversity of coral reefs as emergent properties found only at the level of the reef community.[50] The

Eniwetok experience corroborated his conviction that "the whole is greater than the sum of its parts."

The Odums were in the ecological vanguard in 1954 in their rejection of the West's traditional conceptual order, but their belief in ecosystem equilibrium would be challenged by ecologists of the next generation. In the 1970s, several influential studies appeared to disprove the long-standing assumption that succession leads to equilibrium, and to lend support to a nonecosystem ecology centered on Darwinian competition among organisms and rooted in genetics.[51] By 1990 Daniel Botkin was calling the belief that nature returned to a state of balance and harmony after disturbance "an ancient theme of nature" that could not be verified by observation.[52] By 1998 Gene himself had modified his views in response to the developments in his discipline. In *Ecological Vignettes* he stated: "We now understand that, while there are very important balances in nature, such as the balance between atmospheric oxygen and carbon dioxide that has persisted for aeons, there is no such thing as a central control device (like a thermostat) that keeps nature as a whole in equilibrium."[53]

But in 1954 few ecologists questioned the concept of equilibrium, which was actually the linchpin not only of the Odums' science but also of their environmentalism. Equilibrium was the determinant of an ecosystem's maturity and the marker of a stable relationship between humans and their nonhuman environment. Departure from equilibrium signaled danger for an ecosystem's inhabitants, both human and nonhuman. For the Odums and a generation of environmentalists influenced by ecosystem ecology, stability was the standard by which to measure an ecosystem's health.

The Odums moved easily between science and environmentalism, both in their Eniwetok study and in their later writings. Their approach to nature — their focus on energy flow rather than on individual organisms, and their attention to the whole rather than its parts — allowed them to gain an understanding of ecosystem functions that was unavailable through traditional approaches and that was conducive to environmentalist lessons. For example, the Odums used the interdependence of coral and algae, which they discovered by looking at the reef as a whole and tracking its energy flow, as an emblem of the interdependence of humans and the natural environment. From within the traditional Western Cartesian model of nature, in which scientists looked at the parts first, the interdependence was not evident. But from within the holistic model, in which the Odums looked at energy flow first, the interdependence was indeed evident. And such interdependence indicated the vulnerability of an ecosystem to disturbance by human actions, signaled by disequilibrium.

The coral reef article brought the scientific community's attention to Eugene Odum and Howard T. Odum as a powerful intellectual team, brothers who were united in their motivations and complementary in their fields of expertise. And it brought the brothers' attention to the fruitful possibilities of collaboration. According to Gene, he and H. T. had a marvelous summer together, despite having left their families behind in San Francisco when they boarded the military cargo plane that took them to the Marshall Islands. They lived on the marine base, where they enjoyed good food, convivial relations with the military personnel, and laboratory facilities; and they received free helicopter rides to and from the atoll whenever they wished, day or night. They alternated between working on the atoll, where they would sample the water at different times of the diurnal cycle and explore the reef, and working in the laboratory on base. Their greatest fun came from their nighttime underwater excursions into the reef, Gene said, when with their flashlight they could swim through the canyons and see the coral polyps extending their tentacles to catch plankton "like people waving handkerchiefs from the windows of city buildings." They carefully avoided the deadly stonefish, whose camouflage made its spines difficult to spot, and the moray eels and sharks prowling the canyons, but they were often stung by the tentacles of the coral.

Gene Odum took away from Eniwetok an environmental ethic that he expounded in one book after another to the end of the century. The coral community answered for him the question of how to prosper in a world of limited resources. In *Ecological Vignettes*, published in 1998 when he was eighty-five years old, he wrote:

> We can now say that *close encounters of the mutual kind* are the basis for the coral reef's success in overcoming resource limitation. Producers and consumers

(plants and animals) live in intimate contact and aid each other. There is little waste that is not used or recycled by some member of the community. Sunlight and water flow are efficiently used as energy sources. The diversity of species insures that all the "jobs," or ecological niches, necessary for an efficient and regenerative "economy" will be carried out by some critter or group of critters.

The lesson we learn can be stated as follows: *When things get tight and resources are scarce, it pays to cooperate for mutual benefit.* Or, we might even say, *we have to work together in order to survive.*[54]

Atoms for Peace

In 1955, for two weeks, Gene Odum attended the Conference on the Peaceful Uses of Atomic Energy in Geneva as an official delegate of the United States. There he heard the conference chair, Homi J. Bhabha of India, proclaim the commencement of a new era for humankind. In the use of energy, Bhabha said, human civilization had passed through the ages of "muscle power" and "fossil fuels" and was now entering "the atomic age."[55] According to Odum, Bhabha predicted that by 1975 electricity generated by atomic plants would be so cheap that utility companies would simply charge a flat fee for its use and not bother to meter it. Since "the atom is everywhere," nations would enjoy equality in their access to energy. When Odum and a few others asked about nuclear waste disposal, they were assured that it would be a minor engineering problem.[56]

In his own address at the conference, a collaboration with H. T. titled "Consideration of the Total Environment in Power Reactor Waste Disposal," Gene Odum elaborated the problems he foresaw with nuclear energy. He gave particular attention to waste disposal, stating that "safe disposal of radioactive waste products resulting from large scale uses of atomic energy for power or other peaceful purposes involves not only the protection of individuals from direct effects, but also an understanding of the long term influences of low level radiations on aquatic and terrestrial environments into which the by-products may be released."[57] Ecosystems, Odum said, have "unique characteristics which are additional to those of the individual organisms or units making up the functional entity." Accordingly, every large atomic power plant should have a radiation ecologist to study the effects of radiation on the surrounding biotic community. The existing practice of studying radiation's effects on cells, tissues, and individual organisms, "while valuable," would not yield the knowledge of radiation's total impact on the "higher levels of biological organization as represented by the population, the biotic community and the biogeochemical cycles vital to the functioning of world ecological systems." [58]

The following January, Odum vigorously attacked the use of an "experimental animal monitor" for radiation testing in a paper he presented at the Conference on Radioactive Isotopes in Agriculture in Michigan. That practice, he said, would not reveal the potential for the radiation's concentration at different stages in the food chain and its harm to a variety of organisms in the ecosystem. In the atomic age, problems of waste disposal would "shift from last to first consideration." To determine the potential harm to humans and other organisms, ecologists would have to develop methods of assaying radiation's "total effects on ecosystems." [59]

In the early years of the atomic age, President Dwight D. Eisenhower, who had conceived the idea for the Geneva "atoms for peace" conference, had high hopes for atomic power, and Americans of all walks of life were eager to learn about its benefits. Consequently, the United States government funded all kinds of research — both basic and applied — that could be related in some way to atomic power, as Gene Odum was quick to notice. Odum was to profit personally from the national obsession, first in the form of government grants to investigate succession at the Savannah River Plant site; next in the form of a fellowship to develop expertise in radiation; and finally, in the late 1960s, in the form of public interest in ecosystem ecology and enthusiasm for environmentalism. That enthusiasm, in part driven by the "Ban the Bomb" movement and the fear of nuclear contamination, drove up the sales of his textbook. Ecosystem ecology flourished in the atomic age because nuclear energy provided the incentive to understand how radiation could permeate a biotic system, the tools — radionuclides — to carry out the investigation of the whole, and the money to do it.

Frank B. Golley, Odum's longtime associate at the Savannah River Plant in the 1950s and at the Institute of Ecology thereafter, explained in his *History of the Ecosystem Concept in Ecology* that before the escalation of the Vietnam War, American ecologists perceived no problem in a close relationship with the military. The scientists "tended to accept the cold war as a fact of life and welcomed the opportunities military research made available." The government offered generous grants for studying the accumulation of radioactive material in organisms in the vicinity of nuclear explosions and for studying the transfer of radioactivity through food chains.[60] For that reason, according to Golley, the United States became the world leader in ecosystem ecology. The AEC's interests in baseline conditions at atomic energy plants, in the assimilation into the environment of radioactive materials produced by weapons testing, and in the effects of ionizing radiation on biological systems propelled governmental funding of research at the ecosystem level, reinforcing the dominance of ecosystem ecology within the broad discipline of ecology.[61]

Odum returned to the University of Georgia after the Geneva conference realizing that he knew little about the effects of atomic waste on the environment. So he applied for and received a National Science Foundation Senior Postdoctoral Fellowship for 1957–58 to study atomic energy and to complete the second edition of *Fundamentals of Ecology*, with a new chapter on "radiation ecology." He obtained a leave of absence from the University of Georgia to spend four months each in Los Angeles, California, working in the UCLA library and at the UCLA Energy Project; in Richland, Washington, at the Hanford Atomic Energy Plant; and in Oxford, England, in the laboratory of Charles Elton.

Odum went to UCLA for several reasons: the university had a number of scientific journals in its library that the University of Georgia did not have, and it had a radioecology laboratory that had been monitoring the effects of atomic explosions at the Nevada Proving Grounds. That fall, Odum joined UCLA biologists and ecologists on their frequent three-hour train trips from Los Angeles to Las Vegas to observe the open-air tower tests and to sample the fallout from the mushroom clouds.

Odum wrote his colleagues back home a long letter about life in Mercury, Nevada, where the tests took place:

Life at Mercury revolves around a little pole in the center of the great cluster of one-story buildings; on this pole little flags fly by day and a light shines by night. If flag or light is blue then a dawn test is "on," if red it is off and if white none are scheduled. "Shots" as each "device" is called can only be completed when upper winds are blowing in such a way as not to carry the "fallout" over any of the small towns. Thus the weather boys control the schedule and they will often postpone test at the last minute. Actually the predictions are quite accurate and the path that will be taken by the fallout cloud can be charted in advance with great precision which in turn enables the biological teams to get their sampling devices out directly under the path a few hours before the fallout comes down. At 10 PM there is a weather briefing if a shot is scheduled; if favorable winds are predicted then everything rolls into high gear and mankind takes on a reversed diurnal rhythm; cafeterias open at 2 AM for breakfast and mobile units of coffee and doughnuts move into field areas 30–40 miles to the north. Even offices and labs not directly concerned with actual test operate on a different schedule during test days, working at night and sleeping by day. At 3 AM the final weather briefing takes place; often the test is called off then, but everyone is resigned to it, even the biological teams who may have traveled 200 miles out into the desert to get into position only to have to turn around again and do it all over the next night. If the blue light is still on then the pattern of activity accelerates. At about 4:30 everyone at the base who is not already in the field hops into available cars, trucks or buses and starts for the observation ridge overlooking Yucca Flats where the "bomb" is waiting silently in the dark of the night. It is quite a sight to see a string of little red tail lights many miles long stretching out over the desert. No matter how many tests there have been everyone who can wants to see each one; there is a kind of inner excitement which seems not to be dulled by repeated occurrences since each one is different and often highly experimental so that one is never *quite* sure what will happen. Like ships, the shots are given names and come to have a "personality" of their own (the present series is named after mountains,— Whitney, Rainier, etc.). On reaching the observation ridge cars park in well-ordered government-type rows . . . and everyone gets out to stand or sit on bleachers under searchlights. At 30 minutes before scheduled explosion a voice begins to count off the minutes — 30 minutes before zero, 29 minutes before zero, etc. At five minutes the seconds are counted, and at one minute everyone is instructed to put on dark goggles or turn and face the other way (The light for the first few seconds is so bright that one could be blinded). Then the countdown 10 . . . 9 . . . 8 . . . 7 . . . 6 . . . 5 . . . 4 . . . 3 . . . 2 . . . 1 . . . 0. At this instant someone in the buildings just above throws that last of an incredibly complicated series of electronic gadgets which will not only detonate the device but equally important will also start the hidden camera and other recording devices which will later form the highly secret record of what happened that no eye could follow. Then, 30 miles away the fireball silently appears incredibly bright even thru extremely thick goggles. As the fireball rises and draws up with it the familiar stem of the "mushroom" one waits and braces for the shock wave. It seems ages before the hot breath passes by and the "boom" can be heard. In wide open spaces distances are deceptive so that while it is 30–40 miles away from the explosion it seems much closer. I should point out, of course, that the position on the observation ridge is an entirely safe one in so far as radioactivity is concerned; the intense radioactivity all goes up in the cloud and unless the weather boys should really goof one knows that the cloud will move off in some other direction! Some of radioactive material, of course, will fall back to the "ground zero" but practically none will be found for more than a couple miles radius; instead most of it goes off and is deposited in an unbelievably narrow line (not more than five miles wide with high activity only about a mile wide) strung out for many miles. This midline is charted carefully by airplanes which immediately follow the cloud (at a respectable distance). Also, as [the radioactive] cloud reaches into maximum height and before it begins to move off, fiery little rockets appear out of nowhere and pass thru the cloud taking a sample as they go; then little planes appear out of nowhere and begin chasing the rockets to find out exactly where they fall to the ground; later, when it is light enough helicopters come and pick up the rockets. By this time, the sun is beginning to rise over the mountains and the ominous cloud becomes a beautiful pink (if one wanted to be poetic or rather corny, he could speak of an "atomic sunrise"!). In other words the whole thing is quite a show.[62]

The day before the early-morning tests the UCLA scientists would ride out across the desert along the line the mushroom cloud was supposed to follow downwind and put out trays with little plastic bottles to collect the fallout. When the nuclear tests were postponed, the scientists would have to collect the trays to keep for the next attempt. Sometimes the tests were postponed three or four times in a row, Odum recalled. When a bomb was to be detonated, the scientists would position themselves on a hill five or ten miles upwind from the tower to watch the blast. After the explosion, they would go back across the desert to collect the trays along with a few wild animals, such as jackrabbits and small rodents, to see what the animals along the fall line had picked up. What they discovered was alarming: the animals a hundred miles downwind from the blast were more radioactive than those nearby. The small particles carrying strontium 90, formed late in the fission reaction, traveled farther than the heavier particles, which fell immediately to the ground. Consequently, the danger of radioactive fallout entering the food chain, in the form of the small soluble particles carrying the strontium 90, was greater a hundred miles away from ground zero than two miles away. Later the scientists learned that some of the light particles entered the stratosphere and traveled around the world.[63]

The experience of working with the UCLA radioecologists in the Nevada Proving Grounds did much to prepare Odum for writing the chapter on radiation ecology, and so did his visits to the Hanford Atomic Energy Plant and Oxford. At the Hanford plant, Odum became acquainted with the concept of biological magnification, or food chain concentration, which scientists there had discovered through studies on the Columbia River. In his textbook Odum described in detail the phenomenon whereby a radioactive isotope released into the environment at a seemingly harmless level becomes increasingly concentrated at each step in the food chain. Recognizing the potential danger of even tiny dosages, he declared: "In other words we could give 'nature' an apparently innocuous amount of radioactivity and have her give it back to us in a lethal package!"[64]

At Oxford University Odum met Charles Elton, author of the 1927 textbook *Animal Ecology,* and worked in his laboratory and in his Bureau of Animal Populations. Elton had contributed to the discipline of ecology the paradigm of the natural community as a simplified economy operating on the basis of four principles: the food chain; food size, or the relation of optimum food size to its consumer; the "pyramid of numbers"; and the "niche," which he defined as the status or occupation of the organism in the biotic community—its job in the economy of nature.[65] While at Oxford, Odum joined one of Elton's students in research on population density in a species of underground ant, for which they used a radionuclide tracer.[66] He also spent many hours talking with Elton himself, usually at morning coffee or afternoon tea (for which he made an appointment ahead of time), and succeeded in persuading Elton to read the draft he had completed there of the second edition of *Fundamentals of Ecology*.[67]

In the preface to the second edition Odum triumphantly claimed victory for an ecology devoted to function: "Until comparatively recently, ecologists were content to describe how nature 'looks' (sometimes by means of fantastic terms!) and to speculate on what she may have looked like in the past or might look like in the future. Now, an equal emphasis is being placed on what nature 'does,' and rightly so, because the changing face of nature can never be understood unless her metabolism is also studied!" The attention to the food chain that Elton had called for and which radionuclide tracers had facilitated had effected the revolution from structure to function that Odum had advocated for so long.

In the textbook's chapter "Radiation Ecology," Odum explained the danger to humans of radiation in the natural environment through the concept of an organism's niche in a complex biotic system:

> Should a system receive a higher level of radiation than that under which it evolved, nature will not take it "lying down," so to speak; adaptations and adjustments will occur along with the elimination of sensitive strains or species. So long as the eliminated component is replaced by a similar component which "does the same job" in the community, not much overall effect on the system may result (assuming the eliminated component is not man!). If, on the other hand, the components in question are different or belong to different trophic levels, a considerable total effect might result, which would disturb the adjustment of the system.[68]

A reductionist examination of radiation's effect on individual organisms or species would not reveal the potential damage to the ecosystem as a whole. Even using human beings to test for radiation tolerance, Odum pointed out, would not provide adequate knowledge of a safety threshold, because radioactive isotopes may concentrate in some components of the environment — such as bird eggs — more than others. Odum concluded the chapter with a section on nuclear waste disposal, which he warned would pose a far greater problem to human society in the future than fallout, in the absence of atomic war. And he made a plea for the involvement of ecologists in decisions regarding the release of waste material into the environment.

By the time he was ready to leave Oxford, Odum had accomplished all that he had intended during his sabbatical from the University of Georgia. The writing of the chapter on radiation ecology, which he could not have done without his interaction with the scientists at UCLA, Hanford, and Oxford, symbolized for him a turning point in the development of both his own intellect and the field of ecosystem ecology, for which he was now recognized as a leading proponent. His career was going well, and the University of Georgia had honored him the previous spring by appointing him Alumni Foundation Distinguished Professor of Zoology.

Throughout his life Gene exploited every opportunity possible to have his family with him on long trips. He had brought Martha and Bill with him to the Geneva conference, taking them through Italy, Spain, France, and Switzerland before the meeting and through England afterward. During his sabbatical year he did the same. In the fall, Martha and Bill joined him in Los Angeles, where Bill, always an excellent student, enrolled in Samuel High School, whose open campus and international student body provided a sharp contrast with the public high school he attended in Athens. Martha's father had died the preceding year, so Gene and Martha invited her mother, Bernice Huff, to join them for Christmas in Santa Monica. In January, Gene, Martha, and Bill moved on to Richland, Washington, where Martha learned that she had breast cancer in an early stage. Never one to complain, she recovered from her surgery, a lumpectomy, in time for Gene to take her, Bill, and her mother across the Atlantic.

Gene and Martha included Martha's mother on almost all of their long trips thereafter, and Bernice was an enthusiastic traveler. That summer the four of them flew to Norway and then traveled through Sweden, Denmark, Finland, Holland, Belgium, Scotland, Wales, and England before reaching their destination in Oxford. Once Gene was settled in Oxford, Martha took Bill and her mother on what she described as a "fast, hectic jaunt" through Switzerland, Italy, and France, then back to Oxford, where they lived for the rest of the summer in an apartment with Gene.

The following summer, in 1959, Odum resumed his five-year appointment as instructor in charge of the marine ecology course at the Marine Biological Laboratory at Woods Hole, Massachusetts. He had visited the prestigious laboratory for the first time in August 1956, when he and Martha and Bill had traveled through New England on their way to Rensselaerville, New York, for the anniversary of the founding of the E. N. Huyck Preserve. Gene was surprised to be asked to return to Woods Hole as a member of the staff, since at the time he felt that he knew little about marine ecology. But he accepted the appointment with pleasure. So, with the exception of the year 1958, when H. T. substituted for him while he was at Oxford, Gene and his family spent summers from 1957 through 1961 on Cape Cod. Bill fished with the marine biologists, and Martha "painted like mad," recalled Gene, and had numerous exhibitions of her work.

For Gene Odum, Woods Hole was a "crossroads of science." The world's leading scientists offered summer courses there in invertebrate zoology, physiology, embryology, marine botany, and marine ecology. Odum found the gathering of these great thinkers from many different countries with many different ideas both extraordinarily stimulating at the time and valuable to him for the rest of his life. Woods Hole dramatically expanded his intellectual expertise, which heretofore had been in terrestrial ecology; brought him into contact with individuals from many nations, with whom he later traded invitations to lecture and give seminars; and acquainted him with new trends.

Odum liked the team-teaching approach, and taught his course with three colleagues from different disciplines associated with marine ecology. Focusing on a marine pond, he would have his students study the major components—such as phytoplankton, zooplankton, bottom fauna, decomposers, fish, and nutrients — "in terms of their composition in various habitats and in relation to basic cycles of matter and the flow of energy." Marine experts passing through Woods Hole whom Odum could persuade to join the class offered their own perspectives on the function of that ecosystem. Odum himself instructed his students in the "fundamentals" of ecology.[69]

Odum tried to convince the administration of the Woods Hole laboratory to establish a center for ecosystem ecology, but he was unsuccessful. So he turned his attention back to the University of Georgia.

The Institute of Ecology

By the early 1960s the Atomic Energy Commission had funded large-scale environmental programs not only at the Savannah River Site but also at Oak Ridge, Tennessee; Brookhaven, New York; Argonne, Illinois; Hanford, Washington; and Puerto Rico.[70] Radioecology was thereby becoming an important subdiscipline of ecology, and the scientists at the Savannah River Ecology Laboratory were contributing significantly to its development. SREL was well represented at the First National Symposium on Radioecology held at Colorado State University in Fort Collins in September 1961. Odum gave two papers, one of them with Frank Golley on the use of radioactive tracers to measure energy flow in an ecosystem.[71] The time was ripe to create an institute for the study of radiation ecology at the University of Georgia.[72]

In 1961, Odum and his colleagues began planning an Institute of Radiation Ecology that "would be independent of any department and which could, therefore, promote and administer off-campus and other team research that must involve staff and students from many disciplines."[73] Seeing little need to await approval from the Board of Regents, they organized the institute themselves and operated it informally for several years, with Odum as its director, before submitting a formal proposal.

In 1966 the Board of Regents granted approval, initially for the Institute of Radiation Ecology, and then, after University of Georgia ecologists asked to have "Radiation" removed from the title, for the Institute of Ecology. The university located the institute in Rock House, originally called Lumpkin House because it was once the home of Governor Wilson Lumpkin of Georgia. Rock House was a small three-story building located south of the football stadium where the university was situating its new science buildings. The ecologists were delighted with the space. Odum became the institute's official director, and in 1967 Frank Golley became its executive director.[74]

As Golley recalled, Odum "by self admission, was not interested in day to day administration. He was more interested in observing trends and patterns and then taking advantage of opportunities. He was uninterested in managing faculty or researchers and in discussing and debating alternatives for the Institute administration or research programs."[75] Odum left the management of the institute to Golley, who later succeeded him as its director.

Gene Odum was an impassioned competitor both within the university and without. While always looking for instances of cooperation in nature, he demonstrated a marked inclination to view his colleagues outside the institute as rivals for resources. His philosophical antagonism toward reductionists developed in part because of the campaigns he had to wage against them, first to get ecology recognized as a legitimate science, and then to get the discipline to focus on the ecosystem. But part of the antagonism arose because of the battles he had to fight for financial support for ecologists at the University of Georgia both against other departments and against the administration. In both realms, from his standpoint, the reductionists presented primary obstacles to his aspirations. It was reductionists who dismissed ecology in the 1940s as lacking principles; it was reductionists who questioned ecosystem science for its inexactitude; and it was reductionists who seemed—at least until the mid-1960s—to capture most of the in-state funds available to biological scientists.[76] Thus, while Odum was a commanding intellectual leader, a formidable proponent of ecosystem ecology, and a great representative of the institute abroad, he was a less-than-gifted administrator at home.

Odum liked the institute's organization: it was an affiliation of faculty from several academic departments who had expertise not only in ecology but also in a particular branch of the biological sciences, such as zoology or botany. From his perspective, the synergy generated by ecologists trained in different disciplines working together constituted an advantage in the development of new ideas that the interaction of scientists trained in the same discipline did not have. However, the arrangement proved not fully satisfactory in that the institute's administration had no authority over the hiring or tenuring practices of the academic departments and consequently had no assurance that the institute could increase, or even maintain, the number of ecologists on campus. The institute had difficulty getting funding within the university because of its success in obtaining funding from outside; it was required to use much of its soft money for its own administrative expenses.[77]

Despite internal setbacks, however, by the mid-1960s the institute was thriving. Faculty, staff, and graduate students associated with the institute had research programs under way at the Savannah River Ecological Laboratory; the Marine Institute on Sapelo Island; the Coweeta Hydrological Laboratory in Franklin County, North Carolina; and the tropics. But none were conducting programs in the nearby piedmont region of Georgia. In 1965, concerned that University of Georgia ecologists had no opportunities to conduct research near Athens, Odum, Golley, and their colleagues began seeking such a site on which to do long-term ecological studies. They discovered that the College of Agriculture was abandoning the Horseshoe Bend area on the North Oconee River, only a mile from campus, and Odum persuaded the university administration to reassign the tract to the Institute of Ecology. Odum's Ph.D. student Gary Barrett worked with Steve Pomeroy, a master's student, and Ron Pulliam, an undergraduate, on the site's first ecological research project: a mesocosm study of the effect of the insecticide Sevin on the entire aboveground community of a planted millet stand. Barrett and Pulliam later returned to the university as faculty members and served stints as director of the institute.[78]

The institute continued to grow in size and reputation, attracting to the University of Georgia ecologists Dac Crossley and Bill Wiebe, and systems theorist Bernard Patten to the departments of Entomology, Microbiology, and Zoology, respectively. In 1970 the institute established a Ph.D. in ecology. In 1974 the institute moved into a beautiful new facility, acquired through a large grant from the National Science Foundation secured by Don Scott, who was then the chair of the university's Division of Biology, and supplemental funds supplied by the state. The one-story building, designed by Golley, Odum, and the institute's Executive Committee with Atlanta architects Peter Norris and Morris Hall, was organized on the principle that "the built environment influences how humans act and work."[79] Circling a courtyard, the glass-walled edifice with its wall-less common rooms allowed ecologists and students to enjoy the experience of being outside among the trees while working inside. In its foyer, which served as a gallery for exhibitions by local artists, Martha Odum had several shows of her watercolors.

Howard Thomas (H. T.) Odum, Edmund Taylor, Eugene (Gene) Odum, and Arnold Breckenridge looking at a bird's nest in Chapel Hill in 1934.

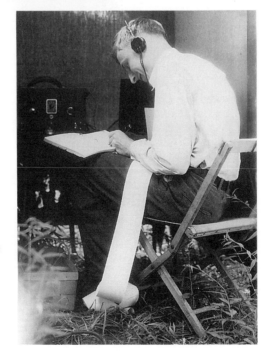

Eugene Odum recording the heartbeats of small birds at the Baldwin Bird Research Laboratory in Gates Mills, Ohio, in 1937.

Right: Eugene Odum in the make-shift laboratory of the Edmund Niles Huyck Preserve in Rensselaerville, New York, in 1939.

Below: Victor Shelford, Jane Dirks, and Eugene Odum on a University of Illinois Easter field trip in Reelfoot Lake, Tennessee, in 1938.

Eugene Odum at the Eniwetok Atoll in the South Pacific in 1954.

Eugene Odum in the field with fellow ecologists as cordirector of a training program in radiation ecology for the Oak Ridge Associated Universities in 1962.

Eugene Odum and Martha Huff Odum at their wedding on November 18, 1939.

Eugene Odum and President
Jimmy Carter at the University
of Georgia in 1981.

Mrs. Howard Thomas (Betty) Odum, Mrs. Eugene (Martha) Odum, Howard
Thomas Odum, Queen Silvia, Eugene Odum, and King Carl XVI Gustaf of
Sweden when the Crafoord Prize for Ecology was awarded to H. T. Odum and
Gene Odum in Stockholm in 1987.

Eugene Odum in his office at the University of Georgia in 1987. (Photograph by Frank Charles Winstead.)

Eugene Odum examining grasses at the Savannah River Ecology Laboratory in 1987.

Martha and Eugene Odum in 1989.

Ecologists Gene Likens, Howard Thomas Odum, Eugene Odum, and
William Odum in the late 1980s.

Eugene Odum in his garden in Athens examining the blueberry blossoms in 1996. (Photograph by Betty Jean Craige.)

4   The Age of Ecology

After the second edition of *Fundamentals of Ecology* was published in 1959, ecosystem ecology became mainstream ecology. For two decades *Fundamentals* remained the only textbook in biology that approached the study of nature ecosystem first, and Eugene Odum's long-running crusade to shift ecologists' attention from structure to function was effective. By 1970, combined sales of the first and second editions totaled 112,000.[1] The textbook was educating a second generation of students in ecosystem theory, and Odum was preparing the third edition.

But it was not simply *Fundamentals of Ecology* that made the ecosystem concept central to ecology in the 1960s. Nuclear energy had produced both the stimulus to investigate ecosystems — the need to understand the effects of radiation on the natural environment — and the means to do so. The building of atomic weapons and atomic energy plants raised questions about fallout and waste disposal that only ecosystem ecologists seemed prepared to address. The discovery of biological magnification made the ecosystem appear the appropriate level for ecological studies of radiation. The availability of radionuclides allowed ecosystem ecologists to track material through food chains and thereby learn how ecosystems function. And United States government grants funded radioecology research projects and the training of future ecosystem ecologists involved in those projects.

The discipline of ecosystem ecology was strengthened by a resistance to "atoms for peace" as well. The enthusiasm of some Americans for nuclear energy engendered an increasingly strong opposition from others in the form of a movement to ban the bomb and stop the construction of nuclear power plants. In 1958, plant physiologist Barry Commoner and other scientists organized the Committee for Nuclear Information, which included increasing numbers of biologists, to alert the general public to the dangers of nuclear fallout and waste disposal.[2] After the United States Senate banned atmospheric testing of nuclear weapons in 1963, Commoner renamed the organization the Committee for Environmental Information and extended its scope to include the dangers of chemical-based fertilizers and detergents to the natural environment.[3]

The nuclear protest movement, which included both pacifists and conservationists, fed into the growing environmentalist movement, whose ranks swelled after the publication in 1962 of Rachel Carson's *Silent Spring*. Carson's exposure of the concentration of the insecticide DDT in the food chain and its potential for contaminating all of nature had sounded an alarm that was heard throughout the country and had raised the visibility of ecology as a discipline positioned to address the dangers. By 1969, according to *Time* magazine, *ecosystem* was a household word.[4] In January 1970, *Newsweek*, in an issue devoted to "the ravaged environment," announced the dawning of "the Age of Ecology." Ecology "examines the precarious relationships between living things and their surroundings," *Newsweek* reported, and "to understand ecology, and the present dilemma that man has created for himself, one must first understand the concept of 'ecosystem.'"[5]

In their stories about civilization's pollution of "the web of life," the periodicals to some extent conflated ecology and environmentalism by focusing on the way ecologists could help to solve the environmental crisis. And the articles profiled ecologists who had been "moved to action" by their knowledge of the negative aspects of technology.[6] In the political climate of the late 1960s, in which antiestablishment young people were rebelling not only against atomic weapons testing, the Vietnam War, and social oppression, but also against technology and the spoiling of wilderness, these ecologists appeared to be the long-sought saviors of the planet.

Both *Time* and *Newsweek* featured Odum as an ecologist and environmental activist. Odum himself did not fail to emphasize the environmentalist implications of his science. To *Newsweek* he explained that the word *ecology* derives from the Greek *oikos*, meaning "house," and that therefore ecology means "the study of houses or, in a broader sense, environments." After Darwin's discovery that species adapt to habitats, he said, there was "a simultaneous recognition throughout the world that the whole is not just the sum of its parts, that the forest is more than a collection of trees."[7] Odum repeated his frequent observation that preserving environmental health requires long-range thinking, something Americans were unaccustomed to doing: "The American creed is get rich today and to hell with tomorrow."[8] To *Time* he said, "We have got to stop thinking of ourselves as being in the growth stage of civilization and realize that we are in the mature stage. Up to now we have been a consumptive, destructive civilization. We must now learn to recycle and reuse."[9] For Odum, ecosystem ecology *was* ecology. And after the awakening of the American public to the possibilities of planetary pollution, ecosystem ecology became a foundation for environmentalism.

A Trip to Japan in 1962

As the ecosystem concept became better known abroad in the early 1960s, largely through *Fundamentals of Ecology*, Odum began to receive invitations from other countries to explain the principles of ecosystem ecology. The textbook had been published in Japanese translation in 1956, and one of Odum's first foreign invitations came from the Ecological Society of Japan.

Odum accepted the invitation to spend two months in Japan in the spring of 1962 lecturing at the ten imperial universities, and he took with him on the trip Martha, Bill, and Martha's mother, Bernice. According to Martha's newsletter, the family had a glorious time sightseeing, staying at both Western hotels and Japanese inns, where they felt they were treated like royalty, and visiting friends made previously at conferences and at Woods Hole. As they followed the blossoming of the cherry trees from the southern part of the country in April to the northern part in May, Martha painted almost fifty watercolors. The Odums traveled in comfort, for their extraordinarily generous Japanese hosts had deposited one million yen in a bank account to cover the cost of the trip for the four of them.

Odum later recalled that Japanese ecology was reductionist at the time, but the Japanese ecologists were extremely interested in learning about his approach to the study of nature. Still recovering from the devastation wrought by the atomic bombs in Nagasaki and Hiroshima, they had not been thinking about "atoms for peace," though they were eager to learn about the use of radionuclides to study the food chain.

On 4 April, at the Ninth Annual Meeting of the Ecological Society of Japan, Odum delivered a major address titled "Relationships between Structure and Function in the Ecosystem." [10] In it he defined *ecology* exclusively as ecosystem ecology. Rejecting the conventional definition of ecology as the study of interrelationships between organisms and their environment, Odum said that he preferred to define it as "the study of the structure and function of ecosystems. Or," he added, "the study of structure and function of nature." [11] The subject of his lecture was actually ecological succession.

In the lecture Odum explained the significance of the P/R relationship — the ratio of the ecosystem's gross production to its respiration — to succession theory in ecosystem ecology. Respiration (R) is the expenditure of energy by a living system to maintain itself; gross production (P) is the amount of energy it converts from sunlight into food or other organic materials; and energy is "the ability to do work." [12] When the biological community converts more solar energy into food than it needs to maintain itself, its gross production is greater than its respiration (P > R) and it is in a growth stage of its development. When the biological community's respiration equals its production, it has achieved maturity and "homeostasis" (P = R).[13]

Odum argued that "the basic pattern of functional change in ecological succession is the same in all ecosystems, but that the species composition, rate of change and duration of succession [are] determined by the physical environment and the resultant community structure."[14] In other words, ecosystems develop, and all ecosystems follow the same path toward "a functional homeostasis."[15]

Odum had recently begun using the term *homeostasis* to refer to an ecosystem's internal equilibrium. It was a term he had imported into ecology from physiology, specifically from a 1932 book by Walter B. Cannon called *The Wisdom of the Body*.[16] Odum adopted the term because he found it more descriptive of the ecosystem's "physiology" than the term *steady state*. Just as an organism or a cell tends to maintain its internal equilibrium — of temperature, fluid content, etc. — by regulating its physiological processes and by making automatic adjustments to the external environment, his theory said, so an ecosystem maintains an internal equilibrium in its mature state, when P equals R.[17] Although Odum had rejected his predecessors' organicist metaphor of the "superorganism," he continued to use physiological vocabulary to describe ecosystems, even while analyzing them as physical systems.

Odum was giving his Japanese audience a functional criterion for determining when an ecosystem was in its growth stage and when it had reached maturity, and homeostasis. To adherents to the older structural ecology, in which the species structure of the biological community indicated the stage of its succession, Odum's ideas were new and important, as was his terminology.

Before Eugene and H. T. Odum presented a functional account of an ecosystem's climax state in their 1955 Eniwetok study, most ecologists employed structural criteria to assess the stages of an ecosystem's succession. They defined succession as a relay or a replacement of species, and climax in terms of the species in the biological community. Frederic Clements and

Victor Shelford had assumed that succession leads to a state of equilibrium, and they had instilled that assumption in Gene. But Gene and his brother had recognized that the structural definition, which they disparaged as "descriptive," was applicable only to terrestrial communities and not broadly generalizable because of each community's uniqueness. By focusing on the P/R ratio of the coral reef, the Odums established functional criteria for identifying the state of equilibrium. The principle they proposed — that when P is equal to R an ecosystem is in equilibrium — they believed was applicable universally. And their "black box" method for analyzing the energy flow through a system could be used on all ecosystems, including marine ones, without extensive information about the particular species composition.

Gene Odum was introducing the Japanese to a new discipline, an ecology based on energetics. By defining the climax state in terms of energy, the Odums and their colleagues had shifted ecology from predominantly structural description of biological communities to predominantly functional analysis of ecosystems.

It was by focusing primarily on the function of ecosystems — the relation of P to R — that Gene Odum arrived at the conclusion in 1962 that all ecosystems display the same pattern of functional change. And it was by focusing on function that Odum could generalize his conclusion beyond terrestrial and marine ecosystems to human social systems, as he was to do in his interview with *Time* in 1969. Odum employed the P/R ratio not only to determine the proximity of an ecosystem to homeostasis, but also to evaluate the health of a human social system. He looked at the P/R ratio as an instrument that could measure the viability of any living system. It could show when a system — such as a city or a university — was in its growth stage and when it had reached maturity and was using all its energy simply to maintain itself. The ratio could also warn that a system was in decline and in need of repair. Although in 1962 Odum was still using the vocabulary of the structural ecologists, he would soon follow Clements and substitute *development* for *succession* in his representation of ecosystem change in order to emphasize the ecosystem's orderliness, interactivity, and directionality in its transition from one stage to another.[18]

The Strategy of Ecosystem Development

In 1964, the year he became president of the Ecological Society of America, Eugene Odum announced in *BioScience* the establishment of "a new ecology" that had risen "to a front-line position in man's thinking [as] a consequence of the exploitation of atomic energy, the exploration of outer space, and the human population explosion." In the same essay Odum defined the new ecology as a "systems ecology" dealing with "the structure and function of levels of organization beyond that of the individual and species." And he laid out its premises: the ecosystem is "the basic unit of nature with which [ecologists] must ultimately deal"; biological diversity increases ecosystem stability; "homeostasis, or biological regulation, is equally important at all levels in the spectrum from molecules to ecosystems"; the whole is greater than the sum of its parts; and therefore reductionist scientific methods cannot adequately explain living systems.[19]

These were the premises on which Odum had based his science from the beginning and with which he was always thereafter identified. All would occasion debate in the 1970s and 1980s, but perhaps none more than his mantra, that the whole is greater than the sum of its parts. Odum saw in each level of organization in nature characteristics resulting from the interactivity of its components. The analysis of the components can produce an adequate understanding of the structure of the larger whole, he would say, but not an adequate understanding of their interactivity, or the function of the whole. To look at a complex living system's function is to see interactivity that is not predictable from examination of its structure alone. When complex systems are viewed from the standpoint of function, the whole appears greater than its parts. Odum's impatience with reductionism developed largely out of his zeal to convert the discipline of ecology into a study of nature's function at the ecosystem level.

Odum's campaign on behalf of ecosystem ecology reached its broadest audience with his 1969 essay "The Strategy of Ecosystem Development," which was published in *Science* and became a "citation classic." It was cited so frequently because Odum's argument—that succession in an ecosystem is orderly, directional, and predictable; results from interaction between the biotic community and its physical environment; and culminates in homeostasis—was controversial, as was his use of the word *strategy*.[20]

In "The Strategy of Ecosystem Development" Odum refined and elaborated the ideas he had presented in Japan and provided empirical data to support them. The "strategy" of succession, wrote Odum, is "increased control of, or homeostasis with, the physical environment in the sense of achieving maximum protection from its perturbations."[21] He cited an article by H. T. Odum and R. C. Pinkerton showing that succession involves a decrease in energy relegated to production and an increase in energy relegated to maintenance. Accordingly, he asserted, the P/R ratio should be "an excellent functional index of the relative maturity" of an ecosystem.[22] Odum presented laboratory evidence of a microcosm's stages of succession toward maturity and delineated the characteristics of young and mature ecosystems in a lengthy table.

Odum's twofold purpose in writing the essay was to lay out the pattern of ecosystem development and then to show its applicability to resolving the "environmental crisis" presently threatening humankind.[23] Each ecosystem develops in a similar way. In its early stages the ecosystem's components are mainly species with high reproduction and growth rates that are capable of competing successfully in uncrowded conditions—that is, "*r*-selected species." At maturity the components are mainly species with lower growth and reproductive potential that are capable of surviving under "equilibrium density"—that is, "*K*-selected species." The difference between *r*-selected species and *K*-selected species, concepts Odum had taken from Robert MacArthur and Edward O. Wilson's 1967 book *The Theory of Island Biogeography*, Odum designated as "quantity versus quality."[24] In the course of the ecosystem's development toward "equilibrium density," Odum said, symbiosis becomes increasingly prevalent and the ecosystem expends an increasing amount of its energy on maintenance.[25]

Odum summarized the pattern of ecosystem development as follows:

While one may well question whether all the trends described are characteristic of all types of ecosystems, there can be little doubt that the net result of community actions is symbiosis, nutrient conservation, stability, a decrease in entropy, and an increase in information. The overall strategy is . . . directed toward achieving as large and diverse an organic structure as is possible within the limits set by the available energy input and the prevailing physical conditions of existence (soil, water, climate, and so on).[26]

In the ecosystem model presented in "The Stragegy of Ecosystem Development," the forces of undisturbed nature move in the direction of equilibrium, which is achieved by increased cooperation among organisms as their environment becomes more crowded and the energy costs of maintenance rise. That is the strategy whereby nature achieves "balance."

All of these aspects of ecosystem development had implications for environmentalist action, to which Odum devoted at least half of his essay. Human beings have upset nature's balance, he noted, by cultivating crops for high productivity and ignoring the other functions of ecosystems beneficial to the maintenance of the whole, such as gas exchange, water purification, and nutrient cycling. We have treated the landscape as our "supply depot," he said, forgetting that it is also our home. Society needs to develop a "systems analysis procedure" to discover "when we are getting 'too much of a good thing'" and damaging the ecosystem of which we are part. Once we see that the ecosystem is an interactive whole of which we are part, he insisted, we will recognize the inadequacy of the "one problem, one solution approach." He concluded: "In the pioneer society, as in the pioneer ecosystem, high birth rates, rapid growth, high economic profits, and exploitation of accessible and unused resources are advantageous, but, as the saturation level is approached, these drives must be shifted to considerations of symbiosis (that is, 'civil rights,' 'law and order,' 'education,' and 'culture'), birth control, and the recycling of resources."[27] At present, he ended, human beings show little awareness of the need to adapt to our ecosystem's "ultimate equilibrium-density stage."[28]

With his usual optimism for solving problems, Odum proposed a tripartite strategy for "resolving man's conflict with nature": the use of nonchemical pest-control agriculture; the implementation of a "compartment model" for landscape zoning, which would be supported by "landscape lawyers"; and a reorientation of society's goals, to be accomplished by instruction in eco-system ecology beginning in elementary school. The underlying aim of the strategy was to avoid upsetting nature's balance. That required humans to understand the functioning of ecosystems, recognize the work done by sup-posedly unproductive parts of the whole, and build a civilization that would protect the natural environment from human exploitation. Odum's circular chart of the environmental zones that civilization needs for its well-being, defined by their function, showed the interaction of productive environ-ments (growth systems), urban-industrial environments (nonvital systems), compromise environments (multiple-use systems), and protective environ-ments (mature systems). Computer simulations would allow ecologists to determine the optimum size and capacity of each compartment.[29] "The preservation of natural areas," Odum declared, "is not a peripheral luxury for society but a capital investment from which we expect to draw interest."[30]

The Challenge to Ecosystem Ecology

The philosophical implications of the ecosystem model as the Odums defined it became increasingly evident with the criticism of "The Strategy of Ecosystem Development." In his essay Odum had defined *ecosystem* as "a unit of biological organization made up of all of the organisms in a given area (that is, 'community') interacting with the physical environment so that a flow of energy leads to characteristic trophic structure and material cycles within the system."[31] In 1973 William Drury and Ian Nisbet, ecologists as-sociated with the Massachusetts Audubon Society, published an article titled "Succession" which challenged the basic premises of ecosystem ecology, in-cluding the ecosystem concept itself.

The Odums had developed ecosystem ecology out of Frederic Clem-ents's model for climax formation in plant communities. Drury and Nisbet promoted an alternative model, one first articulated fifty years earlier by Henry A. Gleason that reflected the Darwinian emphasis on species com-petition in natural selection. The two models — ecosystem ecology and com-munity ecology — generated a debate that continued through the end of the century over the central suppositions of ecosystem ecology: ecosystem development and emergent properties.

Gleason had published "The Individualistic Concept of the Plant Association" in 1926 to counter the concept of the climax that Clements had advanced in his influential 1916 book *Plant Succession*. Clements defined the climax as the major unit of vegetation and the final stage of succession; each climax association is a response to and an expression of the climate of its region. Clements called the climax association a "superorganism."

Gleason opened his essay with a suggestion that synecology—that is, the study of community structures—belonged to a classification of knowledge that was not supported by the actual vegetation data being collected by ecologists. Questioning Clements's basis for defining plant associations, Gleason assembled evidence showing that "an association is not an organism, scarcely even a vegetational unity, but merely a *coincidence*." An area's vegetation, he said, "is merely the resultant of two factors, the fluctuating and fortuitous immigration of plants and an equally fluctuating and variable environment." [32]

> Every species of plant is a law unto itself, the distribution of which in space depends upon its individual peculiarities of migration and environmental requirements. . . . Plant associations, the most conspicuous illustration of the space relation of plants, depend solely on the coincidence of environmental selection and migration over an area of recognizable extent and usually for a time of considerable duration. A rigid definition of the scope or extent of the association is impossible, and a logical classification of associations into larger groups, or into successional series, has not yet been achieved. [33]

In other words, as historian Donald Worster summarized Gleason's position, there is no climax community, no steady state, no organized wholes, no "cooperation" in nature; there is only competition. [34]

Drury and Nisbet took up Gleason's individualistic critique of synecology with an argument against the concept of community properties. They showed that according to recently reported field studies, many plant communities did not conform to the succession criteria set forth by Eugene

Odum and Robert Whittaker, whose work they considered in the mainstream of contemporary ecosystem ecology. They quoted a paragraph from Odum's 1969 "Strategy of Ecosystem Development" in which Odum had described ecosystem development as "an orderly process of community development that is reasonably directional and, therefore, predictable" and that culminates in homeostasis; and a paragraph from Whittaker's 1970 *Communities and Ecosystems* in which Whittaker stated that the "end point of succession is a climax community of relatively stable species composition and steady-state function, adapted to its habitat and essentially permanent in its habitat if undisturbed."[35] And they reproduced Odum's table of "trends to be expected in the development of ecosystems."

Drury and Nisbet examined hypotheses by Odum, Whittaker, Ramón Margalef, and other ecosystem ecologists regarding bioenergetics, soil development, sequence of vegetation types, diversity, stability, and reproductive strategies in relation to field evidence that contradicted them. The common feature of ecosystem theories, Drury and Nisbet said, is their attribution of succession to properties of the community. And because of their concern with adducing community properties, ecosystem ecologists neglected to consider adequately the effect of natural selection on individual species and organisms in their theories of succession.[36]

Drury and Nisbet presented an "alternative explanation": "most of the phenomena of succession can be understood as consequences of differential growth, differential survival (and perhaps also differential colonizing ability) of species adapted to growth at different points on environmental gradients." There is no "strategy of ecosystem development," they said, because there is no community control over the process of succession. They concluded: "A comprehensive theory of succession should be sought at the organismic or cellular level, and not in emergent properties of communities."[37] They were thus questioning Odum's concept of the ecosystem, in which "a flow of energy leads to characteristic trophic structure and material cycles within the system," and the concept of the whole and its emergent properties. Instead they advocated a reductionist methodology for the pursuit of a comprehensive succession theory, a bottom-up approach to the study of nature instead of the top-down approach that Odum had employed in his textbook.

Other critiques of Odum's 1969 essay followed. In 1977, Joseph H. Connell and Ralph O. Slatyer presented data that undermined the ideas of succession and climax formations by showing that succession does not stop. They explained that the apparent discoveries of emergent properties were premised on Clements's and Odum's assumption that the mature community is a highly organized stable system protected from environmental perturbations. Odum's "strategy" theory was based on an embryology analogy, they said, which lacked empirical support: "Since there is no evidence that so-called mature communities are internally controlled in a steady state," the characteristics Odum had listed as attributes of a mature ecosystem could not be deduced from the communities.[38] In other words, there is no homeostasis in nature, no equilibrium, no "ecosystem."

In 1979, two biophysicists from the University of Kentucky mounted another attack on the concept of the ecosystem as an integrated whole. J. Engelberg and L. L. Boyarsky published an article titled "The Noncybernetic Nature of Ecosystems," in which they claimed that ecosystems are not cybernetic systems — they do not function through feedback processes, do not possess information networks, and therefore are not integrated wholes.[39] Odum and his University of Georgia colleague Bernard Patten rebutted the argument in an article titled "The Cybernetic Nature of Ecosystems," in which they questioned Engelberg and Boyarsky's criteria for a cybernetic system and their expectation that a cybernetic system must be goal-oriented. Odum and Patten distinguished between "set-point" controls, such as a thermostat, and "feedback controls." In an ecosystem, they wrote, "the interplay of material cycles and energy flows, under informational control, generates self-organizing feedbacks with no discrete controller required."[40]

Two Models of Nature

Apparent in the two models of nature — the holistic model and the atomistic, or individualistic, model — are not only two different understandings of the way nature works but also two different ideologies and, by extension, two different environmentalist programs. The different ideologies can be traced back to *On the Origin of Species*, in which Darwin laid out a history of nature in his theory of evolution by natural selection. In the late nineteenth century, Anglo-American advocates of laissez-faire capitalism extracted social Darwinism from Darwin's theory of competition, and philosopher Herbert Spencer coined the phrase "survival of the fittest," which Darwin used in later editions of the *Origin*. In 1899, Andrew Carnegie extolled the virtues of competition in his essay "The Gospel of Wealth," in which he argued that competition is the means by which society advances. Although the law of competition might be hard on some individuals, he said, "it is best for the race, because it insures survival of the fittest in every department."[41]

In 1902, the Russian Petr Kropotkin, a prince-turned-anarchist, published *Mutual Aid: A Factor of Evolution* to challenge what he perceived to be Darwin's individualist description of nature. Kropotkin, who believed that Darwin's followers were actually more fixated on competition than Darwin himself, whom he admired, compiled a large set of examples to show that the "fittest" in nature are not those organisms continually at war with one another, but rather those with habits of "mutual aid" that permit them to live long enough to bear progeny. Natural selection, Kropotkin believed, favors cooperation and the formation of sociability. Kropotkin did not fail to make clear the social implications of the individualist interpretation of the *Origin of Species*:

> Science loudly proclaims that the struggle of each against all is the leading principle of nature, and of human societies as well. To that struggle Biology ascribes the progressive evolution of the animal world. History takes the same line of argument; and political economists, in their naïve ignorance, trace all progress of modern industry and machinery to the "wonderful" effects of the same principle. The very religion of the pulpit is a religion of individualism, slightly mitigated by more or less charitable relations to one's neighbours, chiefly on Sundays.[42]

Ecology, "the study of all those complex interrelations referred to by Darwin as the conditions of the struggle for existence," according to Ernst Haeckel, who named the discipline, became a science split between adherents to atomistic methods and theories and adherents to holistic methods and theories. Yale ecologist G. Evelyn Hutchinson, in his 1978 *Introduction to Population Ecology*, described the two methods as "merological" and "holological." Scientists employing the merological approach, which is based on the assumption that population phenomena determine the properties of higher levels of organization, focus on populations of independent organisms. Scientists employing the holological approach, such as the Odums, focus on the flow of materials and energy through an ecosystem without considering the ecosystem's component organisms. The former reflects a demographic view of nature; the latter reflects a physiological view.[43] Odum picked up Hutchinson's terminology and in his 1983 *Basic Ecology* defined *holological* (from *holos*, meaning "whole") as an approach "in which inputs and outputs are measured, collective and emergent properties of the whole are assessed, and then the component parts are investigated as needed"; and *merological* (from *meros*, meaning "part") as an approach "in which the major parts are studied first and then integrated into a whole system."[44] Although Hutchinson's terminology was not widely adopted, his characterization of the two approaches remains apt for population ecology and ecosystem ecology.

In the individualist tradition characterized by emphasis on competition and attention to populations, Darwin is followed by Gleason, Drury and Nisbet, Connell and Slatyer, and a host of population ecologists, evolutionary biologists, and geneticists who employ reductionist methods for the investigation of succession and evolution. To these ecologists, for whom the concept of a "whole" is specious, the so-called emergent properties occupying the attention of the holists can be explained and predicted by analysis of a system's individual components. From their perspective there are no emergent properties. Nor is there any homeostasis or climax state.

In the holistic tradition, which is characterized by emphasis on organismal interaction and cooperation, Kropotkin, whose book Eugene Odum read and admired in the 1980s, is followed by Clements, Shelford, W. C. Allee, Leopold, the Odum brothers, and the school of ecosystem ecologists who employ a top-down approach to the investigation of natural systems. Although many of these ecologists study succession in order to understand the history of nature, they are less interested in the evolution of species than in the evolution of ecosystems. Some of them, including Eugene Odum, accept the controversial hypothesis of coevolution, which Odum defined in his 1971 edition of *Fundamentals of Ecology* as a type of community evolution "involving reciprocal selective interaction between two major groups of organisms with a close ecological relationship," and group selection, which he defined as "natural selection between groups of organisms not necessarily closely linked by mutualistic associations."[45]

Although causal relationships between scientific hypotheses and political trends are difficult to corroborate, the political correlatives to these scientific traditions are obvious. Scientists themselves may be little influenced by the dominance of one political ideology or another, but the reception of their ideas may be greatly influenced by politics. Gleason published his paper in 1926, in the heyday of unconstrained capitalism, but during the Great Depression his criticism of Clements's theory of the interaction of organisms in community succession was largely ignored. In the 1930s, in the period of President Franklin Roosevelt's New Deal, Clements and Shelford focused on the "co-action" of plants and animals in biomes, and their ideas achieved great prominence. In the 1930s Leopold wrote "The Land Ethic," in which he described an ethic as "a limitation on freedom of action in the struggle for existence" for the welfare of the group as a whole.[46] Published with other essays in *A Sand County Almanac* in 1949, "The Land Ethic" was hailed in the 1960s as a cornerstone of the environmentalist movement, whose membership was largely anticapitalist. Odum, inheriting from his left-of-center sociologist father a propensity to look at the whole of a system and to attend more to cooperation than to competition, absorbed Clements's and Shelford's theory of community succession, took over the ecosystem concept expounded first by Tansley, and wrote a textbook that required students to look at the ecosystem first. At the end of the 1960s, when the youth rebellion against capitalism and individualism was at its peak, the ecosystem concept was promulgated by environmentalists, and the ecosystem became a basis on which to measure harm to the environment inflicted by technology and the military.

In the final decades of the twentieth century, as free enterprise became once more the dominant cultural ideology and genetics moved into a privileged position in science for its explanatory power in organismal development and behavior, challenges to ecosystem ecology became increasingly effective in both political and scientific circles. Drury and Nisbet were only the first of what Worster called "post-Odum" ecologists, who regard nature "as a landscape of patches . . . changing continually through time and space, responding to an unceasing barrage of perturbations." [47] These new ecologists see nature as a giant complex system in which change is continuous, events unpredictable, and equilibrium nonexistent. Daniel Botkin, in his 1990 book *Discordant Harmonies*, drew environmentalist implications from the understanding of nature as continuous change. Instead of attempting to preserve a state of equilibrium in protected areas, Botkin said, society should design policies that allow for change, in the recognition that "nature in the twenty-first century will be a nature that we make." [48] As ecosystem ecology lost some of its authority, political attacks on ecosystem environmentalists such as Alston Chase's *In a Dark Wood* became commonplace.

Yet just as skeptics of ecosystem ecology were gaining in numbers, Lynn Margulis and James Lovelock were putting forth a compelling holistic idea. The earth, they said, constitutes a single planetary ecosystem in which biosphere, atmosphere, hydrosphere, and lithosphere all interact with one another and thereby maintain the planet in a more or less steady state. It was an idea first suggested in 1958 by Alfred Redfield in his article "The Biological Control of Chemical Factors in the Environment," which Odum endorsed enthusiastically in his 1971 *Fundamentals of Ecology* and in the textbooks that followed. [49] Lovelock and Margulis named that system Gaia in their 1973 article "Atmospheric Homeostasis by and for the Biosphere: The Gaia Hypothesis." [50] Lovelock elaborated the hypothesis in his 1979 book *Gaia: A New Look at Natural History*. In 1998 Lynn Margulis published *Symbiotic Planet (A New View of Evolution)*, in which she described Gaia as "an emergent property of interaction among organisms, the spherical planet on which they reside, and an energy source, the sun," and argued that "most evolutionary novelty arose and still arises directly from symbiosis." [51] The view appealed deeply to Gene Odum, who brought Margulis to the University of Georgia several times to speak at the Institute of Ecology.

Odum devoted a section of his 1983 *Basic Ecology* to the Gaia hypothesis, from which he extracted an environmentalist lesson: If individual microorganisms by their concerted action have produced a stable environment hospitable to humans by adapting the geochemical environment to their biological needs over geologic time, then humans jeopardize our survival as a species if we modify that environment to satisfy our own immediate wants. "Besides striving to reduce pollution by every means possible," Odum wrote, "human beings must also preserve the integrity and the large scale of the life-support buffer system."[52]

The concept of equilibrium has been at issue since the beginning of the twentieth century in the scientific debates between reductionist and holist ecologists. But its definition appears to be relative to the scientist's object of attention, whether an old field, an ecosystem, or the planet; the scientist's methodology, whether descriptive or functional; and the scientist's time frame, whether a hundred years or a million years. The concept of emergent properties, also at issue in the debates between representatives of the two models of scientific practice, may likewise be defined according to perspective. From the perspective of the reductionists, emergent properties are inconceivable because the components possess the potential, in their own properties, for interactions that would produce the so-called emergent properties. From the perspective of the holists, emergent properties are features of a system that develop out of interactions among the system's components and are not present at a hierarchical level lower than the system under consideration. The properties are new simply because they emerge from interactions.

In 1979, ecosystem ecologist George Salt published a commentary on the term *emergent properties*, over which, he said, there was semantic confusion. Seven years earlier, R. Harré had given the following explanation of the term: "Many groups or aggregates have properties that are not properties of the individuals of which they are a collection. Such properties are called 'emergent properties.'"[53] Salt proposed a new operational definition: "An emergent property of an ecological unit is one which is wholly unpredictable from observation of the components of that unit." A corollary would be: "An emergent property of an ecological unit is only discernable by observation of that unit itself." Salt distinguished between "emergent properties" and "collective properties." "Collective properties" of a population can be determined by statistical, algebraic, or categorical summaries of the behavior of a system's components. "Emergent properties" are those properties that the population develops when behaving as a unit or a system.[54] Odum cited Salt's article in *Basic Ecology* and explained in his definition of emergent properties that "new properties emerge because the components interact, not because the basic nature of the components is changed. Parts are not 'melted down,' as it were, but integrated to produce unique new properties."[55]

Agreement on the definition of the terms *equilibrium* and *emergent properties* was critical to the debate over the reality of the ecosystem, a debate that began with the differences between Gleason and Clements, Salt said. At center was the question, "Is the community (or ecosystem) an entity in the real world, or is it an abstraction which exists only in the mind of ecologists?" Salt wrote: "The concept of emergent properties appears to provide ecologists with an operational method for deciding these questions. If these ecological entities have an existence in the real world, then natural selection can be presumed to have acted on them as a unit. If it has, then they should exhibit emergent properties in addition to the collective properties derived from their component units."[56]

Salt's clarification of the meaning of *emergent properties* to ecosystem ecologists, while useful, did not end the debate. The two perspectives—the "merological" and the "holological"—are incompatible from the perspective of the proponents of one methodology or the other. Outsiders may deem them complementary, however, each valuable for the particular understanding of nature it facilitates. Historian Joel Hagen concluded that

> an observer's position determines how objects appear in relation to one another and, with the possible exception of cubist paintings, it is difficult to visualize objects simultaneously from two perspectives. In a similar way, intellectual perspectives influence the way ecologists think about the relationships between natural units such as populations, communities, and ecosystems. While it is possible for some ecologists to shift back and forth between perspectives, it is difficult (perhaps impossible) to employ both simultaneously.[57]

Since the ecosystem concept depends on the concept of the whole, which itself depends on the concept of emergent properties, reductionist skepti-

cism of emergence logically extends to skepticism of the ecosystem concept. Ecosystem ecologist and historian Frank Golley, like Hagen, ascribed that skepticism, with particular reference to the position of Engelberg and Boyarsky, to the following viewpoint: "If one focuses on components or individual organisms as a biologist would tend to do, you have a very different systems perspective than if you focus on the flows of energy, matter, and information directly."[58] Golley stated, however, that paleoecologists' discovery in the 1980s that populations of organisms move across the land individually and at different rates of speed, indicating that the complement of species composing an ecosystem does not remain constant over long periods, had brought about a "new form of ecosystem theory," in which equilibrium is considered in relation to the ecosystem's resilience to disturbance. The ecosystem must be defined relativistically, rather than deterministically, and considered as a "response system" in a dynamic relation with its environment. It is therefore a "weak whole," he said, lasting only as long as it is resistant to disturbance.[59]

The Coastal Marshlands Protection Act

The ideological tension between individualism and holism that divided ecologists reflects a timeless political tension that divides the electorate between emphasis on the private good and emphasis on the public good. Eugene Odum always acknowledged the dynamic relationship between the two positions, saying that too much attention to the private good at any given time will be corrected by a renewed attention to the public good, and vice versa. A Democrat all his life, Odum generally supported the public good rather than the private good, in keeping with his propensity to look at the big picture and to consider the long term. He invariably supported efforts to preserve wilderness areas for the benefit of the whole against arguments for individual rights.

During the late 1960s, a conflict between the rights of the individual and the rights of the whole erupted when land developers and a mining firm threatened the survival of the wetlands along the coast of Georgia. Odum, who had helped acquire Sapelo Island for use by the University of Georgia in the early 1950s, became a political activist and joined a citizens' group in a campaign to save the "marshes of Glynn." His success in convincing the public that the marshes were worth more to the state as undeveloped wetlands than their appraised value for real estate or mining purposes catapulted him to fame in Georgia as an environmentalist.

Scientists associated with the Institute of Ecology had long been interested in the coastal wetlands as a marine ecosystem.[60] In 1961, Odum had published "The Role of Tidal Marshes in Estuarine Production," pointing out that "estuaries are among the most naturally fertile areas of the world because of efficient nutrient exchange, flowing water, accessibility to light, and year-around primary production."[61] Employing a functional analysis of the ecosystem, Odum showed that the net production of the estuarine ecosystem was approximately four times its respiration.[62] The article made several arguments: that the marshes, flats, creeks, and bays of the estuary comprised a single ecosystem; that the estuarine ecosystem's function needed to be more fully studied; that because of the estuary's fertility, humans seeking benefits should utilize what it produced naturally rather than attempt to increase its production; and that humans should think in terms of "biological engineering" with respect to preserving the estuary's fertility. He warned that the one-crop harvest practices so often used for terrestrial agriculture would imperil the ecosystem's stability, which was maintained by its enormous diversity of organisms.[63]

By 1968 Odum was warning that the sea's most important function, from the human perspective, is not its production of food but its regulation of the atmosphere. "The protective and regulatory 'open space' function of the seascape (as indeed for all the landscape) can be seriously impaired if we try to manage it only as a food supply depot," he said. Odum predicted that eutrophication — or fertilization — of estuaries would cause large-scale increases in oxygen demand, creating gaseous imbalances in the atmosphere, which was already stressed by industrial energy consumption. Odum, that is, was looking beyond the estuary itself as an ecosystem; he was looking at the relationship of the ocean to the air. Applying Redfield's theory of the biological control of chemical factors in the environment, Odum noted that the fertile estuaries, with their "nutrient traps," contribute to the productivity of off-shore waters in a phenomenon Odum named "outwelling," and the waters govern the content of the air.[64]

In 1967, the Kerr-McGee Corporation, which had purchased twelve thousand acres on islands off the coast near Savannah, discovered a rich lode of phosphate beneath the marshes and petitioned the state for leases to strip-mine underwater land belonging to the state. Governor Lester Maddox's Advisory Committee on Mineral Leasing, which Maddox appointed to review the request, learned that Kerr-McGee intended to remove thirty-six million cubic yards of marsh each year to obtain a yield of three million tons of phosphates. The committee reported that while Kerr-McGee would return to the state two million dollars annually, the mining would would destroy the marshes.

The committee, of which Odum was a member—along with his colleague E. L. Cheatum, director of the university's Institute of Natural Resources—stated that the dredging operations might puncture the aquifer and contaminate the state's water supply, and urged Governor Maddox to deny the petition. In 1969, Odum was quoted in *Life* magazine as saying, "It is no longer a luxury item to save our estuaries. It is a scientific necessity. Right now we need to hold the line so that our great natural resource is not frittered away here and there for the quick gain. We need to hold the line until we have time to come up with an overall plan."[65] Governor Maddox denied Kerr-McGee's petition. The committee also recommended that Georgia create a new state agency to control the development of the wetlands "before great damage is done." Meanwhile, a resort developer was revealing plans to develop Cumberland Island to the south, which angered residents near Brunswick.[66]

The environmentalists' protest provoked declarations of individual rights in response, such as that of Georgia representative Robert Harrison Jr., from the town of St. Marys on the southern coast, who stated that "private people . . . should be allowed to do with their land what they want." Harrison promptly sponsored a bill that would help developers do what they wanted with land under their control.[67]

By 1969, environmentalists recognized that unless the legislature passed a bill to protect the wetlands, private individuals and corporations would damage them beyond recovery within a few years in pursuit of financial gain. Clifford and Sandy West produced a film about the marshes titled *The Untitled Film: A Search for Ecological Balance*, in which they had Odum speak about ecosystem preservation. Students at the University of Georgia, many of them associated with the Institute of Ecology, formed the Save Our Marshes Committee and recruited Odum to help them explain the function of the ecosystem to Georgia voters. Odum wrote a fact sheet describing the salt marshes as "nursery grounds" for marine animals and listing what the marshes provided for human beings: food, recreation, erosion control, open space, and income. And he converted the marshland resource into dollars to show its economic value to the state. "The most productive agricultural crops in the world can produce no more total organic matter than the Georgia marshes where the tide does the work of fertilization and cultivation — free!" he said. The marshes should be valued at a minimum of $2,000 per acre, he continued, because indirectly the marshes produced a yearly income (in 1970 dollars) of $100 per acre, totaling $40 million per year for the whole coast. "It would take almost $1 billion in the bank to produce an income equal to the yearly income from your marshes."

Between November, when *Life* made coastal development in Georgia a national conservation issue, and February the Save Our Marshes Committee organized a massive drive to educate Georgia citizens on the dangers of failing to protect the wetlands. The students distributed ten thousand copies of Odum's fact sheet across the state, printed six thousand "Save Our Marshes" bumper stickers and buttons, and worked with other conservation groups to mobilize a letter-writing campaign. The conservationists won the *Atlanta Constitution* to their side. Odum was in his element, working with students on a cause he held dear, teaching the public about ecosystems, talking with legislators, and testifying at public hearings. At a "Conservation Teach-in" held in late January at the University of Georgia, Odum concluded his lesson on the value of the saltwater wetlands with a comment that was widely quoted. Filling in the Georgia marshes or "allowing them to be whittled away," he said, "is as senseless as filling in San Francisco Bay."[68]

On 6 February 1970, the Georgia Senate, whose members had sided with developers the preceding year, passed unanimously a marshlands protection bill—prepared by Representative Reid Harris of Brunswick with the aid of Odum and other institute ecologists—that established the Coastal Marshlands Protection Agency to monitor development of the wetlands. The following Monday, 9 February, the House of Representatives by a vote of 103 to 21 approved the Senate's bill. Governor Maddox signed the Coastal Marshlands Protection Act of 1970 into law soon afterward.

In an essay titled "Turning Points in the History of the Institute of Ecology" Odum wrote: "So we learn [from the marshlands campaign] that when the public speaks with a loud voice politicians act."[69] For Odum, success in this political crusade represented a "turning point" in the life of the Institute of Ecology in that it publicized the willingness of University of Georgia ecologists to serve the state. From then on, the Institute of Ecology fulfilled all three of the missions of the University of Georgia: research, teaching, and public service. It was a turning point in Odum's own life as well. Odum was adept at explaining science to nonscientists, as he had demonstrated in his textbooks, and he appreciated the increasingly numerous opportunities to address groups of all kinds, such as the eighteen hundred women at the Twenty-Second Virginia Woman's forum held in Richmond that November, where, on a panel with well-known ecologists Ruth Patrick and Robert Testin, he spoke of the need to legislate environmental control.[70] He became an environmental activist, accepting invitations to speak to Rotary Clubs, high school and grade school classes, medical associations, citizen committees, and church congregations to motivate them to preserve the natural environment. Odum used the marshlands campaign frequently as an example of the importance of educating the public, because, he would say, "politicians don't lead, they follow." He also learned from the experience, as did H. T., the need to factor into the economy the value to human beings of nonmarket resources.

The National Academy

In 1970, fifty-six-year-old Gene Odum was a busy man and a well-known and respected public figure. According to Newsweek, the "Age of Ecology" had arrived, and Eugene Odum appeared to be the person who could best explain it to the world. As the director of the University of Georgia Institute of Ecology and the Alumni Foundation Distinguished Professor of Zoology, Odum—who was named Georgia Scientist of the Year for 1967 by the Georgia Science and Technology Commission and quoted in *Time, Life,* and *Newsweek*—was suddenly elevated to local celebrity status. He received attention in the media for his science, his environmentalism—and his tennis. He had won the Athens Men's Singles and Doubles Championships. He was interviewed for the 1970 University of Georgia student yearbook, *Pandora.* His wife, Martha, received newspaper coverage for her work as president of the Athens Art Association. Martha had become adept at sculpture, enameling, glassblowing, and silversmithing, as well as painting.

In the spring of 1970, Gene and Martha traveled to Vancouver, British Columbia, to visit their son Bill. After obtaining his Ph.D. in ecology from the University of Florida with a dissertation on the mangroves of Florida Bay, Bill had accepted a one-year postdoctoral position at the University of British Columbia in Vancouver.[71] While in Bill's apartment looking out over the water, Gene and Martha received a telephone call informing them of Gene's election to the National Academy of Sciences in the Applied Biology section.[72] Gene, the first member of the academy from the University of Georgia, was completely surprised. Shortly after his return to Athens, the Institute of Ecology paid tribute to him with a two-day symposium attended by forty-seven of his former students.

Election to the National Academy represented another turning point in Eugene Odum's career. After 1970 Odum devoted more and more of his time to converting the principles of ecosystem ecology into principles of ecosystem environmentalism. The success of the campaign to save the marshes increased his desire to teach the general public how to make a better world.

5 Ecosystem Environmentalism

In 1969, American society was in upheaval. The Vietnam War continued without abatement, and war protestors were joining ranks with civil rights activists, feminists, and environmentalists in a rebellion against the expansion of the "military-industrial complex" and the values of the middle class. Intellectuals began drawing connections between those values and the military actions of the United States government, between racism and United States foreign policy, between patriarchy and oppression of the weak, between the economics of growth and environmental degradation. Rachel Carson's *Silent Spring*, published in 1962, showed how chemical insecticides could contaminate the entire planet and armed the "back to nature" movement with an understanding of the circulation of materials through food chains. Lynn White's celebrated essay, "The Historical Roots of Our Ecologic Crisis," published in *Science* in 1967, attributed the oppositional relationship between Western human society and nonhuman nature to the Judeo-Christian myth that God had created man in his own image and had made all of nature for man's benefit. *The Population Bomb*, by Paul Ehrlich and Anne Ehrlich, published in 1968, sounded an alarm about the consequences of overpopulation on a global scale. On the first Earth Day, 22 April 1970, Barry Commoner, Paul Ehrlich, and René Dubos rallied college students nationwide to the environmentalist cause. They were joined in the celebration of nature by Ralph Nader, Benjamin Spock, Allen Ginsberg, and activists of various kinds eager to criticize the value system that had made the planet unhealthy.[1]

Eugene Odum's *Fundamentals of Ecology* had been teaching students since 1959 to see the world in terms of interrelated systems and to look at "the big picture." On Earth Day students were indeed looking at the big picture and expressing dissatisfaction with what they saw. Odum interpreted their mounting concern for human rights and environmental preservation and their antagonism toward the keepers of the technological society as a sign of the need "to develop new strategies adapted to the mature system."[2] Although Athens was not a hotbed of unrest in the late 1960s, Odum realized that he now had receptive audiences for his ideas outside the academy as well as inside. The media attention to global pollution inspired by Neil Armstrong and Buzz Aldrin's photographs of the earth had sensitized Americans to the dangers of environmental degradation. Ever competitive, Odum plunged into the missionary work of converting a nation to environmental ethics.

The Total Environment

In 1969, Odum had reached the pinnacle of his scientific career. *Fundamentals of Ecology* remained the only textbook that focused on the ecosystem, and through its translations it was training students throughout the world to study nature from the top down. With his brother, Gene had led the way in the transformation of ecology from the description of ecosystem structure to the analysis of ecosystem function with the award-winning study of the Eniwetok Atoll. He had been instrumental in the founding of the Savannah River Ecology Laboratory and the University of Georgia Institute of Ecology. With his controversial essay in *Science* on the strategy of ecosystem development he had made ecosystem development the central issue of his discipline. And he had been singled out by the media for his prominence in a field of research that promised to save the planet. He could afford to devote some of his abundant energy to trying to change people's behavior toward nature.

Odum knew that he was good at speaking persuasively to nonscientists. The campaign to save the coastal marshlands had stimulated his enthusiasm for explaining ecosystem theory to the general public and his optimism that such explanations could enlarge the public's environmentalist conscience. But the marshlands campaign had also taught him that if environmentalists could not show the *economic* importance to society of preserving a significant part of the biosphere in a natural state, they would lose future battles.

Meanwhile, H. T., who had returned to the University of Florida in 1970, was moving in the same direction, attempting to find a way to convert into dollars the work that nature did in "man's total environment." In his 1972 essay "Energy, Ecology, and Economics" H. T. explained that "even in urban areas more than half of the useful work on which our society is based comes from the natural flows of sun, wind, waters, waves, etc., that act through the broad areas of seas and landscapes without money payment; an economy, to compete and survive, must maximize its use of these energies, not destroying their enormous free subsidies; the necessity of environmental inputs is often not realized until they are displaced." [3] In *Environment, Power, and Society,* published in 1971, H. T. had recommended that the ratio of gross national product (GNP) to national power consumption be used to convert calories to dollars.

In 1972 the Odums collaborated on a paper delivered — in their absence by Gene's colleague E. L. Cheatum — at a North American Wildlife and Resources Conference and published as "Natural Areas as Necessary Components of Man's Total Environment."[4] In it they argued that human society's "natural environment" and "developed environment" interact with each other to constitute a single "life-support" system whose "true value" cannot be determined by measuring the worth of the two components separately. In other words, the "true value" is an emergent property of the system. The "natural environment" they defined as "that part of man's life-support system that operates without energetic or economic input from the power flows directly controlled by man." The "developed environment" they defined as that part of man's life-support system that is "structured and maintained by large auxiliary power flows from fossil or other concentrated fuels that supplement or replace the natural energy flow of the sun." The natural environment and the developed environment should be recognized as comprising a single system, they said, because the self-maintaining natural environment performs certain functions supportive of the developed environment, such as recycling wastes on a continuous basis, without appreciable cost to human society in the market economy.[5]

In their paper the Odums proposed an inclusive conception of the economy, one appropriate to the acknowledgment that "man is a part of, not apart from, the environment." In the marshlands campaign Gene Odum had derived the economic value of the Georgia marshes to the state by calculating the annual income the marshlands produced indirectly; that is, he converted into dollars the work that the natural environment did for the developed environment. But by 1972 he and H. T. realized that the more important calculation was the proportion of the natural environment to the total environment required to maintain the developed environment. If the developed environment outgrows the natural environment that maintains it, then the natural environment is unable to perform its life-support functions, and the productivity and the quality of both decline. Once the ratio is determined for a given area, the Odums said, a land-use plan must be adopted "with sufficient legal and political sanction to counteract the overdevelopment syndrome."[6]

Overdevelopment, in the context of the total environment, yields a precipitous rise in pollution and disorder for the developed environment. The

Odums presented a new principle that they had appropriated from a mathematical discovery about networks: "Developed systems generate economic wealth, but the economic cost of maintenance increases as a power function of the intensity of development." In other words, doubling the size of a city more than doubles the cost of maintaining the same degree of order.[7] In 1950, a scientist at Bell Laboratory had observed that as the number of telephone calls went up at switchboards, the number of needed switches went up by a power factor of 2. He proved that a diseconomy of scale was an intrinsic feature of networks.[8] The Odums took this discovery as support for the theory that an ecosystem's maintenance costs rise faster than its productivity as the system develops, until the system reaches homeostasis, or equilibrium (P = R).

Although in a natural system productivity can never be less than the energy required for maintenance, in a developed system, pushed by population growth and technology, it can, though not for long. When productivity is less than the energy required for maintenance (P < R), the developed system ceases to be self-sustaining. It has grown beyond equilibrium, and, in H. T.'s terminology, can no longer "pump out its disorder" sufficiently to prevent its deterioration. At that point, Gene Odum would say, the system should "stop growing bigger and start getting better." Thus every complex system has an optimal size which can be determined by the P/R ratio. Rapid population growth and technological development accelerate the conversion of natural environment to developed environment. Only legislation, the Odums realized, could slow the process and protect the natural environment as an indispensable resource for human society.

"Natural Areas as Necessary Components of Man's Total Environment" introduced the idea that the natural environment and the developed environment must be regarded as a single system in the computation of P and R. The Odums also began advocating ways to compute wealth that would reflect the combined market and nonmarket resources, since the free market pricing system does not sustain unpriced environmental services such as air, water, and waste treatment. H. T. proposed using as a theoretical currency "eMergy"—a contraction of "embodied energy," the sum of all the energy used to produce any product or service — to give equal value to the goods and services of humans and nature. Gene proposed instituting a "dual capitalism" whereby the government would charge polluters for environmental damage they caused and businesses would factor environmental costs into the prices they charged consumers.[9]

By 1977 Gene Odum was calling the natural environment and the developed environment "the two houses of man," the former powered by the sun and the latter by fossil fuel. Agriculture, a "fuel-subsidized, solar-powered agroecosystem," links the two, but to the extent that agricultural machinery uses more and more auxiliary fuel energy to make fertilizers and pesticides, to irrigate, and to transport and process food, the agroecosystem comes to resemble the industrial system in its impact on the natural environment. Unfortunately, because technology obscures human society's dependence on the natural environment and because society's economic system does not incorporate nature's work, humans have come to ignore the dependence of the "man-made house" on the "house of nature," our life-support system.[10]

Odum told an interviewer in 1979 that he thought the South should set aside about one-third of its area as greenbelts of natural and agricultural land for life-support buffers. He also told her, "Thank goodness for the energy crisis. . . . We become temporarily blinded by the prospect of short term wealth which can be obtained by exploitation. A good energy crisis can wake us up to the fact that there is a tomorrow."[11]

When he spoke during the 1980 Earth Day celebration on the streets of Athens, Georgia, he stressed the importance of greenbelts:

> We need now to give special attention to the life support buffer provided by natural and semi-natural ecosystems. It is the forests, prairies, lakes, rivers, estuaries, and oceans that make it possible for cities and industries to function, because sooner or later natural solar-powered processes act as the ultimate treatment plant and recycler for degradable wastes. We must work hard to be sure that sufficient areas of natural systems and good farmland are preserved for this very important task. Every city must have a very large "green belt" to provide these life-support

services and also outdoor recreation. This means there must be a much greater effort in environmental-use planning at all levels — local, state, national, and global.[12]

From Ecosystem Development to Environmentalism

In a 1969 essay in *BioScience* titled "The Attitude Lag," Eugene Odum declared that society needed a basic reorientation in its attitude toward the natural environment. He urged his colleagues to write more popular articles; address more civic groups; attend more public hearings for resource, pollution, and zoning issues; and offer their services to planning and legislative groups. They must convince their listeners that the "war-like approach to nature" that benefited humans in the growth stages of social systems would be increasingly disadvantageous in the mature stages. He urged a slowdown in growth: "In cybernetic language, we are faced with the problem of going from the positive transient state, when everything is growing and expanding at a great rate, to the steady state when growth rates approach zero and enough is enough, so to speak."[13]

Unlike most scientists, who distinguished clearly between their investigation of nature and their support for political causes, Odum had shown in his articles and books the relevance of ecosystem science to environmentalism. Now he began to apply his theory of ecosystem development to society. And he employed the theory consciously or unconsciously for the rest of his life to account for social change.

Odum had explained in "The Strategy of Ecosystem Development" that ecosystems mature. In their "youthful" stages they grow fast, with their component organisms competing aggressively with one another for space, but in time, as crowding forces organisms to develop relationships of cooperation, they approach a homeostasis which they maintain over long periods. Homeostasis is desirable for human society as well, Odum believed, and humans can achieve it by controlling the size of their social systems. Just as ecosystems, which are characterized by high birth rates, high productivity, rapid growth, and exploitation of accessible resources during their pioneer stages, acquire stability by an increase in symbiotic relationships and a decrease in growth, so does human society. Odum put into the category of symbiosis civil rights, law and order, education, and culture. In Odum's view, the natural development of ecosystems toward equilibrium provides a model that human social systems should emulate in order to achieve optimal efficiency. Equilibrium is the ideal for both nature and society.

In a foreword he wrote to the 1970 *Environmental Law Review* in which he declared that human society is evolving from "a transient, youthful state to a mature (and we hope) enduring state," Odum compared a developing ecosystem to human society:

> As the population density approaches the saturation level, the ecological system matures in the sense that a greater proportion of the available energy is shifted to *maintenance* of the complex structure that has been created. Organisms adapted to the mature system, then, are those with low birth rates, longer life spans, the ability to recycle and reuse resources, and the capability of developing mutualistic relationships with each other. A parallel, of course, exists in the development of human society . . . because man and environment do constitute an ecological system.[14]

Odum associated diversity with stability in both natural and social systems. The increase in diversity that accompanies the shift in the ecosystem's development from its early stages to its mature stages helps maintain the ecosystem's stability. Therefore, he said, to enhance the stability of the total environment, humans should diversify society's sources of energy as well as its food supply, even while recognizing that low diversity yields higher productivity. He warned in 1975 that while humans had prospered materially during the twentieth century by exploiting fossil fuel, society's 90–95 percent dependence on that single source of energy made it unstable because society could not maintain itself with that rate of fossil fuel consumption.[15]

Odum considered the evolution from high productivity to maintenance a shift from emphasis on quantity to emphasis on quality. A better quality of life for human beings in the mature social system—a city, for example—would be effected by "a peaceful co-existence of man and nature," which would involve birth control, recycling of resources, and regulation of land use.[16] In the crowded conditions of the mature social system, cooperative relationships would prove more advantageous to the system's components than competitive relationships, because cooperative relationships would give the system stability. So would the increased diversity he recommended, because it would reduce the risk of any one component group bringing disorder to the whole by its demise. For Odum, to "stop growing bigger and start getting better" would require cooperation, more harmonious relationships among human beings, greater diversity of energy and food sources, and a more harmonious relationship between humans and the natural environment.

Odum spoke again and again about the same issues, addressing different audiences, refining his arguments, and assembling more evidence in their favor—sometimes in response to new information, occasionally in response to criticism. In 1975 Odum spoke at a Yale University conference titled "Beyond Growth." In his talk, "Harmony between Man and Nature," he declared that "if the physical growth of society does not level off at an optimum size in terms of the resources and life-support system on which it depends, the continued improvement of the quality of human life will be more and more threatened by cancerous growth that becomes lethal when it can no longer be supported by the system of which it is a dependent part." That would be the situation in which P is less than R for the "total environment."[17] Odum said that economists' goal of continuous growth would destabilize economic and social systems not only because of environmental deterioration but also because of internal disorder. "As the size of a system increases," he told his audience, referring to the theory of the diseconomy of scale he and H. T. had explored, "the cost of maintenance of a network of services increases as some kind of power function."[18]

Odum observed that as an ecosystem matures, parasitism naturally tends to evolve into mutualism; parasites that fail to make that transition end up destroying their hosts and consequently themselves. Human society must make the same transition, he said, from exploitation of the natural environment to harmonious interaction with it.[19] The danger of destroying our host, the planet earth, was new because until recently neither the size of the human population nor the extent of humans' technological manipulation of the environment had been great enough to affect "regional and global balances."[20]

To avoid killing the host, Odum said, society could "get better," and he listed the substitutes for growth in size that would be features of a "mature stage of harmony between man and nature":

1. Increases in efficiency in the use of energy.
2. Increases in efficiency in the use of resources.
3. Increases in turnover rate of components (repair before deterioration occurs).
4. Increase in rate and efficiency of recycling of materials.
5. Increase in proportion of energy devoted to maintenance.
6. Increase in diversity of components.
7. Increase in stratification.
8. Increase in quality of components (continual improvement of existing superior components rather than proliferation of more inferior ones).[21]

The mature social system would require a new set of values. In "the pioneer stages of civilization," Odum said, it was proper that the greatest economic rewards and the strongest legal protection be given to those citizens who produced and exploited "nature's riches," because "man must subdue and modify his environment in order to survive in it." Now that society has reached maturity, however, economic rewards and legal protection must be given to the people, professions, and industries that endeavor to maintain the quality of human life by recycling and reusing resources — those practicing environmental ethics.[22] Incentives must be provided for cooperation "between man and nature" and among individuals.

The strategy for human societal development would thus be the same as that of the ecosystem, though humans would adopt the strategy intentionally: "increased control of, or homeostasis with, the physical environment in the sense of achieving maximum protection from its perturbations."[23] Odum concluded the third edition of *Fundamentals of Ecology*, which in 1971 alone sold almost forty-two thousand copies, with the statement: "The time has come for man to manage his own population as well as the resources on which he depends, because for the first time in his brief history he is faced with ultimate, rather than merely local, limitations."[24] By understanding ecosystem theory, Odum believed, human beings could manipulate the forces of societal development to establish a sustainable equilibrium that would improve the quality of human life.

In the ethics he was deriving from the concept of ecosystem development, Odum incorporated Aldo Leopold's idea that interdependence leads to cooperation and the development of an ethical community. Leopold said that "an ethic, ecologically, is a limitation on freedom of action in the struggle for existence," a restraint of competition. In the early stages of civilization, an ethical community, defined by the interdependence of its members, was typically no larger than the tribe, but as its members developed relationships of interdependence with individuals outside their tribe, their ethical community expanded. Within the expanded ethical community competition would give way to cooperation. Eventually, as they recognized their relationship of dependence on the land, humans would develop a "land ethic" and live in harmony with the land. The basic premise of the land ethic, as of all ethics, said Leopold, is that "the individual is a member of a community of interdependent parts." [25]

The environmental ethic that the Odums elaborated in the 1970s, in the Leopoldian tradition, was holistic in its focus on the total environment as a system whose components—human and nonhuman, organic and inorganic—were interdependent, and in its attention to emergent properties, such as the diseconomy of scale. The Odums had long talked about human beings as part of "complex 'biogeochemical' cycles with increasing power to modify the cycles." [26] They were unapologetically anthropocentric—unlike Arne Naess and his fellow ecocentric environmentalists—in their aim to preserve ecosystem stability for the survival of humans, and they recognized the need for humans to "manage" ecosystems to enable total environments to be self-sustaining. They viewed sustainable total environments as conducive to both the physical health and the economic health of individuals. Having acquired from their father, Howard Washington Odum, a deep commitment to social justice, Gene and H. T. saw "harmony between man and nature" not only as a prerequisite for harmony among humans but actually as a means to achieve among humans a more equitable distribution of the world's resources.

In 1972 H. T. Odum told an audience in Stockholm, where his ideas were popular, that "high quality of life for humans and equitable economic distribution are more closely approximated in steady state than in growth periods":

> During growth, emphasis is on competition, and large differences in economic and energetic welfare develop; competitive exclusion, instability, poverty, and unequal wealth are characteristic. During steady state, competition is controlled and eliminated, being replaced with regulatory systems, high division and diversity of labor, uniform energy distributions, little change, and growth only for replacement purposes. Love of stable system quality replaces love of net gain. Religious ethics adopt something closer to that of those primitive peoples that were formerly dominant in zones of the world with cultures based on the steady energy flows from the sun. Socialistic ideals about distribution are more consistent with steady state than growth.[27]

Gene Odum often said that "when resources are scarce in terms of need or demand, then it pays to cooperate."[28] The increase in cooperation in the "community of interdependent parts" would bring about an increase in stability that would in turn benefit the community's individuals. If individuals could be made to see their interdependence with one another and their dependence on the land, Odum believed, they would work together to preserve their ecosystem.

Proselytizer of Holism

Gene Odum used every opportunity to train students in his classes and readers of his textbooks, scientific articles, and popular essays to "look at the big picture" — to deal with large-scale complexity by searching for overriding simplicity, whether in the study of nature or in the study of "man in nature."[29] As he became increasingly involved in the study of man's relation to nature, Odum became aware that the understanding of large-scale, complex "real world problems" would require, in addition to a holistic methodology, collaboration among individuals with different skills and perspectives. Since specialization inclines not only science but also society toward reductionist approaches to problems, collaboration would enable teams of individuals to see the big picture. The goal was to understand the functioning of the total environment, a task he knew could not be accomplished except at the highest levels of organization.

Because he had competed with reductionist scientists for both practical resources and scientific credibility throughout his academic life, Odum always saw reductionism as the opponent of holism, just as he saw molecular biologists as the opponents of ecosystem ecologists. As he and the ecosystem ecology he promulgated gained in stature, Gene had to defend the concept of emergent properties against attacks by molecular biologists, community ecologists, and evolutionary ecologists who considered the concept mystical. His brother H. T., having invented a model for understanding energy as the common currency for the total environment, was similarly frustrated in his campaign to persuade scientists and policy makers to look at the big picture.

Odum believed, probably correctly, that in his advocacy of holism he was representing a minority viewpoint. His extraordinary drive to convert people to that viewpoint was motivated by his conviction that a holistic approach would facilitate the solution of many of the world's intellectual, environmental, and social problems.

In June 1975 Gene and H. T. were jointly awarded the prestigious Prix de l'Institut de la Vie, which they accepted at a banquet at the Conciergerie in Paris held in conjunction with a week-long meeting at Versailles. In his acceptance speech Gene took the opportunity to explain why "the time has come to give equal time, and equal research and development funding, to the higher levels of biological organization in the hierarchical sequence."

> Science and technology during the past half century have been so preoccupied with reductionism that supraindividual systems have suffered benign neglect. We are abysmally ignorant of the ecosystems of which we are dependent parts. As a result, today we have only half a science of man. It is perhaps this situation, as much as any other, that contributes to the current public dissatisfaction with the scientist who has become so specialized that he is unable to respond to the larger-scale problems that now require attention.[30]

The existence of emergent properties makes it necessary to employ a holistic approach to larger-scale problems, Odum stated. Problems emerge as a result of the interaction of a system's components, and they may be understood only by examination at the same hierarchical level in which they appear.[31]

Odum prefaced his call for a holistic approach to the solution of real-world problems with an acknowledgment of the value of reductionist science in the prevention and cure of cancer at the organism level and in genetic engineering at the population level. But he went on to say that reductionism is inadequate for such problems as population overgrowth, social disorder, pollution, "and other forms of societal and environmental cancer."[32] Reductionism characterizes not just science but society as well, he argued, because it is an inevitable consequence of professional specialization. If only specialists are available to resolve problems, the problems will necessarily be viewed as divisible into parts and will be addressed by the piecemeal "one-problem/one-solution" method. Odum regarded the increasing social disorder of the 1970s as proof that the Cartesian method of studying the parts before the whole is inapplicable to large-scale systems.

Ecologists should forge links with social scientists, with economists, and with politicians to address multifaceted problems, Odum told his audience in Paris. As an example of the need for such collaboration he cited environmental impact statements, which usually included environmental and economic assessments prepared by environmentalists and economists separately. By working independently rather than together, each group evaluated the situation according to its own criteria for natural and developed environments, "ignoring the fact that it is the interaction between these systems that is of paramount importance."[33] "Decision-making cannot be based on one discipline alone," he told an interviewer from the *Atlanta Journal-Constitution* Sunday magazine. "You might say that environment is too important to leave to environmentalists alone, engineering is too important to leave to engineers alone, economics is too important to leave to economists alone."[34] At about the same time H. T. was noting the dangers to the world if its leaders were "mainly advised by specialists who study only one part of the system at a time."[35]

The "big picture" has a temporal as well as a spatial dimension. The inability of governments at any level to plan for the long term when their officials are elected for the short term is obvious. The short-range view common to such officials often results in the passage of bills that are beneficial to current voters and detrimental to future voters. In 1982 Gene's son Bill Odum applied economist Alfred E. Kahn's theory of "the tyranny of small decisions" to environmental issues, calling it "the tyranny of small decision effects." Long-term environmental damage may occur not because voters decide a particular ecosystem is not worth preserving but because over a long period many different people — politicians, planners, developers, etc. — make a series of seemingly insignificant decisions that have a cumulative effect on the whole. Each of these people is concerned with only a piece of the whole; no individual or group looks at all of it. In this way more than 50 percent of the wetlands along the coast of Connecticut and Massachusetts were destroyed between 1950 and 1970. Bill pointed out in his essay, "Environmental Degradation and the Tyranny of Small Decisions," that the reward process in political, scientific, and academic institutions forces people in decision-making positions to address specific problems as if they were not part of a larger system and to seek solutions to those problems alone. Specialization impedes large-scale, long-term planning.[36]

Gene Odum found the "tyranny of small decisions" useful as an explanation for the dominance of reductionism in science and society, and shortly after Bill had published his essay Gene began referring to "a tyranny of small technologies." The efficiency of small technologies in fixing components of large-scale problems results in "the quick fix," he would repeat, such as the construction of a taller smokestack to take smoke out of town, instead of a system to produce less polluting waste in the first place.[37]

Private interests always impede planning for the public good. However, Odum said, the political pendulum in democracies swings between interest in the individual good, which he called "the conservative stance," and interest in the public good, which he called "the liberal stance" — between attention to the part and attention to the whole. "When diminishing returns of one approach set in, people tend to turn their attention to the other."[38] Odum, ever the optimist, viewed this situation as acceptable because "the parts (individual) and the whole (public) get attention, but not at the same time."[39]

The Pulsing Paradigm

While he never lost his belief in the stability of mature ecosystems and the desirability of stability in human socioenvironmental systems, Odum did modify his views on ecosystem homeostasis. In the late 1980s and early 1990s, after ecologists had accumulated substantial evidence against the notion that ecosystems evolve into equilibrium states, he abandoned the concept of ecosystem homeostasis and began using the term *homeorhesis* to describe the functioning of a mature ecosystem. *Homeorhesis*, derived from the Greek word *rheos*, for "stream" or "current," means "maintenance of a flow." Odum employed the term to designate the maintenance of a flow of energy through a system.[40]

Odum's work on cybernetics in 1981 with his colleague Bernard Patten influenced his understanding of ecosystem stability. Unlike organisms in which "set-point controls" such as the thyroid gland regulate metabolism and thereby maintain the organism's homeostasis, or engineered mechanical systems, in which, for example, a thermostat regulates temperature, ecosystems acquire stability by "non-set-point controls," that is, by using positive and negative feedback from subsystems.[41] Accordingly, as natural and social systems reach limits to their growth or evolution, they "pulse" around some kind of mean, because of their feedback system. A system that continues to expand with a negative productivity-to-cost ratio, for example, will eventually disintegrate.

Because they lack set-point controls, Odum said, social systems, such as cities, may exhibit a growth pattern of "boom and bust." Typically following a sigmoid curve, a social system grows slowly at first, and then more rapidly, and eventually the growth rate pulses back and forth around a mean. If it stays too long in its rapid-growth phase, the system grows beyond its ability to maintain itself and must reduce its size drastically in order to survive. The pulsing is an effect of the diseconomy of scale and one of the causes of the swinging of the political pendulum. Odum applied this model to all kinds of social systems, including the University of Georgia, where he tried again and again to convince administrators of the drawbacks of continued enrollment growth.[42]

Although Odum modified his understanding of ecosystem development in the face of new evidence, he never abandoned his conviction that the whole is greater than the sum of its parts. In his 1983 textbook *Basic Ecology* Odum stated that the "old folk wisdom about the forest being more than just a collection of trees is indeed a first working principle of ecology." But he endorsed Ervin Laszlo and H. Margenau's assertion that the history of science shows an alternation of reductionist and holistic thinking. Odum said, in keeping with his observations on the political pendulum, that the law of diminishing returns might be operative in science, with excessive effort in one direction necessitating a turn in another direction.[43]

Odumology

In using ecosystem theory for environmentalist purposes, Eugene Odum developed an idiosyncratic way of speaking about nature and society that his students called "Odumology." Odumology was, as one student said, "ecology according to Odum." It was the ecosystem ecology Gene and H. T. had worked out together, and it extended into the Odum brand of ecosystem environmentalism. A characteristic of Odumology was the metaphorical description of nature that some of Odum's fellow ecologists viewed as anthropocentric, even teleological. At the same time that he was creating with his brother a sophisticated "new ecology" founded on black-box analyses of energy flows through ecosystems, Gene Odum was describing scientific processes in language that elicited criticism for being unscientific. In his zeal for relating ecological concepts to environmental issues in language intelligible to the general public, Odum may not have fully realized the extent to which his speech was metaphorical.

He also had a tendency to incorporate terms from other disciplines. Odum had come to ecosystem ecology from the study of animal physiology. He often said that in the course of his early career he went from studying the "metabolism of birds" to studying the "metabolism of ecosystems." Although *metabolism*, defined in the *American Heritage Dictionary of Science* as "the sum of the physiological processes by which an organism maintains life," is a word that scientists normally reserve for description of the function of organisms or cells, Odum borrowed it and used it to refer to the function of the ecosystem.[44] He intended no organicism in his use of the word, as he had long ago discarded Clements's discredited notion of the superorganism, but he found it applicable to the ecosystem for its reference to the process by which a living whole sustains itself.

Having employed the metabolism metaphor in his description of ecosystem function, Odum quite naturally found also applicable to ecology the concept of homeostasis when he read Cannon's *Wisdom of the Body* in the late 1950s. That word, too, had been used mainly to describe the ability of organisms or cells to maintain an internal equilibrium, but Odum used it to describe the tendency of a "mature" ecosystem to maintain a steady state. The *Oxford English Dictionary* legitimates Odum's employment of the word in its definition of *homeostasis* as "maintenance of a dynamically stable state within a system by means of internal regulatory processes that counteract external disturbance of the equilibrium; the state so maintained."[45] Both *metabolism* and *homeostasis* imply the maintenance of a whole by the interaction of its component parts—and Odum's usage was therefore subjected to criticism by nonecosystem ecologists who questioned the very concept of the whole.

Odum's rhetoric for ecosystem development in general might be criticized as metaphorical if not actually organicist. Odum stated in "The Strategy of Ecosystem Development" that he was substituting the term *development* for the standard term *succession* to emphasize the interaction—the formation of relationships of organismal cooperation—that takes place in ecosystem succession. He went on to describe development as the ecosystem's "strategy" to achieve homeostasis.[46] Although Odum was not attributing any purpose to nature, his choice of words invited criticism that his scientific argument alone might not have received. All of the definitions the OED gives for *strategy* include the notion of rational planning toward a goal. By his language, then, Odum unintentionally personified nature.

Odum's portrayal of ecosystems as developing "from youth to maturity" constitutes another metaphor that might be more fitting for developed environments than for natural environments. In his 1975 talk at Yale University, Odum quoted economist Kenneth Boulding, whose ideas expressed in a 1972 essay echoed his own: "One might even have an optimistic image of the present period of human expansion as a kind of adolescence of the human race in which man has to devote a large portion of his energy to sheer physical growth. Hence we could regard the stationary state as a kind of maturity in which physical growth is no longer necessary and in which, therefore, human energies can be devoted to qualitative growth—knowledge, spirit and love."[47] Odum and Boulding were making the same argument with the same metaphor. When asked about its origin, Odum replied that the idea was in the air at the time and he did not know its source.[48] Since Boulding was older than Odum, the source was probably Frederic Clements.[49]

Odum cited Boulding to make a point about the difference between organisms' life spans and systems' life spans: "Development at the ecosystem level differs from development at the individual level in that aging and death do not inevitably follow achievement of maturity, as is the case in the individual organism."[50] But Odum extended the individual life-span metaphor in characterizing excess growth as "cancerous."

Odum's advice to "stop growing bigger and start getting better" was a value-laden allusion to the transformation of an ecosystem's component organisms, in his words, "from quantity to quality." But the latter expression is itself a value-laden metaphorical reference to the shift in ecosystem development from the predominance of organisms with high reproductive rates, rapid growth potential, and the ability to exploit unused resources to the predominance of organisms with lower reproductive rates, slower growth potential, and greater inclination to form symbiotic relationships—that is, the shift from the predominance of r-selected species to the predominance of K-selected species. A skeptic would ask, What does "quality" mean? From whose viewpoint may a population of organisms be described as high quality? Does "quality" refer to the population of organisms or to the ecosystem itself? What constitute the criteria for "quality"? Is not "quality" a value judgment? From Odum's standpoint, "getting better" meant increased "cooperation" among the system's component organisms, and consequently increased stability. "Getting better" also meant staying at a social system's optimal size, when P is equal to R. To Odum, it signified the recognition of the limits to growth imposed by the law of the diseconomy of scale and the adoption of measures to preserve the total environment. A system was "better," in his view, if it enabled its individual human components to thrive.

Odum found the concept of cooperation, used in ecology since Darwin's time as a category for relationships of interdependence, apt for a comparison of the basis for stability in both ecosystems and human societies.[51] Metaphorical in reference to nonhuman organisms, *cooperation* means, according to the OED, "working together for the same purpose or in the same task" — that is, purposeful interaction. Symbiosis in nature, because it enables certain organisms to survive, resembles cooperation among humans in society, but without intentionality. For Odum, ecosystems provided a lesson that humans should follow: symbiosis among the system's components keeps a system stable.

Ecologists Jim Porter and Karen Porter, Odum's colleagues at the University of Georgia, were graduate students at Yale in 1975 sitting in the audience at the "Beyond Growth" symposium when Odum delivered "Harmony between Man and Nature." Well acquainted with G. Evelyn Hutchinson, who was Karen's major professor, they and their fellow students were startled by Odum's style, which contrasted sharply with that of the urbane and aristocratic British scientist. Odum was unlike any of the scientists they had met at Yale, the Porters said. He seemed like a country preacher from the South with his pronounced North Carolina accent, his casual dress, and his folksy manner of speech. Yet the left-leaning students who believed that ecology would enable them to "save the earth" liked Odum's environmentalist message, populist political posture, vision of nature as inherently orderly, and desire for a peaceful and harmonious society in which humans would cooperate with one another rather than compete. They could see the applicability of ecosystem ecology to environmental ethics.

Ecology students at the University of Georgia also appreciated Odum's message. Odum taught them that beginning the study of nature by examining its parts first was "ridiculous." In an account he published in 1957 of his ecosystem-centered course he wrote:

We would not first bring the student the liver of the frog (or the stamen of the plant), have him study that, then next day bring him the isolated stomach or each individual muscle one by one — and finally during the last week of the course attempt to assemble all the parts into a frog. For one thing we would probably find that there was not enough time to study all the parts. Our poor frog would be most incomplete and probably bear little resemblance to the real frog when we tried to assemble the parts we did study! Yet amazing as it may seem many attempt to teach ecology using this backwards "parts-before-the-whole" procedure.[52]

By instructing his students in holism, Odum gave them a conceptual framework for thinking about the world that served them, as it did him, as a powerful tool.

Odum's students were well aware that their professor's pedagogical style was out of the ordinary. Joe Pechmann, who had been an undergraduate at Hamilton College in New York before coming to the University of Georgia to take his master's degree in ecology from Odum in the mid-1970s, described Odum's classroom performance as lively:

> As a classroom teacher Dr. Odum was very animated, full of ideas. He would spend part of the class time talking about the subject for the day and then he'd relate that to whatever was on his mind. If he'd just been on a trip somewhere, like to California, then he'd say what he thought about California, politics, the research site, etc. It was like having lunch with him. Students didn't get impatient, because they knew what they were getting into. He taught a class called "Principles of Ecology," which students called "Odumology." The students called it "Odumology" because it was ecology according to Odum. Dr. Odum made no pretense of providing a balanced view of other ecologists' opinions. He presented his own views. Gene was popular with students, and not a particularly difficult teacher. He didn't put great emphasis on grades.[53]

Wyatt Anderson, an undergraduate ecology student in the 1950s who later obtained his Ph.D. from Rockefeller University in genetics and returned to the University of Georgia, described Odum's lecture style as stimulating for its "cascade of ideas." Note taking was difficult, Anderson said, because Odum often began a new idea before finishing his explanation of the previous one. But the classroom was exciting, and so were the field trips. Odum was an excellent naturalist, capable of identifying an enormous number of birds, plants, insects, reptiles, and mammals. He impressed students with his "keen eye in the field" and keen ear, and he communicated his love of field-work to his students. But he walked so fast that students sometimes had a hard time keeping up. He was "awe-inspiring," said one former student, because he was both a great naturalist and a great ecologist. "He was a sage," said another.

Odum had a reputation for giving students high priority among his many responsibilities. He always enjoyed talking with students, and he listened to them as well. Pechmann recalled that one day when a secretary interrupted a discussion Odum was having with students to say that a senator wanted to speak with him on the phone, Odum asked her to tell the senator to call back because he was with students.

Odum gave students plenty of his time, but he was reluctant to select thesis topics for his graduate students or tell them what to do. Carolyn Lee Thomas, who worked with Odum for her master's degree in the late 1970s, relished the freedom Odum allowed his students, but said that not all students were equally appreciative. Some wanted Odum to give them more guidance and supervision, and some wanted him to travel less and stay in his office more. In the 1970s Odum was traveling a great deal, serving on national panels, receiving prizes, and "promoting his cause—the holistic theory of ecology." Thomas did not mind his absences because she thought his cause was important. She chose him as her major professor, she said, because he made her feel that she was at no disadvantage for being a woman. "He respected good ideas, no matter who brought them in. And he was very much a gentleman."

Thomas and others described Odum as a powerful thinker but not intimidating, generous with his ideas, good at explaining difficult concepts, good at arguing, "creative," "energetic," "approachable," "kind," and "never arrogant." He was a missionary, remembered one of them, "trying to convert people and help people to understand ecology." "He made us look at the big picture."

Odum regarded his undergraduate students as future voters, policy makers, economists, politicians, teachers, journalists, and scientists. He expected them to use what they learned about ecology from him as citizens making decisions affecting the total environment.

Odum regarded his graduate students as future ecosystem ecologists who would likewise apply their learning to environmental preservation. He considered them his friends and colleagues as well as his students, and he followed their careers after they left the University of Georgia. The graduate students all came to know Martha, who invited them home for tea from time to time. When students received their degrees, Homer Sharpe recalled, Martha would present them with a painting as a graduation gift.

Honors

The election to the National Academy of Sciences in 1970 was the first of many honors Eugene Odum was to accumulate in the 1970s. In November 1970 he accepted on behalf of the Institute of Ecology a commemorative telephone from Southern Bell marking the installation of its two-millionth phone. At the luncheon, Southern Bell screened a film that it had produced in collaboration with the Instructional Resources Center at the University of Georgia titled *Ecology—A Need for Understanding*. The film featured Odum discussing the need to regulate environmental resources and proposing ways in which the communications industry could help solve environmental problems.[54]

In 1971 Odum was named an Outstanding Educator of America by Outstanding Educators of America. He was also awarded a medal by the architects of Georgia for preserving the environment and was appointed to the Governor's Citizen Council for the Environment. In 1973, having been Alumni Foundation Distinguished Professor of Zoology for twenty years, he was granted the additional title of Callaway Professor of Ecology at the University of Georgia. He was elected president of the Ecology Section of the American Society of Zoologists for the 1973–74 academic year. He was appointed to the advisory committee of the Technological Assessment Commission established by Congress. In 1974, he was given the Eminent Ecologist Award of the Ecological Society of America and was elected an honorary member of the British Ecological Society. The following year, he was elected a fellow of the American Academy of Arts and Scientists.

In 1975, Eugene Odum shared with his brother, H. T., the $80,000 Prix de l'Institut de la Vie. In January 1976, the Georgia General Assembly passed a resolution expressing appreciation for his "many distinguished contributions." Later that same year he was named Conservationist of the Year by the Georgia Wildlife Federation and was given the Gold Seal Award by the National Council of the State Garden Clubs.

In 1977, Eugene Odum received Pepperdine University's $150,000 John and Alice Tyler Ecology Award, which honors individuals or teams of individuals "whose accomplishments have been recognized as conferring the greatest benefit on mankind in the fields of Ecology and Environment." When presenting the prize to Odum, President Jimmy Carter said, "Gene, I'm proud of you." Odum responded, "Jimmy, I'm proud of you, too." Odum donated the $150,000 to the University of Georgia's Institute of Ecology as a challenge grant to establish an endowment fund for research and education in ecology. Accompanied by Martha, he then traveled to Pepperdine University in Malibu, California, for a second award ceremony and a Hollywood reception at the Beverly Wiltshire hosted by Art Linkletter. Afterward, Gene and Martha went up the coast to Carmel so that Martha could paint.

On 12 October 1977, the new Ecology Building at the University of Georgia, built in part with funds from a grant from the National Science Foundation, was dedicated. Secretary of the Interior Cecil Andrus came to Athens for the event, and Congressman Doug Bernard entered a tribute to Odum in the *Congressional Record*.

By the end of the decade Odum had won the University of Georgia's Blue Key Award for being an "Outstanding Georgian," the University of Georgia's Alumni Society Faculty Service Award, and the University of North Carolina's Distinguished Alumnus Award. He had been made an honorary member of the Southeastern Estuarine Research Society and had been appointed a trustee of The Nature Conservancy and of the Conservation Foundation. He had received the Distinguished Service Award from the American Institute of Biological Sciences and the Meritorious Teaching Award from the Association of Southeastern Biologists. He was a member of the Environmental Advisory Committee of the United States Department of Energy. Odum was now being called "the father of modern ecology."[55]

Throughout this period, Gene and Martha enjoyed many opportunities to combine their interests in ecology and art. Their marriage had always been a happy one, and they used Gene's professional conferences in different parts of the world as occasions to travel together—throughout the United States including Hawaii and Alaska, to Japan, to Canada, to Europe, to Africa. Martha's illustrated Christmas newsletters, initiated in 1955 and continued with few interruptions until 1994, right before her death, recounted not only the sequence of honors Gene acquired during the year but also the trips they made and the projects they took on at home. The annual newsletters constituted a family diary, and the approximately three hundred watercolors she left on her death constituted a history of their travels.

One project Martha described in her 1971 Christmas newsletter was the purchase of Spring Hollow, a "small, complete watershed with many springs, diversified forest, and rare wildflowers," to which she and Gene moved a 150-year-old log cabin. The watershed, located fifteen miles north of Athens in a very rural part of the state, covered 90 acres. The two-story cabin was twenty-eight feet by eighteen feet, with square-hewn logs joined by wooden pegs and hand-made nails, and fieldstone chimneys at either end. At the bottom of the newsletter Martha depicted—in caricature—the house-moving caravan: the police vehicle leading the way with its lights flashing, the truck towing the log cabin "minus roof and chimneys," and her own car bringing up the rear for the twenty-mile journey to Pocataligo, Georgia. The drawing showed a large branch resting on the cabin, with Martha's words underneath: "We hit a big tree and snapped a wire!"[56] Gene built a small laboratory for himself not far from the cabin and had a pond constructed. Martha and Gene often drove out late in the afternoon to the cabin, which they nicknamed "Pokey," and sometimes spent the night. It was on a weekend there that they rescued and adopted Bo, a terrier puppy that had belonged to a neighbor who shot him for killing a chicken. They later added two additional pieces of land to their property, for a total of 150 acres.

Martha reported in the same Christmas newsletter their delight over their son Bill's engagement to Maria Bogatta from Long Island. Bill had joined the faculty of the Environmental Science Department at the University of Virginia in January 1971, and he was married in July 1972.

The Odums loved the sea, and in the mid-1980s they bought a contemporary house, under construction at the time, on Fripp Island, near Beaufort, South Carolina. "Sandcastle," as Martha named the house, was situated on the marsh side of the island rather than on the ocean side, because Gene disapproved of developers' efforts to control the erosion patterns of the beach. The reason they gave their friends for their purchase was that they wanted to take Bo with them to the beach, and Bo was not welcome in the condominiums. They bought several additional undeveloped lots near Sandcastle, not all of them contiguous, in order to preserve habitat for birds as the rest of the island was filling up with new houses.

In the course of the next few years Gene and Martha spent many long weekends at Sandcastle, reading, swimming, walking on the beach, playing croquet — with fierce competitiveness — and exploring the island, which was populated with abundant wildlife, including alligators. They were always accompanied by their dog, first Bo, and then, after Bo died, Phoebe, a spitz–basset hound mix. From their screened porch, where they ate most of their meals during the warm months, they could watch the activities of the island. Deer crossed the marsh; egrets nested down the lagoon from their house and flew out at dawn and in at dusk; raccoons came up to the house for scraps in the early evening; and fishing boats went out to sea and returned. Gene kept binoculars handy so that he could identify the birds. Martha decorated the house, which had floor-to-ceiling windows and a fireplace, with poster-size reproductions of Georgia O'Keeffe paintings in the living room and all three bedrooms. And she installed six symmetrically arranged easy chairs because she wanted no hierarchy in the seating arrangement when guests joined them for weekends.

Gene and Martha became passionate croquet players during their last years together, and they joined the Fripp Island Croquet Club and the Lake Oconee Croquet Club. The enthusiasm and skill they had displayed for tennis when their knees still allowed them to compete in tournaments was transferred to croquet. Martha created a six-wicket half court on their property in Athens, next to Gene's vegetable garden. Gene was proud of his handicap of 16, in a scale of 1 to 25, and his name was listed in the 1999 Directory of the United States Croquet Association/Croquet Federation of America. Shortly before she died, Martha said to him, "Don't forget that the last time we played croquet I beat you."

6 The Big Picture

In June 1984 Gene Odum retired from the University of Georgia — "kicking and screaming," one of his friends said — leaving his posts as director of the Institute of Ecology, Alumni Foundation Distinguished Professor of Zoology, and Callaway Professor of Ecology. Georgia law required state employees to retire at seventy, and Odum had reached that age on 17 September 1983. On his seventy-first birthday, the Institute of Ecology celebrated Odum's career by unveiling a bronze bust of him, created by sculptor William Thompson of the university's Art Department, which stands in the foyer of the institute's new building. Inscribed in the sculpture's base is the sentence: "The ecosystem is greater than the sum of its parts."

Although his colleagues knew that Odum had retired, as they had attended the numerous events in his honor, they noticed little evidence of his emeritus status. He continued to come to his office daily; he continued to work with graduate students; he continued to accept committee assignments for the university; he continued to have lunch with fellow ecologists, graduate students, and undergraduates; he continued to influence hiring decisions at the Institute of Ecology, to the pleasure of some and to the frustration of others; he continued to teach as a guest lecturer in classes across the university; he continued to travel professionally; he continued to revise his textbooks; and he continued to publish his thoughts in every possible venue. He maintained close ties with researchers at the Savannah River Ecology Laboratory and at the Marine Institute on Sapelo Island. He served on the advisory committee of Biosphere 2.

Nevertheless, Odum's position in the Athens community had changed; he was now an elder statesman. He was consulted by politicians about pollution; by planners about land use; by transportation officials about freeway routes; by university administrators about environmental literacy requirements; and by newspapers, magazines, and radio stations about local legislation and development. He spoke to civic organizations, church groups, and high school and grade school classes about ecological principles and environmental preservation.

In 1999, when the University of Georgia initiated its "Vision 2010" strategic planning project, the vice president for strategic planning and public affairs asked Odum to compose a brief essay. Odum complied with "The Environment in 2010," in which he used his usual strategy of depicting what might be possible if people would only behave sensibly. In the year 2010, Odum envisioned,

large landfills and toxic wastes dumps are a thing of the past as waste-reduction and elimination at the source has been accomplished by a balance between governmental regulation and incentives (the "stick and carrot" approach), aided by new waste reduction technology. Beginning with the year 2000, environmental quality was a major issue in federal and state as well as local elections for the first time ever. Fuel prices have risen to where they ought to be in terms of long-term costs, so the one-driver large vans and oversize trucks are a thing of the past. Cars are smaller, more fuel efficient, and there are many more bicycles and small motor scooters. More people and goods move by rail. There is more use of renewable energy sources such as solar. Village cluster developments are gradually replacing sprawl; one no longer has to use a car to shop or go to a movie, or to go to school or college.[1]

The scenario Odum presented was not completely optimistic. He forecast deteriorating environmental quality because of the increasing human biomass and the increasing per capita consumption of the earth's life-support resources. "Climate instability and change, rising sea levels, increasing ozone holes, too-rapid urbanization, ethnic and religious wars, local famines and so on will continue to escalate until we recognize that achieving a global society requires cooperation, rather than confrontation, for the common good," he said. He predicted that the greatest challenge of the twenty-first century would be the closing of the "dangerous" gap between the rich and the poor, which could be accomplished only by a reduction in the consumption of resources and energy by the rich.[2]

At the age of eighty-five, Odum enjoyed a reputation at home and abroad as a left-of-center futurist willing to address groups of all kinds. Wherever he spoke he expressed enthusiasm for progress being made toward environmental health and social justice, and instead of focusing on the failures of society he emphasized the possibilities for ameliorative change. His favorite subject was the future, and he never tired of translating ecological principles into lessons for the preservation of the natural environment and the maintenance of the developed environment. Odum was known to all of his friends and colleagues as a man of astounding energy, high spirits, perseverance, and optimism. He was not known as philosophical, self-reflective, or introspective.

Few of his friends and colleagues were aware of the personal tribulations

Gene and Martha had suffered during his extraordinarily productive career. In 1987 their son Tommy passed away after spending forty years in an institution because of his severe physical and mental retardation. Gene and Martha almost never mentioned him, for Martha could not do so without shedding tears. On 3 April 1991, their other son, Bill, died suddenly of liver cancer. He had just stepped down from the chair of the Department of Environmental Sciences at the University of Virginia. On his deathbed Bill said to his mother, "In the big picture it was a great life, and this dying is just a small part of it." At his memorial service, held in a garden at the University of Virginia, Gene and H. T. both gave eulogies, as did many of Bill's friends and students, including one undergraduate, who said that Bill had changed her life. The Estuarine Research Federation honored Bill with the William E. Odum Memorial Symposium, organized by Linda K. Blum, at the organization's annual meeting in November 1993 on Hilton Head Island, South Carolina. Gene and H. T. jointly delivered the keynote address, titled "Nature's Pulsing Paradigm," by Eugene P. Odum, Howard T. Odum, and William E. Odum. Published in 1995, it was the Odum, Odum, and Odum paper Gene had always dreamed of producing.[3]

On 29 June 1995, Martha, Gene's beloved wife of fifty-six years, died of cancer. On her deathbed she repeated Bill's words, "In the big picture it was a great life, and this dying is just a small part of it."

Having been diagnosed twenty years before with congestive heart failure, Gene had never expected to outlive Martha and Bill in good health. Yet he seldom talked of the loneliness he obviously felt after their deaths. Instead he busied himself with writing; gardening; spending time in his office talking with colleagues and students; dining with friends; speaking to local groups; accepting the awards that the world continued to bestow upon him; and, as he put it, "entering Martha into art history."

Writing for the World

The essay Gene Odum contributed to Vice President Donald Eastman's booklet *Vision 2010: Strategic Planning for the 21st Century* reflected his belief that social stability requires not only a harmonious, mutually supportive relationship between the developed environment and the natural environment but also social justice within the developed environment. By the time he published *Ecological Vignettes*, at the age of eighty-five, Odum had fully explored the implications for social interaction of his model of nature.

Odum had spent his career writing and revising his textbooks, and he continued to do so into his old age. In 1989 he published *Ecology and Our Endangered Life-Support Systems*, "a citizen's guide to the principles of ecology as they relate to today's threats to earth's life-support systems," for which he produced second and third editions in 1993 and 1997.[4] His lifelong ambition had been to write a book that would enable ordinary people to understand ecological principles. Since *Ecology and Our Endangered Life-Support Systems*, lively and informative as it was, did not fulfill that ambition, Odum tried again with a book he called *Ecological Vignettes: Ecological Approaches to Dealing with Human Predicaments*. Filled with instructive cartoons by Sidney Harris and Tom Hammond, it was a book he thought should be sold in airports. It was not, because he had added to the humorous and easily intelligible "vignettes" almost two hundred pages of "Essays and Commentaries for Further Reading." The essays were mostly his own, but they included a few by his brother; his son; and a sociologist, William R. Catton Jr., who discussed the differential impact of humans on the environment with respect to their consumption levels. Immediately after its publication Odum asked his publisher to issue a "vignettes-only" second edition that could be sold in airports, and he began working on additional vignettes for it.

Odum organized the vignettes around adages and maxims: "To grow or not to grow is not the question; the question is when to stop getting bigger and start getting better." "When things get tough, it pays to cooperate." "Don't put all your eggs in one basket." "Count on scientists to recognize problems but not to solve them." "Money is a very incomplete measure of wealth." "The whole is greater than the sum of its parts." The last vignette focused on environmentalists' critique of the Bible's exhortation to be fruitful, to multiply, and to take dominion over the earth (Genesis 1:28), which

Odum interpreted in keeping with Aldo Leopold's model for the emergence of ethics out of interdependence and his own model for ecosystem development.

> In the early stages of civilization, taking dominion over the environment and exploiting resources (clearing the land for crops, mining the earth for materials and energy, etc.) as well as high birth rates were necessary for human survival. As our society becomes crowded, ever more resource-demanding, and technologically complex, there is less need for large families and child labor, and, more important, various limitations are reached that force us to think and act as stewards. It is now very much in our interests as individuals to begin to do so.[5]

The message appealed to the church groups that invited Odum to speak about environmental preservation.

Ecological Vignettes, composed of reader-friendly lessons from ecology and more challenging scientific essays, encapsulates Odum's environmentalist obsessions. At the end of his life, with his intelligence as keen as ever, Odum continued to find new ways to express, again and again, the lessons he took from ecosystem ecology. He gave lots of advice but cheerfully understood that the time was not right for much of it.

Eugene Odum was not inclined toward philosophy. He read widely in the sciences and social sciences, but with the exception of Smuts's book on holism, not in philosophy. Nor was he inclined to express abstractly his vision of nature and culture, philosophically coherent as it was. His social philosophy might nevertheless be summarized as follows: The degree to which the interdependent components of a social system form nonexploitative bonds of cooperation, preserve the natural environment that supports their system, and ensure the continuance of diversity in both the natural environment and the social system is the degree to which the system will acquire stability. The interdependence of the system's components makes cooperation advantageous to all of the components, because their individual well-being depends on the stability of the whole.

An article Odum published in *BioScience* in 1992, "Great Ideas in Ecology for the 1990s," synthesizes his understanding of the discipline. In it he set forth the principles he considered most important to ecosystem ecology:

the ecosystem is a thermodynamically open system; ecosystems maintain stability by internal feedback; natural selection can occur at the level of the group, and it involves mutualism as well as interorganismal competition; mutualism increases when resources are scarce; ecosystem development is a two-phase process in the second stage of which the ecosystem is "self-organized"; and "since the beginning of life on earth, organisms have not only adapted to physical conditions but have modified the environment in ways that have proven to be beneficial to life in general." Among these ecological principles Odum interspersed a few environmental precepts: the calculation of the carrying capacity of a socioenvironmental system must take into account both the number of users and the intensity of per capita use; input management is the only way to reduce nonpoint pollution; the gaps between human-made and natural life-support goods and services and between nonsustainable short-term and sustainable long-term management must be bridged; and "a parasite-host model for man and the biosphere is a basis for turning from exploiting the earth to taking care of it."[6] Central to Odum's ecological, social, and ethical visions is the conviction that "a species that benefits its community has survival value greater than a species that does not," for which Odum cited studies by D. S. Wilson on evolution at the level of communities, R. Axelrod and W. D. Hamilton on the evolution of cooperation, and S. J. Gould on the expansion of evolutionary theory.[7]

At the end of the twentieth century Odum's model for ecology seemed to fit the new global society, for national governments worldwide acknowledged the imperative for cooperation among the world's interdependent nations. In a June 1988 commencement address at the University of Georgia Odum had proclaimed: "In human society, we see the beginnings of worldwide recognition of the need to shift from military confrontation to mutual aid in the dramatic changes that are occurring in the relationships between the superpowers—the United States and the Soviet Union."[8] His prediction was accurate. The Soviet Union disintegrated, as Odum said it would, because its maintenance costs, which included the costs of military confrontation, exceeded its productivity.[9] The old hierarchical assumption that dominance assures well-being began to give way, at least in the United States, to the more holistic notion that the well-being of a nation, even the most powerful nation, depends on the stability of the geopolitical system of which it is a part. In terms of the Odum "strategy for ecosystem development," the global community of nations appeared to be moving out of its pioneer stage, in which nations struggled rapaciously against each other for resources and dominion, and into a mature stage in which increased diversity and the proliferation of relationships of mutualism would bring equilibrium to the whole. Eventually, according to that strategy, the global society will achieve a pulsating stability.

Eugene Odum's grand theory provides both guidelines and a rationale for the preservation of part of the planet as a natural environment to support the developed environment. His explanation of the ecosystem, in textbooks used around the world in many translations, has helped make the environmentalist movement a transnational effort to protect natural areas, slow population growth, eliminate sources of pollution, and recycle waste. Odum has had a powerful influence on the emergence of a holistic political vision among environmentalists and, to some extent, on the emergence of a holistic ecological vision among ordinary citizens who learn about ecosystems through newspapers and television.

But the challenge to the Odum model of ecosystem development has also gained strength. "Post-Odum" ecology presents a universe that is not self-organizing but is characterized by continuous, unpredictable change. Unlike ecosystem ecology, which came to be indistinguishable in the public mind from environmentalism, post-Odum ecology has no easily discernible environmentalist corollary. The new ecology has introduced fundamental questions that environmentalists of the twenty-first century will have to face, such as: If unattended natural areas evolve continuously, what constitutes environmental "preservation"? How may human interference in natural systems be measured? Historian Donald Worster asked, What does "environmental damage" mean in a world of natural chaos? [10] Ecologist Daniel Botkin, who pointed out that "nature in the twenty-first century will be a nature that we make," said that the real issue is the degree to which our molding of nature will be intentional or unintentional, desirable or undesirable. [11]

The phrase "post-Odum ecology" did not appeal to Gene Odum; nor did the science it represented. To the end of his life Odum saw the universe as orderly. But he did not disagree with Botkin's observation that humans must now manage nature in order to maintain an adequate proportion of the planet as a life-support system. Although he did not claim to be optimistic about the future for human civilization, Odum always described himself as "hopeful" that the human species, always clever — however late — in solving life-threatening problems, would finally effect a "harmony between man and nature."

Entering Martha into Art History

Gene and Martha Odum were in love with each other the whole of their long marriage. They celebrated their fiftieth wedding anniversary on 18 November 1989 with two parties, the first a dinner in their home for forty of Gene's relatives, most of whom came from North Carolina; the second a candlelit dessert reception-dance at the Georgia State Botanical Garden for two hundred of their friends. In her Christmas letter Martha reported that it was a "magical, happy evening." "There were table covers of gold lamé, bouquets of daisies and ferns (like my wedding bouquet), and our own pottery and wood bowls and candlesticks," she wrote. "We danced to a wonderful band, 'The Professors,' playing 'the golden oldies.'"

Three years later Gene watched Martha put together a jewelry exhibition and symposium at the Georgia Museum of Art in honor of a close friend, the talented silversmith Ann Orr Morris, who had been stabbed to death in Athens by a psychotic vagabond. Martha collected the pieces for the exhibit from owners of Ann Orr jewelry living all over the Southeast and oversaw the photography for the exhibition catalog, *Ann Orr: Silversmith, Goldsmith & Enamelist*. William Eiland, director of the Georgia Museum of Art at the University of Georgia, who worked with her, described Martha as "single-minded in her determination, generous in her support, and visionary in her leadership of the project."[12] Gene thus learned from Martha that the way to enter an artist into art history is to organize an exhibition and create a catalog for it.

When Martha passed away, leaving in her studio almost three hundred finished watercolors, Gene went to Eiland to arrange an exhibition of them.

At that time the university was constructing a large new building for the Georgia Museum of Art, and in honor of Gene's significant donation, it established the Martha H. and Eugene P. Odum Gallery on the second floor. The gallery opened in January 1997 with a show, curated by Jennifer De-Prima, of Martha's watercolors, silver goblets, and silver and gold jewelry. The accompanying catalog, titled *Martha Odum: Watercolors*, featured sixty-five of her paintings, with an introduction by Gene and short essays by Ei-land, DePrima, Edward Lambert, and Betty Jean Craige.[13] In the introduction Gene wrote: "Art and ecology have been a partnership in the Odum family for more than fifty years. Martha, in addition to being a gifted designer and craftsperson, was a landscape painter who was able to capture the 'essence of place' in her watercolors. Along with our son and my brother, I am a landscape ecologist who studies the 'essence of function' of landscapes as living, pulsing ecosystems." Gene wrote that after his retirement he had accepted lecture invitations generally only for places where Martha wanted to paint.[14]

Martha Odum influenced the cultural life of Athens for more than fifty years. Generous with her time and money, she served her friends as artistic adviser, interior designer, florist, carpenter, landscape architect, and promoter. Highly energetic and full of zeal for uniting local artists, she encouraged her fellow Athens art lovers to form galleries that would bring notice to the city as a developing art center, and in 1967 and 1968 she served as president of the Athens Art Association. When she was in her seventies, she often said that she had achieved her adolescent ambition of creating art for the sake of art alone, and she was happy with what she had accomplished. Without the obligations that employment as a commercial artist would have entailed, she had been able to travel with Gene and to paint whatever she liked. Between 1941 and 1990, when she exhibited her watercolors for the last time in the gallery of the Institute of Ecology, she had ten one-woman shows. It was her desire that on her death her paintings be distributed as gifts to relatives, friends, and institutions.[15] Gene implemented her wish.

At the age of eighty-five Gene decided to make another book of Martha's watercolors. He had 150 of her on-the-spot sketches of places where they had been together arranged in a photo album, which he sent to Eiland along with a proposal that the Georgia Museum of Art publish fifty of the sketches with commentaries he would write. The book, which he would subsidize, would be called "Essence of Place, with Watercolors by Martha H. Odum and Ecological Commentaries by Eugene P. Odum."

More Honors

In 1987 Gene and H. T. traveled to Stockholm with their wives, Martha and Betty, to accept the Crafoord Prize in Ecology, which was awarded to the brothers by the Royal Swedish Academy of Sciences in Stockholm. Gene used his share of the prize, $125,000, to establish a private foundation for the promotion of research and education in ecology.

The last years of Gene's life were filled with accolades. Between 1980 and 2000 he was given six honorary doctorates, from Hofstra University; Ferum College; the University of North Carolina, Asheville; la Universidad del Valle, Guatemala; Ohio State University; and la Universidad de San Francisco, Quito, Ecuador. He was recognized for his contributions to science by the Ecological Society of America, the Philadelphia Academy of Sciences, and the International Association of Landscape Ecology. He was recognized for his contributions to environmental preservation by the United States Departments of the Interior and Energy, the National Wildlife Federation, the Georgia Environmental Council, the Society of Environmental Toxicology and Chemistry, and the Georgia Conservancy. He was honored at a conference on ecosystem processes organized by Larry Pomeroy and at numerous other events at the University of Georgia. He was the subject of a short film, *Eugene Odum: An Ecologist's Life*, written by novelist and science journalist Philip Lee Williams, directed by David Silvian from the Georgia Center for Continuing Education, and aired on Georgia Public Television; and he was interviewed on a CNN *Future Watch* program.[16] He received the Estuarine Federation Lifetime Achievement Award jointly with H. T. and, posthumously, Bill.

For many years Gene and Martha had saved Gene's salary and had lived on his textbook royalties. Uninterested in thinking about their personal financial situation, they were surprised to discover, about the time Gene and

H. T. won the Crafoord Prize, that they had accumulated a great deal of wealth, some of it in landholdings, the rest in savings and retirement accounts. So they began giving it away. Gene had already donated his Tyler Prize money to the University of Georgia Foundation to create an endowment for the Institute of Ecology and had established the Odum Lecture Series at the institute, which David C. Coleman inaugurated in November 1985. He provided an initial gift of $25,000, with a promise to match an additional $25,000, to establish the Odum-Kendeigh Fellowship Fund for the Department of Ecology at his alma mater, the University of Illinois. He gave the University of North Carolina the thirty acres in Chapel Hill of the old Odum farm that he had inherited from his father, worth approximately $750,000, to endow the Howard W. Odum Professorship, and gave additional funds to the UNC School of Social Work his father had founded. He gave a large gift to the William E. Odum Fund at the University of Virginia and willed the university one of his lots on Fripp Island appraised at $150,000. At the University of Georgia he contributed to the Center for Humanities and Arts; the Center for Latin American and Caribbean Studies; and Sphinx, a student honor society. And he deeded over to the Institute of Ecology Spring Hollow, his 150-acre watershed at Pocataligo, Georgia, for which he provided funds for an endowment to support research there for a long time to come. He made major gifts to the Eugene P. Odum Professorship that the College of Arts and Sciences was creating and to the Georgia Museum of Art. And he regularly sent checks to environmental preservation groups. In all, Odum gave away $1.5 million. In his will he left the University of Georgia much of the remainder of his estate — the million-dollar twenty-five-acre plot of forested land, now in the middle of an elegant Athens neighborhood, on which he and Martha had spent their lives.

After Martha's death Gene Odum put great importance on socializing with colleagues and friends, and he seldom missed his midday trip to the university. He often ate lunch with Frank Golley, Dac Crossley, Ron Pulliam, Gary Barrett, and Mack Rawson, as well as graduate students, faculty from other departments, visiting lecturers, and visiting politicians. He enjoyed talking with fellow institute ecologists Carl Jordan, Ron Carroll, Dave Coleman, Bud Freeman, Larry Pomeroy, Patty Gowaty, Paul Hendrix, Judy

Meyer, and Gene Helfman; and with Savannah River Ecology Laboratory scientists Mike Smith, Lehr Brisbane, Whit Gibbons, and Becky Sharitz, when they came up to Athens from Augusta. Whenever he had the opportunity he dined out and attended concerts with friends—with Bobbie Epting, Fausto and Elena Sarmiento and their family, Brenda Stewart, Gary and Terry Barrett, and Betty Jean Craige. And wherever he ate he asked for a doggy bag to take home a meaty treat for Phoebe.

At home, when not reading or writing, Gene could be found with Phoebe in his "reduced tillage, chemical, and water usage vegetable garden," which covered a quarter of an acre of the land adjacent to his croquet court. He wrote up a description of his agroecological practices for his friends:

> The garden area is rototilled once a year in the fall and planted in crimson clover (a cool-season nitrogen-fixer crop), which grows slowly over winter and forms a green mat by spring. Summer crops (squash, tomatoes, etc.) are planted directly into this mat without further tillage. Mulch ($7 pickup truck–load from local landfill) and wheat straw ($2 a bale) are used liberally. All of this suppresses weed growth and builds up soil quality. Small amounts of mineral fertilizer are applied to root zone, and watering is restricted to root zone by use of submerged pots and cans (the "jug irrigation" system used for centuries in arid countries). (We have a lot to learn from traditional agriculture practiced in underdeveloped countries.) For the most part no pesticides are needed. If pesticides are needed, only short-lived pesticides, such as Sevin and Rotonone, are used. A bamboo lattice fence enclosing bean area keeps out deer. Crops are kale and collards in the winter, snap peas in the spring, and pole beans squash, tomatoes, potatoes, and blueberries in the summer.

In his late eighties, after the publication of *Ecological Vignettes* in 1998, Gene Odum embarked on three new writing projects: "Essence of Place," which would display his fifty-year partnership with Martha in ecology and art; a new edition of *Basic Ecology*, on which he was working with Barrett; and another book, "Southeastern Songbirds: Their Ecology and Their Contributions to the Human Quality of Life." And he kept up his lifelong practice of rising early, feeding the birds, walking his dog, and writing for two hours before driving to his office "to socialize."

Days after his eighty-sixth birthday, Gene underwent surgery for the first time in his life to remove a bone spur in his neck that was pressing on his spinal cord and causing numbness in his extremities. Surrounded by attentive and devoted friends, he lacked nothing he needed—but patience. Housebound for several weeks after the operation, with his neck in a brace, he found recovery slower than he had anticipated and he chafed at the doctor's order that he refrain from driving. But remembering his father's admonition not to waste time, he busied himself with writing.

At the end of his life Gene Odum has remained very busy. He is, he says, "racing against time."

The Publications of Eugene P. Odum

The publications are listed in chronological order by year, and alphabetically within
each year.

BOOKS

With Earle R. Greene, Herbert Stoddard, William Griffin, and Ivan Tompkins.
*Birds of Georgia: A Preliminary Checklist and Bibliography of Georgia Orni-
thology.* Athens: University of Georgia Press, 1945.
A North Carolina Naturalist: H. H. Brimley. Selections from His Writings. Chapel
Hill: University of North Carolina Press, 1949.
Fundamentals of Ecology. Philadelphia: W. B. Saunders, 1953.
In collaboration with Howard T. Odum. *Fundamentals of Ecology.* 2nd ed. Phila-
delphia: W. B. Saunders, 1959.

Ecology. Modern Biology Series. New York: Holt, Rinehart and Winston, 1963.

Fundamentals of Ecology. 3rd ed. Philadelphia: W. B. Saunders, 1971.

Ecology: The Link between the Natural and the Social Sciences. 2nd ed. New York: Holt, Rinehart and Winston, 1975.

Basic Ecology. Philadelphia: W. B. Saunders, 1983.

Ecology and Our Endangered Life Support Systems. Sunderland, Mass.: Sinauer Associates, 1989.

Ecology and Our Endangered Life Support Systems. 2nd ed. Sunderland, Mass.: Sinauer Associates, 1993.

Ecology: A Bridge between Science and Society. Sunderland, Mass.: Sinauer Associates, 1997.

With F. O. Sarmiento. *Ecología: el puente entre ciencia y sociedad.* McGraw-Hill/Interamericana Editores, S. A. de C. V. Mexico, 1998.

Ecological Vignettes: Ecological Approaches to Dealing with Human Predicaments. Amsterdam: Harwood Academic Publishers (Gordon and Breach), 1998.

JOURNAL PAPERS, NOTES, ESSAYS, REVIEWS, AND COMMENTARIES

1930

"Back-yard Ornithology." *Bird-Lore* 32 (1930): 419–420.

1931

"Notes on the Nesting Habits of the Hooded Warbler." *Wilson Bulletin* (December 1931): 316–317.

1932

"Notes from Chapel Hill, North Carolina." *Auk* 49 (1932): 362–363.

1933

"A Brewster's Warbler in North Carolina." *Auk* 50 (1933): 116.

"Spring Occurrence of the Tennessee Warbler in North Carolina." *Auk* 50 (1933): 117.

1934

With Edmund Taylor. "1933 Notes from Chapel Hill, N.C." *Auk* 51 (1934): 396–397.

1935

With Edmund Taylor, Coit Coker, and Arnold Breckenridge. "The Birds of Chapel Hill, North Carolina." *Journal of the Elisha Mitchell Scientific Society* 51.2 (1935): 312–341.

1936

"Notes on the History of the Germ Cells in the Toadfish (*Opsanus tau*)." *Journal of the Elisha Mitchell Scientific Society* 52.2 (1936): 235–248.

1938

"Late Nesting Date for Yellow-billed Cuckoo." *Chat* (September–October 1938): 63.

1939

"Variations in the Heart Rate of Birds: A Study in Physiological Ecology." *Ecological Monographs* 3 (1939): 299–326.

With Frank A. Pitelka. "Storm Mortality in a Winter Starling Roost." *Auk* 56 (1939): 451–455.

1940

With S. Charles Kendeigh. "The Cardio-Vibrometer: A New Instrument for Measuring the Heart Rate and Other Body Activities of Animals." *Ecology* 21.1 (1940): 106.

1941

"Annual Cycle of the Black-capped Chickadee 1." *Auk* 58 (1941): 314–333.

"Annual Cycle of the Black-capped Chickadee 2." *Auk* 59 (1942): 518–535.

"Technics in Life History Study." *Jack-Pine Warbler* 21.2 (1941): 1–9.

"Technics in Life History Study." *Oriole* 6.3 (1941): 1–9.

"Winter Homing Behavior of the Chickadee." *Bird-Banding* 12 (1941): 113–119.

With William Ingram. "Nests and Behavior of *Lepomis gibbosus* (Linnaeus) in Lincoln Pond, Rensselaerville, New York." *American Midland Naturalist* 26.1 (1941): 182–193.

1942

"A Comparison of Two Chickadee Seasons." *Bird-Banding* 23.4 (1942): 155–159.

"Annual Cycle of the Black-capped Chickadee 3." *Auk* 59 (1942): 500–531.

"Long Incubation by a Carolina Chickadee." *Auk* 59 (1942): 430–431.

"Muscle Tremors and the Development of Temperature Regulation in Birds." *American Journal of Physiology* 136.4 (1942): 618–622.

"News and Reviews. *Birds of North Carolina.*" *Oriole* (December1942): 36–37.

"Notes from Athens." *Oriole* 7 (1942): 20.

1943

"'Courtship Feeding' in the Black-capped Chickadee." *Auk* 60 (1943): 444–445.

"Long-eared Owl, White-crowned Sparrows, and Prairie Horned Larks at Athens." *Oriole* 8 (1943): 20.

"The Vegetation of the Edmund Niles Huyck Preserve, New York." *American Midland Naturalist* 29.1 (1943): 72–88.

"Some Physiological Variation in the Black-capped Chickadee." *Wilson Bulletin* 55.3 (1943): 178–191.

"Some Possible Range Extensions in North Carolina." *Oriole* 8.1–2 (1943): 6–8.

1944

"Circulatory Congestion as a Possible Factor Regulating Incubation Behavior." (General Notes). *Wilson Bulletin* 56.1 (1944): 48–49.

"A Guide to Bird Watching." Review of *A Guide to Bird Watching,* by Joseph J. Hickey. *Ecology* 25.2 (1944): 256–257.

"Notes on Small Mammal Populations at Mountain Lake, Virginia." *Journal of Mammalogy* 25.4 (1944): 404–405.

"*Sorex longirostris* at Mountain Lake, Va." *Journal of Mammalogy* 25.2 (1944): 196.

"Summer Occurrence of the Oven-bird at Athens." *Oriole* 9 (1944): 35.

"Water Consumption of Certain Mice in Relation to Habitat Selection." *Journal of Mammalogy* 25.4 (1944): 404–405.

1945

"Chuck-will's Widow in Dade County." *Oriole* 10 (1945): 55.

"The Concept of the Biome as Applied to the Distribution of North American Birds." *Wilson Bulletin* 57.3 (1945): 191–201.

"The Heart Rate of Small Birds." *Science* 101.2615 (1945): 153–154.

"A Nest of the Blackburnian Warbler in Pickens County, Ga." *Oriole* 10 (1945): 53.

"Northern Species Summering at the End of the Blue Ridge." *Oriole* 10 (1945): 49–52.

"In Quest of Georgia Mountain Warblers." *Oriole* 10.2 (1945): 15–19.

With G. W. Burton. "The Distribution of Stream Fish in the Vicinity of Mountain Lake, Virginia." *Ecology* 26.2 (1945): 182–194.

1946

With T. D. Burleigh. "Southward Invasion in Georgia." *Auk* 63 (1946): 388–401.

With W. W. Griffin. "Black-throated Green Warbler Definitely Breeding in Pinelog Mountain." *Oriole* 11 (1946): 51.

With W. T. Summerford. "Comparative Toxicity of DDT and Four Analogues to Goldfish, Gambusia, and Culex Larvae." *Science* 104 (1946): 480–482.

1947

"Breeding Bird Populations of Virgin Southern Hemlock Forest; Young Short-leaf–Loblolly Pine Forest; and Climax Southern Oak-Hickory Forest." *Audubon Field Notes* 1 (1947): 197, 203, 213.

"The Breeding of the Least Flycatcher in Rabun County, Ga." *Oriole* 12 (1947): 5.

"Dickcissel at Athens." *Oriole* 12 (1947): 34.

"Marsh Hawks Responding to Peak Abundance of Cotton Rats." *Oriole* 12 (1947): 48.

1948

"Nesting of the Mountain Vireo at Athens, Georgia. Conclusive Evidence of a Southward Invasion." *Oriole* 23 (1948): 17–20.

"*Synaptomys* on the Highlands, North Carolina, Plateau"; and "*Microtus* from the Piedmont of Georgia." *Journal of Mammalogy* 29.1 (1948): 74.

1949

"Heart Rate–Breathing Rate Ratio in Birds and Mammals." Abstract. *American Journal of Physiology* 159.3 (1949): 583.

"Small Mammals of the Highlands (North Carolina) Plateau." *Journal of Mammalogy* 30.2 (1949): 179–192.

"Weight Variations in Wintering White-throated Sparrows in Relation to Temperature and Migration." *Wilson Bulletin* 61.1 (1949): 3–14.

"Woodland Jumping Mouse (*Napaeozapus*) in Georgia." *Journal of Mammalogy* 30 (1949): 200.

With Robert A. Norris. "Effect of DDT on Birds in Georgia Pecan Orchards with a Note on Late Summer Census Methods." *Journal of Wildlife Management* 13.4 (1949): 415–417.

1950

"Bird Populations of the Highlands (North Carolina) Plateau in Relation to Plant Succession and Avian Invasion." *Ecology* 31.4 (1950): 587–605.

"The Vermilion Flycatcher in Georgia." *Oriole* 15 (1950): 13–14.

1951

With David W. Johnston. "The House Wren Breeding in Georgia: An Analysis of a Range Extension." *Auk* 68 (1951) 357–366.

With Jesse D. Perkinson Jr. "Relation of Lipid Metabolism to Migration in Birds: Seasonal Variation in Body Lipids of the Migratory White-throated Sparrow." *Physiological Zoology* 24.3 (1951): 216–230.

1952

"House Wren Nesting at Athens for the Second Season." *Oriole* 17 (1952): 8.

1953

With Milton N. Hopkins. "Some Aspects of the Population Ecology of Breeding Mourning Doves in Georgia." *Journal of Wildlife Management* 17.2 (1953): 132–143.

1954

With R. A. Humphries. "The McKinney's Pond Heronry." *Oriole* 19 (1954): 3–4.

1955

"Consideration of the Total Environment in Power Reactor Waste Disposal." Including work by Howard T. Odum. Abstract of paper presented at the International Conference on Peaceful Uses of Atomic Energy, Geneva, 12 July 1955, 8/P/480.

"An Eleven Year History of a *Sigmodon* Population." *Journal of Mammalogy* 36.3 (1955): 368–378.

With Edward J. Kuenzler. "Measurement of Territory and Home Range Size in Birds." *Auk* 72 (1955): 128–137.

With Howard T. Odum. "Trophic Structure and Productivity of a Windward Coral Reef Community on Eniwetok Atoll." *Ecological Monographs* 25 (1955): 291–320.

1956

"Ecological Aspects of Waste Disposal." Paper presented at the Conference on Radioactive Isotopes in Agriculture at East Lansing, Michigan, 12–14 January 1956.

AEC Report TID-7512: *A Conference on Radioactive Isotopes in Agriculture*, 95–102. Washington, D.C.: U.S. Government Printing Office, 1956.

With Clyde E. Connell. "Lipid Levels in Migrating Birds." *Science* 123 (1956): 892–894.

With D. W. Johnston. "Breeding Bird Populations in Relation to Plant Succession on the Piedmont of Georgia." *Ecology* 37.1 (1956): 50–62.

With James C. Major. "The Effect of Diet on Photoperiod-Induced Lipid Deposition in the White-throated Sparrow." *Condor* 58.3 (1956): 222–228.

With Howard T. Odum. "Corals as Producers, Herbivores, Carnivores, and Possibly Decomposers." *Ecology* 37.2 (1956): 385.

With Henry C. Robert and John M. Teal. "Summer Birds of Sapelo Island, Georgia: A Preliminary List." *Oriole* 21.4 (1956): 37–48.

1957

"Ecology and the Atomic Age." *ASB Bulletin* 4.2 (1957): 27–29.

"The Ecosystem Approach in Teaching of Ecology Illustrated with Sample Class Data." *Ecology* 38.3 (1957): 531–535.

"Environmental Aspects of Nuclear Radiation." *Bulletin of the Georgia Academy of Science* 15 (1957): 127–136.

With John B. Gentry. "The Effect of Weather on the Winter Activity of Old-Field Rodents." *Journal of Mammalogy* 38.1 (1957): 72–77.

With Gordon L. Hight. "The Use of Mist Nets in Population Studies of Winter Fringillids on the AEC Savannah River Area." *Bird-Banding* 28 (1957): 203–213.

With Howard T. Odum. "Zonation of Corals on Japtan Reef, Eniwetok Atoll." *Atoll Research Bulletin* 52 (15 September 1957). Washington, D.C.: Pacific Science Board, National Academy of Sciences, National Research Council, 1957.

With Albert Schwartz. "The Woodrats of the Eastern United States." *Journal of Mammalogy* 38.2 (1957): 197–206.

1958

"Ecology Course at Woods Hole." *AIBS Bulletin* (January 1958): 427.

"The Fat Deposition Picture in the White-throated Sparrow in Comparison with That in Long-Range Migrants." *Bird-Banding* 29 (1958): 105–108.

With Edward J. Kuenzler and Sister Marion Xavier Blunt. "Uptake of P32 and Primary Productivity in Marine Benthic Algae." *Limnology and Oceanography* 3.3 (1958): 340–345.

1959

"The Macroscopic Organism and Its Environment." In *Proceedings of the University of Michigan Biological Station Semicentennial Celebration, June 16–19, 1959,* 53–64.

With Alfred E. Smalley. "Comparison of Population Energy Flow of a Herbivorous and a Deposit-Feeding Invertebrate in a Salt Marsh Ecosystem." *Proceedings of the National Academy of Sciences* 45.4 (1959): 617–622.

1960

"Ecology." In *McGraw-Hill Encyclopedia of Science and Technology,* 1960, 4:388–398.

"Factors which Regulate Primary Productivity and Heterotrophic Utilization in the Ecosystem." In *Transactions of the Seminar on Algae and Metropolitan Wastes, April 27–29, 1960.* Cincinnati: U.S. Public Health Service, Robert A. Taft Sanitary Engineering Center, 1960.

"Lipid Deposition in Nocturnal Migrant Birds." In *Proceedings of the Twelfth International Ornithological Congress, Helsinki, 1958,* 563–576. 1960.

"Organic Production and Turnover in Old Field Succession." *Ecology* 41.1 (1960): 34–49.

"Premigratory Hyperphagia in Birds." *American Journal of Clinical Nutrition* 8 (1960): 261–269.

With Roger W. Bachmann. "Uptake of Zn65 and Primary Productivity in Marine Benthic Algae." *Limnology and Oceanography* 5.4 (1960): 349–355.

With Clyde E. Connell and Herbert Kale. "Fat-Free Weights of Birds." *Auk* 77 (1960): 1–9.

With W. Roland Taylor. "Uptake of Iron-59 by Marine Benthic Algae." *Biological Bulletin* 119.2 (1960): 343.

1961

"Excretion Rate of Radio-isotopes as Indices of Metabolic Rates in Nature: Biological Half-life of Zinc-65 in Relation to Temperature, Food Consumption, Growth and Reproduction in Arthropods." *Biological Bulletin* 121.2 (1961): 371–372.

"The Role of Tidal Marshes in Estuarine Production." *New York State Conservationist* (June–July 1961): 70–79.

With Clyde E. Connell and Herbert L. Stoddard. "Flight Energy and Estimated Flight Ranges of Some Migratory Birds." *Auk* 78 (1961): 515–527.

With Cameron E. Gifford. "Chlorophyll *a* Content of Intertidal Zones on a Rocky Seashore." *Limnology and Oceanography* 6.1 (1961): 83–85.

With A. J. Pontin. "Population Density of the Underground Ant, *Lasius flavus*, as Determined by Tagging with P32." *Ecology* 42.1 (1961): 186–188.

With Claire L. Schelske. "Mechanisms Maintaining High Productivity in Georgia Estuaries." In *Proceedings of Gulf and Caribbean Fisheries Institute*, 75–80. Fourteenth Annual Session, November 1961.

1962

"Relationships between Structure and Function in the Ecosystem." *Japanese Journal of Ecology* 12.3 (1962): 108–118.

With Clyde E. Connell and Leslie B. Davenport. "Population Energy Flow of Three Primary Consumer Components of Old-Field Ecosystems." *Ecology* 43.1 (1962): 88–96.

With R. P. Martin and B. C. Loughman. "Scanning Systems for the Rapid Determination of Radioactivity in Ecological Materials." *Ecology* 43.1 (1962): 171–173.

1963

"Concluding Remarks of the Co-chairman." In *Proceedings of the Second Annual Tall Timbers Fire Ecology Conference, March 14–15, 1963, Tallahassee, Florida,* 177–180.

"Energy Storage in Migrating Birds." Abstract. *ASB Bulletin* 10.2 (1963): 35.

"Primary and Secondary Energy Flow in Relation to Ecosystem Structure." In *Proceedings of the Sixteenth International Congress of Zoology, Washington, D.C., August 20–27,* 1963, 4:336–338.

With Armando A. de la Cruz. "Detritus as a Major Component of Ecosystems." *AIBS Bulletin* 13.3 (1963): 39–40.

With Frank B. Golley. "Radioactive Tracers as an Aid to the Measurement of Energy Flow at the Population Level in Nature." In *Radioecology*, ed. V. Schultz and A. W. Klement Jr., 403–410. Proceedings of the First National Symposium on Radioecology, Colorado State University, Fort Collins, Colorado, 10–15 September 1961. New York: Reinhold, 1963.

With Edward J. Kuenzler. "Experimental Isolation of Food Chains in an Old-Field Ecosystem with the Use of Phosphorus-32." In *Radioecology*, ed. V. Schultz and A. W. Klement Jr., 113–120. Proceedings of the First National Symposium on Radioecology, Colorado State University, Fort Collins, Colorado, 10–15 September 1961. New York: Reinhold, 1963.

With Jiro Mishima. "Excretion Rate of Zn65 by *Littorina irrorata* in Relation to Temperature and Body Size." *Limnology and Oceanography* 8.1 (1963): 39–44.

1964

"Experimental Tests of the Two Channel Energy Flow Diagram as a Working Model Useful for Relating Function and Structure at the Ecosystem Level." Abstract of paper presented at the Tenth International Botanical Congress, Edinburgh, August 1964, 238.

"The New Ecology." *BioScience* 14.7 (1964): 14–16.

"The Role of Tidal Marshes in Estuarine Production." In *Proceedings of the MARCH Conference organized by IUCN, ICBP, and IWRB, Les Saintes-Maries-de-la-Mer, November 12–16, 1962*, pt. I/A: 79–79. IUCN Publications, new series 3, 1964.

With Larry D. Caldwell and Shirley G. Marshall. "Comparison of Fat Levels in Migrating Birds Killed at a Central Michigan and a Florida Gulf Coast Television Tower." *Wilson Bulletin* 75.4 (1964): 428–434.

With David T. Rogers Jr. "Effect of Age, Sex, and Level of Fat Deposition on Major Body Components in Some Wood Warblers." *Auk* 81.4 (1964): 505–513.

With David T. Rogers and David L. Hicks. "Homeostasis of the Nonfat Components of Migrating Birds." *Science* 143 (1964): 1037–1039.

1965

"Adipose Tissue in Migratory Birds." In *Handbook of Physiology—Adipose Tissue*, 37–43. Washington, D.C.: American Physiology Society, 1965.

"Feedback between Radiation Ecology and General Ecology." *Health Physics* 11 (1965): 1257–1262.

"Panel Discussion on Education and Research Training." In *Radioecology*, ed. V. Schultz and A. W. Klement Jr., 643–644. Proceedings of the First National Symposium on Radioecology, Colorado State University, Fort Collins, Colorado, 10–15 September 1963. New York: Reinhold, 1965.

"Summary." In *Symposium on Ecological Effects of Nuclear War*. BNL 917 (C-43), ed. G. M. Woodwell. Upton, N.Y.: Brookhaven National Laboratory, 1965.

With Cameron E. Gifford. "Bioenergetics of Lipid Deposition in the Bobolink, a Trans-equatorial Migrant." *Condor* 67.5 (1965): 383–403.

With Shirley G. Marshall and Timothy G. Marples. "The Caloric Content of Migrating Birds." *Ecology* 46.6 (1965): 901–904.

With John E. Wood. "A Nine-Year History of Furbearer Populations on the AEC Savannah River Plant Area." *Journal of Mammalogy* 45.4 (1965): 540–551.

1966

"Alfred C. Redfield, Eminent Ecologist." *Bulletin of the Ecological Society of America* 47.4 (1966): 166–167.

With L. R. Pomeroy, R. E. Johannes, and B. Roffman. "Flux of 32P and 65Zn through a Salt-Marsh Ecosystem." In *Disposal of Radioactive Wastes into Seas, Oceans and Surface Waters*, 177–188. Vienna: International Atomic Energy Agency, 1966.

With David T. Rogers Jr. "A Study of Autumnal Postmigrant Weights and Vernal Fattening of North American Migrants in the Tropics." *Wilson Bulletin* 78.4 (1966): 415–433.

1967

"Man and the Landscape." *Scientist and Citizen* 9.1 (1967): 12–14. St. Louis: The Greater St. Louis Citizens' Committee for Nuclear Information, 1967.

With Armando A. de la Cruz. "Particulate Organic Detritus in a Georgia Salt Marsh–Estuarine Ecosystem." In *Estuaries*, 383–388. New York: American Association for the Advancement of Science, 1967.

With R. C. Wiegert and J. H. Schnell. "Forb-Arthropod Food Chains in a One-Year Experimental Field." *Ecology* 48.1 (1967): 75–83.

1968

"A. Description and Productivity of Georgia Salt Marsh Estuaries," and "B. Environmental Effects of Proposed Mining." In *University of Georgia System Report on Proposed Phosphate Mining*, ed. E. L. Cheatum, c1–c7, 1968.

"Description and Productivity of Georgia Salt Marsh Estuaries." In *Report on Proposed Leasing of State-Owned Lands for Phosphate Mining*, ed. E. L. Cheatum, c1–c22, 1968.

"Energy Flow in Ecosystems: A Historical Review." *American Zoologist* 8 (1968): 11–18.

"Natural Production in Estuaries, a Source of Food for Oysters." In *Proceedings of the Oyster Culture Workshop*, ed. T. L. Linton, 1–3. Brunswick, Ga.: Marine Fisheries Division, Georgia Game and Fisheries Commission, 1968.

"A Proposal for a Marshbank and the Strategy of Ecosystem Development for the Estuarine Zone of Georgia." Paper presented at the Conference on the Future of the Marshland and Sea Islands of Georgia, October 1968. Brunswick, Ga.: Coastal Area Planning and Development Commission, 1968.

With G. Dennis Cooke and Robert J. Beyers. "The Case for the Multispecies Ecological System, with Special Reference to Succession and Stability." In *Bioregenerative Systems*, 129–139. SP-165. Washington, D.C.: National Aeronautics and Space Administration, 1968.

With John B. Gentry, Marc Mason, Vince Nabholz, Samuel Marshall, and John T. McGinnis. "Effect of Altitude and Forest Manipulation on Relative Abundance of Small Mammals." *Journal of Mammalogy* 49.3 (1968): 539–541.

With H. Ronald Pulliam and Gary W. Barrett. "Equitability and Resource Limitation." *Ecology* 49.4 (1968): 772–774.

1969

"Air-Land-Water = An Ecological Whole." *Journal of Soil and Water Conservation* 24.1 (1969): 4–7.

"The Attitude Lag." *BioScience* 19.5 (1969): 403.

"Comments on the Distribution of Indices of Diversity." In *Statistical Ecology*, 315–365. Proceedings of the International Symposium on Statistical Ecology, Yale University and U.S. Forest Service Research Laboratory, New Haven, Connecticut, 21–28 August 1969. Philadelphia: University of Pennsylvania Press, 1969.

"Ecological Succession." *Science* 166 (1969): 403–404.

"A Research Challenge: Evaluating the Productivity of Coastal and Estuarine Water." In *Proceedings of the Second Sea Grant Conference, 1968*, 63–64. Newport: Graduate School of Oceanography, University of Rhode Island, 1969.

"The Strategy of Ecosystem Development." *Science* 164 (1969): 262–270.

With Alicia Breymeyer. "Transfer and Bioelimination of Tracer 65Zn during Predation by Spiders on Labeled Flies." In *Symposium on Radioecology*, ed. Daniel J. Nelson and Francis C. Evans, 715–720. Proceedings of the Second National Symposium on Radioecology, Ann Arbor, Michigan, 15–17 May 1967. Washington, D.C.: U.S. Atomic Energy Commission Division of Biology and Medicine (TID 4500), 1969.

With Sharon Davis. "More Birds in the Bushes from Shrubs in the Plans." *Landscape Architecture* (October 1969): 36–37.

With Robert W. Gordon, R. J. Beyers, and R. G. Eagon. "Studies of a Simple Laboratory Microecosystem: Bacterial Activities in a Heterotrophic Succession." *Ecology* 50.1 (1969): 86–100.

With William H. Mason. "The Effect of Coprophagy on Retention and Bioelimination of Radionuclides by Detritus-Feeding Animals." In *Symposium on Radioecology*, ed. Daniel J. Nelson and Francis C. Evans, 721–724. Proceedings of the Second National Symposium on Radioecology, Ann Arbor, Michigan, 15–17 May 1967. Washington, D.C.: U.S. Atomic Energy Commission Division of Biology and Medicine (TID 4500), 1969.

With L. R. Pomeroy, R. E. Johannes, and B. Roffman. "The Phosphorus and Zinc Cycles and Productivity of a Salt Marsh." In *Symposium on Radioecology*, ed. Daniel J. Nelson and Francis C. Evans, 412–419. Proceedings of the Second National Symposium on Radioecology, Ann Arbor, Michigan, 15–17 May 1967. Washington, D.C.: U.S. Atomic Energy Commission Division of Biology and Medicine (TID 4500), 1969.

With H. Ronald Pulliam and Gary W. Barrett. "Bioelimination of Tracer 65Zn in Relation to Metabolic Rates in Mice." In *Symposium on Radioecology*, ed. Daniel J. Nelson and Francis C. Evans, 725–730. Proceedings of the Second National Symposium on Radioecology, Ann Arbor, Michigan, 15–17 May 1967. Washington, D.C.: U.S. Atomic Energy Commission Division of Biology and Medicine (TID 4500), 1969.

With Richard G. Wiegert. "Radionuclide Tracer Measurement of Food Web Diversity in Nature." In *Symposium on Radioecology*, ed. Daniel J. Nelson and Francis C. Evans, 709–710. Proceedings of the Second National Symposium on Radioecology, Ann Arbor, Michigan, 15–17 May 1967. Washington, D.C.: U.S. Atomic Energy Commission Division of Biology and Medicine (TID 4500), 1969.

1970

"The Attitude Revolution." In *The Crisis of Survival*, ed. by the editors of *The Progressive*, 9–15. Introductions by Eugene P. Odum and Benjamin DeMott. New York: Morrow, 1970.

Foreword to *Environmental Law Review*, ed. H. Floyd Sherrod. New York: Clark Boardman, 1970.

Interview. *Pandora 1970*. University of Georgia Student Yearbook, 115–116.

"Needed: Land Trusteeship, Not Just Ownership." *Field and Stream* 2 (June 1970): 48–63.

"Optimum Population and Environment: A Georgian Microcosm." *Current History* 58 (1970): 355–359. (Reprinted in condensed form in *The Ecologist* 1.9 [1971]: 14–15; and *Teem* 1.2: 4–9.)

"Questions and Answers." CBS News, New York, Earth Day, 1970. Taped 22 April 1970.

With Michael D. Dahlberg. "Annual Cycles of Species Occurrence, Abundance, and Diversity in Georgia Estuarine Fish Populations." *American Midland Naturalist* 83.2 (1970): 382–392.

With R. G. Wiegert and D. C. Coleman. "Energetics of the Litter-Soil Subsystem." In *Methods of Study in Soil Ecology*, 93–98. Paris: IBP-UNESCO, 1970.

1971

"Ecological Principles and the Urban Forest." In *Proceedings of the Symposium on the Role of Trees in the South's Urban Environment*, 78–81. Athens: Georgia Center for Continuing Education, 1971.

"Ecosystem Theory in Relation to Man." In *Ecosystem Structure and Function*, ed. John A. Wiens, 11–24. Proceedings of the Thirty-first Annual Biology Colloquium. Corvallis: Oregon State University Press, 1972.

"Viewpoint." *Research Reporter* 7.1 (1972): 2.

With Howard T. Odum. "Natural Areas as Necessary Components of Man's Total Environment." In *Transactions of the Thirty-seventh North American Wildlife and Natural Resources Conference, March 12–15, 1972*, 178–187. Washington, D.C.: Wildlife Management Institute, 1972.

1973

"A Description and Value Assessment of South Atlantic and Gulf Coast Marshes and Estuaries." In *Proceedings of the Fish and Wildlife Values of the Estuarine Habitat: A Seminar for the Petroleum Industry*, 23–31. Atlanta: Bureau of Sport Fish and Wildlife, 1973.

"Harmony between Man and Nature: An Ecological View." In *Beyond Growth: Essays on Alternative Futures*, 43–55. New Haven: Yale University School of Forestry Bulletin 88, 1975.

"The Living Marsh." Introduction to *Gaule: The Golden Coast of Georgia*, 19–28. San Francisco: Friends of the Earth, 1973.

"Panel Discussion on the Energy Crisis." Discussion at the annual meeting of the Georgia Conservancy, St. Simons Island, Georgia, 1973.

"The Pricing System." *Georgia Conservancy Magazine* (fourth quarter 1973): 8–10.

With Marsha E. Fanning. "Comparison of the Productivity of *Spartina alterniflora* and *Spartina cynosuroides* in Georgia Coastal Marshes." *Bulletin of the Georgia Academy of Science* 31 (1973): 1–12.

With James G. Gosselink and R. M. Pope. *The Value of the Tidal Marsh.* Baton Rouge: Louisiana State University Center for Wetland Resources LSU-SG-74-03 (1973).

With Steven E. Pomeroy, J. C. Dickinson III, and Kermit Hutcheson. "The Effects of Late Winter Litter Burn on the Composition, Productivity and Diversity of a 4-Year-Old Fallow-Field in Georgia." In *Proceedings of the Annual Tall Timbers Fire Ecology Conference, March 22–23, 1973, 399–419.*

1974

"Diversity as a Function of Energy Flow." In *Unifying Concepts in Ecology.* The Hague: W. Junk, 1974.

"Ecosystem." In *Encyclopaedia Britannica.* 15th ed., 1974, 281–286.

"Ecosystem Theory." In *Encyclopedia of Environmental Science,* 208–218. London: Gordon and Breach, Science Publishers, 1974.

"Environmental Ethic and the Attitude Revolution." In *Philosophy and Environmental Crisis,* ed. William T. Blackstone, 10–15. Athens: University of Georgia Press, 1974.

"Halophytes, Energetics and Ecosystems." In *Ecology of Halophytes,* ed. Robert J. Reimold and William H. Queen, 599–602. New York: Academic Press, 1974.

1975

"Pricing the Natural Environment." *University of Georgia Research Reporter* 9.1 (1975): 10–12.

1976

"The Coming Merger of Ecology and Economics." In *Proceedings of the President's Seminar on Forging the Economic Quality of Life in Georgia,* ed. John Legler, 85–89. Athens: University of Georgia College of Business Administration and Center for Continuing Education, 1976.

"Diversity and the Survival of the Ecosystem." In *Proceedings of the Fiftieth Anniversary of the American Type Tissue Culture Symposium,* 53–55. 1976.

"Earth as a Productive System." Review of *Primary Productivity of the Biosphere*, by Helmut Lieth and Robert Whittaker. *Science* 193 (1976): 138.

"Energy and Ecology." In *Environmental Effects of Energy*, 6–8. Proceedings of the Conference at Savannah, Georgia, 2–3 December 1976. Oak Ridge, Tenn.: Oak Ridge Associated Universities, 1976.

"Energy, Ecosystem Development and Environmental Risk." *Journal of Risk and Insurance* 43.1 (1976): 1–16.

With Gary W. Barrett and George M. Van Dyne. "Stress Ecology." *BioScience* 26.3 (1976): 192–194.

With Gene A. Bramlett, Albert Ike, James R. Champlin, Joseph C. Zieman, and Herman H. Shugart. "Totality Indices for Evaluating Environmental Impacts of Highway Alternatives." *Transportation Research Record* 561: 57–67. Washington, D.C.: National Academy of Sciences, 1976.

1977

"Ecology: The Commonsense Approach." *Ecologist* 7.7 (1977): 250–253.

"The Emergence of Ecology as a New Integrative Discipline." *Science* 195 (1977): 1289–1293.

"The Life Support Value of Forests." In *Forests for People*, 101–105. Proceedings of the Society of American Foresters National Convention. Washington, D.C.: Society of American Foresters, 1977.

With Roger L. Kroodsma. "The Power Park Concept: Ameliorating Man's Disorder with Nature's Order." In *Thermal Ecology II*, ed. G. W. Esch and R. W. McFarlane, 1–9. Proceedings of the Symposium sponsored by Savannah River Ecology Laboratory, Augusta, Georgia, May 1975. ERDA Symposium Series, Conf. 750425, 1977.

1978

"Diversity and the Emergence of Integrative Disciplines in Universities." Address delivered at the Forty-first Annual Meeting of the Southern University Conference. In *Southern University Conference 1978*, 9–13. Birmingham: Birmingham-Southern College, 1978.

"Ecological Importance of the Riparian Zone." Opening address at the Symposium on Strategies for Protection and Management of Floodplain Wetlands and Other Riparian Ecosystems, Callaway Gardens, Georgia, 11–13 December 1978. Georgia General Technology Report WO-12, 410. Washington, D.C.: Forest Service, U.S. Department of Agriculture, 1978.

"Georgia's Institute of Ecology: A Center for Integrating Disciplines." In *The Role of Colleges and Universities in Land-Use Planning and Resource Allocation in the Southeast*, 21–22. Proceedings of the Twenty-ninth Annual Meeting of the American Institute of Biological Sciences, Athens, Georgia, 1978.

"The Value of Wetlands: A Hierarchical Approach." In *Wetland Functions and Values: The State of Our Understanding*, ed. Phillip E. Greeson, John R. Clark, and Judith E. Clark, 1–10. Proceedings of the National Symposium on Wetlands, 1978. Minneapolis: American Water Resources Association, 1978.

With R. Gary Bakelaar. "Community and Population Level Responses to Fertilization in an Old-Field Ecosystem." *Ecology* 59.4 (1978): 660–665.

With Serge González. *Energy: The Common Denominator of an Ecosystem*. University of Georgia Institute of Ecology Series, ed. Lorraine Edwards. Athens: University of Georgia Institute of Ecology, 1978.

1979

"Dedication of a New Wing of Narragansett EPA Laboratory, June 1977." In *Advances in Marine Environmental Research*, ed. Francine Sakin Jacoff, iv–viii. Proceedings of the Symposium on Advances in Marine Environmental Research. EPA-600/9-79-035. Narrangansett, R.I.: Environmental Research Laboratory, Office of Research and Development, U.S. Environmental Protection Agency, 1979.

"Rebuttal of 'Economic Value of Natural Coastal Wetlands: A Critique.'" *Coastal Zone Management Journal* 5 (1979): 232–237. (Reply to a critique by L. Shabman and S. S. Batie in *Coastal Zone Management Journal* 4 [1978]: 231–247.)

With John T. Finn and Eldon H. Franz. "Perturbation Theory and the Subsidy-Stress Gradient." *BioScience* 29.6 (1979): 349–352.

1980

"Alternatives of Sustained Use of Resources." In *Economics, Ethics, Ecology: Roots of Productive Conservation*, ed. Walter E. Jeske, 20–24. Ankeny, Iowa: Soil Conservation Society of America, 1980.

"Ecology and the Future: An Interview with Eugene P. Odum." *EPA Journal* 6.4 (1980): 14–15, 40–41.

"Radiation Ecology at Oak Ridge." In *Environmental Sciences Laboratory Dedication*, 53–57. ORNL–5666. Oak Ridge, Tenn.: Oak Ridge National Laboratory, 1980.

"The Status of Three Ecosystem-Level Hypotheses regarding Salt Marsh Estuaries: Tidal Subsidy, Outwelling, and Detritus-Based Food Chains." In *Estuarine Perspectives*, 485–495. San Diego: Academic Press, 1980.

With James L. Cooley. "Ecosystem Profile Analysis and Performance Curves as Tools for Assessing Environmental Impact." In *Biological Evaluation of Environmental Impacts*, 94–102. Proceedings of the 1976 Meeting of the Ecological Society of America. FWS/OBS-80/26. Washington, D.C.: Fish and Wildlife Service, U.S. Department of Interior, 1980.

With Eldon H. Franz. "Whither the Life-Support System?" In *Growth without Ecodisasters*, ed. N. Polunin, 264–274. Proceedings of the Second International Conference on Environmental Future in Reykjavik, Iceland 1977. London: Macmillan, 1980.

1981

"The Effects of Stress on the Trajectory of Ecological Succession." In *Stress Effects on Natural Ecosystems*, ed. Gary W. Barrett and Rutger Rosenberg, 43–47. New York: John Wiley and Sons, 1981.

Foreword to *Wetlands of Bottomland Hardwood Forests*, ed. J. R. Clark and J. Benforado, xi–xiii. Washington, D.C.: Conservation Foundation, National Wetlands Technical Council, 1981.

"A Functional Classification of Wetlands." In *Proceedings of the U.S. Fish and Wildlife Service Workshop on Coastal Ecosystems of the Southeastern United States, Big Pine Key, Florida, February 18–22, 1980*, ed. Robert Cary and Paul Markovits, 4–9. FWS/OBS-80/59. Washington, D.C.: U.S. Department of the Interior, 1981.

"Looking at the Whole." *EPA Journal* 7.1 (1981): 4–5.

"A New Ecology for the Coast." In *Coast Alert*. San Francisco: Friends of the Earth, 1981.

"Revival of Non-laboratory Science." Walton Distinguished Lecture Series. *ASB Bulletin* 28.3 (1981): 119–121.

With Thomas Eisner, Hans Eisner, Jerrold Meinwald, Carl Sagan, Charles Walcott, Enrst Mayr, Edward O. Wilson, Peter H. Raven, Anne Ehrlich, Paul R. Ehrlich, Archie Carr, and, Carl Gans. "Conservation of Tropical Forests." *Science* 213 (1981): 1314.

With Paul F. Hendrix, Christine L. Langner, and Carolyn L. Thomas. "Microcosms as Test Systems for the Ecological Effects of Toxic Substances: An Appraisal with Cadmium." EPA-600/S3-81-036, 1–4. Washington, D.C.: U.S. Environmental Protection Agency, 1981.

With Bernard C. Patten. "The Cybernetic Nature of Ecosystems." *American Naturalist* 118 (1981): 886–895.

With Kathleen C. Parker and James L. Cooley. *Natural Ecosystems of the Sunbelt.* Report. Athens, Ga.: Institute of Ecology, 1981.

1982

"Diversity and the Forest Ecosystem." In *Natural Diversity in Forest Ecosystems*, 35–41. Proceedings of the Workshop, 29 November–1 December 1982, University of Georgia. Sponsored by USDA Forest Service Southeastern Forest Experiment Station and Southern Appalachian Research/Resource Management Cooperative. Athens: University of Georgia Institute of Ecology, 1982.

Foreword to *The Ecology of a Salt Marsh*, ed. L. R. Pomeroy and R. G. Wiegert, v–vi. Ecological Studies 38. New York: Springer-Verlag, 1982.

With Paul F. Hendrix and Christine L. Langner. "Cadmium in Aquatic Microcosms: Implications for Screening the Ecological Effects of Toxic Substances." *Environmental Management* 6.6 (1982): 543–553.

1983

"Ecology: A New Integrative Discipline." Guest editorial in *Living in the Environment*, 3rd ed., ed. G. Tyler Miller, 80–81. Belmont, Calif.: Wadsworth, 1983.

Foreword to *The Guide to Environmental Organizations in North Carolina*, by Lisa Blumenthal. Raleigh: North Carolina Center for Public Policy Research, 1983.

"Wetlands and Their Values." *Journal of Soil and Water Conservation* 38.5 (1983): 380.

"Wetlands and Their Values." *National Wetlands Newsletter* 5.3 (1983): 2.

With J. B. Birch and James L. Cooley. "Comparison of Giant Cutgrass Productivity in Tidal and Impounded Marshes with Special Reference to Tidal Subsidy and Waste Assimilation." *Estuaries* 6.2 (1983): 88–94.

With John P. Giesy Jr. "Microcosmology: Introductory Comments." In *Microcosms in Ecological Research*, 1–12. U.S. Department of Energy Symposium 52, 1983.

With G. J. House, B. R. Stinner, R. E. Hicks, and D. A. Crossley. "Simulation Models of Nitrogen Flux in Conventional and No-Tillage Agroecosystems." In *Nutrient Cycling in Agricultural Ecosystems*, ed. R. Lowrence, R. Todd, L. Asmussen, and R. Leonard, 569–578. College of Agriculture Experiment Stations, Special Publication 23. Athens: University of Georgia, 1983.

With B. R. Stinner and D. A. Crossley Jr. "Nutrient Uptake by Vegetation in Relation to Other Ecosystem Processes in Conventional Tillage, No-Tillage and Old-Field Systems." In *Agriculture, Ecosystems and Environment*, 10:1–13. Amsterdam: Elsevier Science Publishers, 1983.

1984

"The Mesocosm." *BioScience* 34.9 (1984): 558–562.

"A Message from Eugene Odum." *Intercom* (University of Georgia Institute of Ecology) 15.3 (1984): 2–3.

"Nitrogen Cycling in Conventional and No-Tillage Agroecosystems in the Southern Piedmont." *Journal of Soil and Water Conservation* 39.3 (1984): 194–200.

"Properties of Agroecosystems." In *Agricultural Ecosystems: Unifying Concepts*, ed. R. Lowrance, B. R. Stinner, and G. J. House, 5–11. New York: John Wiley and Sons, 1984.

Review of *Disturbance and Ecosystems: Components of Response. Quarterly Review of Biology* 59 (1984): 498–499.

Review of *The Granite Garden: Urban Nature and Human Design*, by Anne Whiston Spirn. *Landscape Journal* 3.2 (1984): 153–154.

"Wetlands as Vital Components of the Nation's Water Resources." In *The Water Resources of Georgia and Adjacent Areas*, ed. Ram Arora and Lee Gorday, 88–92. Georgia Geologic Survey Bulletin 99. Atlanta: Georgia Department of Natural Resources, 1984.

With Lawrence J. Biever. "Resource Quality, Mutualism, and Energy Partitioning in Food Chains." *American Naturalist* 124 (1984): 360–376.

With G. J. House, R. R. Stinner, and D. A. Crossley Jr. "Nitrogen Cycling in Conventional and No-Tillage Agro-ecosystems: Analysis of Pathways and Processes." *Journal of Applied Ecology* 21 (1984): 991–1012.

With J. E. Pinder III and T. A. Christiansen. "Nutrient Losses from Sandy Soils during Old-Field Succession." *American Midland Naturalist* 111.1 (1984):148–154.

With B. R. Stinner, D. A. Crossley, and R. L. Todd. "Nutrient Budgets and Internal Cycling of N, P, K, Ca, and Mg in Conventional Tillage, No-Tillage, and Old-Field Ecosystems on the Georgia Piedmont." *Ecology* 65.2 (1984): 354–369.

1985

"Biotechnology and the Biosphere." Letter to the Editor. *Science* 229 (1985): 1338.

"Ecology: The State of Our Science." *Bulletin of the Ecological Society of America* 66.1 (1985): 14–15.

"Trends Expected in Stressed Ecosystems." *BioScience* 35 (1985): 419–422.

1986

"Crops as Ecological Systems: Energy Partitioning and Mutualism." In *Nitrogen in Tropical Cropping Systems*, ed. Joann P. Roskoski, 1–6. Proceedings of Workshop at Rodale Research Farm, 13–15 July 1983. Maui, Hawaii: NifTal Project, University of Hawaii, 1986.

"In Defense of Two Georgias." *Georgia Business and Economic Conditions* 46.6 (1986).

"Introductory Review: Perspective of Ecosystem Theory and Application." In *Ecosystem Theory and Application*, ed. Nicholas Polunin, 1–11. New York: John Wiley and Sons, 1986.

With Mary Pitts Diner and Paul Hendrix. "Comparison of the Roles of Ostracods and Cladocerans in Regulating Community Structure and Metabolism in Freshwater Microcosms." *Hydrobiology* 133 (1986): 59–63.

With Paul F. Hendrix, Robert W. Parmelee, D. A. Crossley Jr., D. C. Coleman, and Peter Groffman. "Detritus Food Webs in Conventional and No-Tillage Agroecosystems." *BioScience* 36.6 (1986): 374–380.

With Richard Lowrance and Paul F. Hendrix. "A Hierarchical Approach to Sustainable Agriculture." *American Journal of Alternative Agriculture* 1.4 (1986): 169–173.

1987

"Biotechnology Presents Challenge to Campus." *Columns* 14.16 (26 January 1987): 5–6.

"Early University of Georgia Research, 1952–1962, at the Savannah River Plant." In *The Savannah River and Its Environs: Proceedings of a Symposium in Honor of Dr. Ruth Patrick*, ed. John C. Corey, 43–83. Aiken, S.C.: Savannah River Ecology Laboratory, 1987.

"Global Stress in Life-Support Ecosystems Mandates Input Management of Production Systems." Acceptance speech for the Crafoord Prize in the Biosciences, 1987. Stockholm: Royal Swedish Academy of Sciences, 1987.

"Reduced-Input Agriculture Reduces Nonpoint Pollution." *Journal of Soil and Water Conservation* 42.6 (1987): 412–414.

"Resolution of Respect: S. Charles Kendeigh, 1904–1986." *Bulletin of the Ecological Society of America* 68.4 (1987): 508–509.

With N. Polunin. "Top-Down Management." Abstract. Program of the Fourth Congress of Ecology, August 1987, Syracuse, New York, 259.

1988

Foreword to *Forest Hydrology and Ecology at Coweeta*, ed. W. T. Swank, and D. A. Crossley, v–vi. Ecological Studies 55. New York: Springer-Verlag, 1988.

"Mountain Bill Would Safeguard Valuable 'Life-Support' System." Forum. *Atlanta Journal/Atlanta Constitution*, 21 February 1988.

With Monica Turner. *The Georgia Landscape: A Changing Resource*. Kellogg Interdisciplinary Task Force on Physical Resources (1985–1987): Final Report. Athens: University of Georgia Institute of Ecology, 1988.

With Monica G. Turner, Robert Costanza, and T. M. Springer. "Market and Nonmarket Values of the Georgia Landscape." *Environmental Management* 12.2 (1988): 209–217.

1989

"Bridging the Four Major 'Gaps' that Threaten Human and Environmental Quality." *Bridges* 1.3–4 (1989): 135–141.

"Diversity in the Landscape: The Multilevel Approach." *Georgia Landscape* (spring 1989). Athens: University of Georgia School of Environmental Design, 1989.

"Input Management of Production Systems." *Science* 243 (1989): 177–182.

"Wetland Values in Retrospect." In *Freshwater Wetlands and Wildlife*, ed. R. R. Sharitz and J. W. Gibbons. DOE Symposium Series 61. CONF-8603101. Oak Ridge, Tenn.: U.S. Department of Energy Office of Scientific and Technical Information, 1989.

With F. B. Golley and J. Bellet. "Dynamic Analysis of the Behavior of Two Landscape Systems." *Options Méditerranéennes*. Série Séminares 3 (1989): 253–257.

With R. Thomas James. "Trends in Ground-water Levels and Use in Georgia: 1950–1987." In *Proceedings of the 1989 Georgia Water Resources Conference*, 66–69. Athens: University of Georgia Institute of Natural Resources, 1989.

With Monica G. Turner. "The Georgia Landscape: A Changing Resource." In *Changing Landscapes: An Ecological Perspective*, ed. S. Zonneveld and R. T. T. Forman, 137–164. New York: Springer-Verlag, 1989.

1990

"Field Experimental Tests of Ecosystem-Level Hypotheses." *Trends in Ecology and Evolution* 5.7 (1990): 204–205.

"The Transition from Youth to Maturity in Nature and Society." *Bridges* 2.1–2 (1990): 57–62.

1991

"Earth Stewardship." *Georgia Landscape* (spring 1991): 5. Athens: University of Georgia School Environmental Design, 1991.

"How to Prosper in a World of Limited Resources." 1990 Ferdinand Phinizy Lecture. Athens: University of Georgia, 1991.

"The Savannah River Site as a National Environmental Park." In *Integrated Environmental Management*, ed. John Cairns and T. V. Crawford, 79–85. Chelsea, Mich.: Lewis Publishers, 1991.

With Joseph M. Meyers. "Breeding Bird Populations of the Okefenokee Swamp in Georgia: Baseline for Assessing Future Avifaunal Changes." *Journal of Field Ornithology* 62.1 (1991): 53–68.

1992

Foreword to *Georgia*, by James Randklev. Englewood, Colo.: Westcliffe Publishers, 1992.

"Great Ideas in Ecology for the 1990s." *BioScience* 42.7 (1992): 542–545.

"When to Confront and When to Cooperate." *Georgia Landscape* (1992). Athens: University of Georgia School of Environmental Design, 1992. (Reprinted in *INTECOL Bulletin* 20 [1992]: 21–23.)

With D. C. Coleman and D. A. Crossley Jr. "Soil Biology, Soil Ecology, and Global Change." *Biology and Fertility of Soils* 14 (1992): 104–111.

1993

"Biosphere 2: A New Kind of Science." *Science* 260 (1993): 878–879.

"Body Masses and Composition of Migrant Birds in the Eastern United States." In *CRC Handbook of Avian Body Masses*, ed. John B. Dunning, 313–332. Boca Raton: CRC Press, 1993.

"Essay: Ecology in the 1990s." In *Guide to Developing Secondary and Postsecondary Biology Curricula*, 74–77. Colorado Springs, Colo.: BSCS, 1993.

"How a University Grows." *University of Georgia Research Reporter* 23.3 (1993). (Reprinted in *ISEE Newsletter* [January 1995]: 3–4.)

"Prerequisites for Sustainability." *Biosphere-2 Newsletter* 3.3 (1993): 10–11.

With H. R. Pulliam and Olin S. Allen. "Southward Extension of Breeding Ranges of Passerine Birds in the Georgia Piedmont in Relation to the Reversed Latitudinal Gradient." *Georgia Journal of Science* 51 (1993): 131–140.

1994

"Conservation of Biodiversity." In *Biological Diversity: Problems and Challenges*, ed. S. K. Majumdar, F. J. Brenner, J. E. Lovich, J. F. Schalles, and E. W. Miller, 18–25. Philadelphia: Pennsylvania Academy of Science, 1994.

"Le déclin de la biodiversité." *Le Médecin vétérinaire du Quebec* Numero Special— Environment (Juillet 1994): 29–30.

"Ecology as a Science." In *Encyclopedia of the Environment,* ed. R. A. Eblen and W. R. Eblen, 171–174. Boston: Houghton Mifflin, 1994.

With T. Y. Park and Kermit Hutcheson. "Comparison of the Weedy Vegetation in Old-Fields and Crop Fields on the Same Site Reveals that Fallowing Crop Fields Does Not Result in Seedbank Buildup of Agricultural Weeds." *Agriculture, Ecosystems and Environment* 49 (1994): 247–252.

1995

"The Importance of Federal Environmental Standards and Research in Sustaining the Quality of Life and Economics." *Chattooga Quarterly* (winter 1995): 11–12.

"Profile Analysis and Some Thoughts on the Development of the Interface Area of Environmental Health." *Ecosystem Health* 1.1 (1995): 41–45.

"A Sustainable Georgia." In *Georgians on Sustainability,* ed. O. M. Ivey and G. Lawes, 15–17. Athens: University of Georgia Institute of Ecology, and Atlanta: Georgia Environmental Organization, 1995.

With M. H. Beare, D. C. Coleman, D. A. Crossley Jr., and P. F. Hendrix. "A Hierarchical Approach to Evaluating the Significance of Soil Biodiversity to Biogeochemical Cycling." *Plant and Soil* 70.1 (1995): 5–22.

With H. T. Odum and W. E. Odum. "Nature's Pulsing Paradigm." *Estuaries* 18.4 (1995): 547–555.

With T. Y. Park. "Comparison of Weed Populations in Conventional Till and No-Till Experimental Agroecosystems." *Korean Journal of Ecology* 18.4 (1995): 471–481.

1996

"Conceptual Models Relevant to Sustaining Coastal Zone Resources." In *Sustainable Development in the Southeastern Coastal Zone,* ed. F. John Vernberg, Winona B. Vernberg, and Thomas Siewicki, 75–80. Columbia: University of South Carolina Press, 1996.

"Cost of Living in Domed Cities." *Nature* 382 (4 July 1996): 18.

Foreword to *Ecotoxicology: A Hierarchical Treatment,* ed. M. C. Newman and C. H. Jagoe. Boca Raton, Fla.: Lewis Publishers, 1996.

With Olin E. Rhodes Jr. "Spatiotemporal Approaches in Ecology and Genetics: The Road Less Traveled." In *Population Dynamics in Space and Time,* ed. O. E.

Rhodes Jr., R. K. Chesser, and M. H. Smit, 1–7. Chicago: University of Chicago Press, 1996.

1997

"Can Ecology Contribute to C. P. Snow's Third Culture?" *Bulletin of the Ecological Society of America* 78.3 (1997): 234.

"Commentary: Source Reduction, Input Management and Dual Capitalism." *Journal of Cleaner Production* 5.1–2 (1997): 123.

With G. W. Barrett and J. D. Peles. "Transcending Processes and the Levels-of-Organization Concept." *BioScience* 47 (1997): 531–535.

1998

"Productivity and Biodiversity: A Two-Way Relationship." *Bulletin of the Ecological Society of America* 79.1 (January 1998): 125.

With D. C. Coleman and P. F. Hendrix. "Ecosystem Health: An Overview." In *Soil Chemistry and Ecosystem Health.* Special Publication 52. Madison: Soil Science Society of America, 1998.

1999

"Humanity's Two Houses." In *Field Notes.* Pleasantville, N.J.: U.S. Fish and Wildlife Service, 1999.

Professional Milestones and Honors

1934

A.B., University of North Carolina, with major in zoology and minor in botany

1936

A.M., University of North Carolina, in zoology

Instructor, Department of Biology, Western Reserve University (1936–37)

1939

Ph.D., University of Illinois, in zoology, with major in ecology

Resident naturalist, Edmund Niles Huyck Preserve, Rensselaerville, N.Y. (1939–40)

1940

Instructor, Department of Zoology, University of Georgia

1942

Assistant professor, Department of Zoology, University of Georgia

1945

Associate professor, Department of Zoology, University of Georgia

Fellow, American Ornithologists' Union

1950

Fellow, American Association for the Advancement of Science

1954

Professor, Department of Zoology, University of Georgia

1956

Mercer Award, with Howard T. Odum, for "Trophic Structure and Productivity of a Windward Coral Reef Community on Eniwetok Atoll"

1957

Alumni Foundation Distinguished Professor, Department of Zoology, University of Georgia

National Science Foundation Senior Fellowship

Instructor in Charge, marine ecology course, Marine Biological Laboratory, Woods Hole, Mass. (1957–61)

1961

Director of Institute of Ecology, University of Georgia

1963

President-elect, Ecological Society of America

1964

President, Ecological Society of America (1964–65)

1968

Georgia Scientist of the Year for 1967, awarded by the Georgia Science and Technology Commission

1970

Elected member of the National Academy of Sciences

Recipient, on behalf of the Institute of Ecology, of two-millionth telephone in Georgia in recognition of work for Georgia's environment

1971

Outstanding Educator of America for 1971 (awarded by Outstanding Educators of America)

Award from the architects of Georgia for preserving the environment

1973

Callaway Professor of Ecology, University of Georgia

Member, Advisory Committee, Technological Assessment Commission established by Congress

President, Ecology Section, American Society of Zoologists (1973–74)

1974

Eminent Ecologist Award of the Ecological Society of America

Honorary member, British Ecological Society

1975

Prix de l'Institut de la Vie, shared with Howard T. Odum

Fellow, American Academy of Arts and Scientists

1976

Resolution expressing "appreciation for the many distinguished contributions of Dr. Eugene P. Odum" passed by Georgia General Assembly, January

Conservationist of the Year, Georgia Wildlife Federation

Gold Seal Award, National Council of the State Garden Clubs

1977

John and Alice Tyler Ecology Award

Tribute by Representative Doug Bernard entered in the *Congressional Record*, 12 October

Blue Key Award, University of Georgia, for being "an outstanding Georgian"

1978

University of Georgia Alumni Society Faculty Service Award

University of North Carolina Distinguished Alumnus Award

Distinguished Service Award from the American Institute of Biological Scientists

St. Andrews Medal

Honorary member, Southeastern Estuarine Research Society

1979

Member, Environmental Advisory Committee, U.S. Department of Energy (1979–80)

1980
Honorary Doctor of Letters, Hofstra University

1981
Cynthia Pratt Laughlin Medal, Garden Club of America, Cincinnati, Ohio

1982
Certificate of Appreciation from the Ecological Society of America
Illini Alumni Achievement Award, University of Illinois

1983
Educator of the Year, National Wildlife Federation
Inclusion as "Father of Modern Ecology" in the Museum of Arts and Science in
    Macon, Georgia — on their list of "Notables: Imaginative Georgians and Their
    Discoveries" for Georgia's 250th celebration

1984
Retirement from University of Georgia
Earle R. Greene Memorial Award, Georgia Ornithological Society

1985
Distinguished Associate Award, U.S. Department of Energy
Eugene Odum Coastal Conservation Award established by Sierra Club
Odum Lecture Series established at University of Georgia
Chairman, Kellogg Task Force charged with studying Georgia's needs and statewide
    environmental problems

1986
Honorary Doctor of Humanities, Ferrum College, Ferrum, Va.

1987
Crafoord Prize in Ecology, shared with Howard T. Odum, Royal Swedish Academy
    of Science, Stockholm

1989
Chevron Conservation Award, Washington, D.C.
Silver Trout Award from "Trout Unlimited of Georgia"

1990
Honorary Doctor of Humane Letters, University of North Carolina, Asheville
Honored at the Seventy-fifth Annual Meeting of the Ecological Society of America

1991

Abraham Baldwin Award, University of Georgia

Theodore Roosevelt Distinguished Service Award

1992

Environmental Educator Award from the Society for Environmental Toxicology
and Chemistry

1994

Recipient of the Georgia Conservancy's Distinguished Conservationist Award

Citizens for Nuclear Technology Award

1996

Honorary Doctor, *Honoris en Ecología*, la Universidad del Valle de Guatemala

1997

Lifetime Achievement Award, Georgia Environmental Council

Eugene Odum: An Ecologist's Life, videotape written by Philip Lee Williams and
produced by University of Georgia

Estuarine Federation Lifetime Achievement Award established in honor of
Eugene P. Odum, Howard T. Odum, and William Eugene Odum

1998

Distinguished Service Award, International Association of Landscape Ecology

Award from Philadelphia Academy of Sciences, presented at International Symposium on Concepts and Controversies in Salt March Ecology for "pioneering research in the field of salt marsh ecology and inspiring a generation of coastal
ecologists"

1999

Honorary Doctor of Science, Ohio State University

Alex Little Environmental Award, University of Georgia

Honorary Doctor of Science, *Honoris Causa*, la Universidad San Francisco, Quito,
Ecuador

Notes

Introduction

1. See "Ecology: The New Jeremiahs" and "The Ravaged Environment." Both carried photographs of Eugene Odum.

2. The first edition of *Fundamentals of Ecology*, to which Howard Thomas Odum contributed substantially, was published in 1953, and the second edition came out in 1959. When the third edition appeared in 1971, it was still the only textbook in biology that began with a discussion of the whole — the ecosystem — rather than its constituent parts. Between 1969 and 1971, according to Gene Odum, annual sales of the textbook jumped from approximately 6,200 to almost 42,000.

3. I am indebted to Karen and Jim Porter, who were students of Evelyn Hutchinson at Yale University in the early 1970s when they first met Gene Odum and who became Gene's colleagues at the University of Georgia, for their explanations of the popularity of the ecosystem concept.

4. Charles Darwin, *On the Origin of Species*, 489.

5. Haeckel coined the word *Oecologie* in 1866 in *Generelle Morphologie der Organismen*. His description of the new discipline was translated and is quoted in the preface to *Principles of Animal Ecology*, by W. C. Allee et al. It is quoted also in Frank Golley, *A History of the Ecosystem Concept in Ecology*,207; and Donald Worster, *Nature's Economy: A History of Ecological Ideas*, 192.

The English word *oecology* acquired its modern spelling, *ecology*, after the International Botanical Congress of 1893. Worster, *Nature's Economy*, 192.

6. Tansley, "The Use and Abuse of Vegetational Concepts and Terms," 299–301.

7. In the preface to the first edition of *Fundamentals of Ecology*, Odum wrote: "I am especially indebted to my brother, Howard Thomas Odum, of the University of Florida, who has read and criticized all of the manuscript and has contributed much to the material in Chapters 4 to 7" (vii).

8. Although Tansley characterized the universe, the solar system, the sugar molecule, and the ion or free atom as "organised wholes," he did not subscribe to the philosophy of "holism" as defined in 1926 by Jan Christiaan Smuts in *Holism and Evolution*.

9. Alston Chase, *In a Dark Wood: The Fight over Forests and the Rising Tyranny of Ecology*, 120, 130.

10. Chase, *In a Dark Wood*, 6.

11. *The New Shorter Oxford English Dictionary* defines *ecotage* as "sabotage carried out for ecological reasons."

12. Quoted in Chase, *In a Dark Wood*, 189.

13. Odum called the alternation of individualistic and holistic philosophies, which he saw as a characteristic feature of politics, "political zigzagging." Citing *Cycles of American History*, by Arthur M. Schlesinger Jr., Odum wrote: "What usually happens is that excessive attention to one level leads to neglect of the other level, which brings on a new political regime that promises to deal with the neglected level. So, in a sort of zigzag fashion, humanity strives to achieve a balance between what are viewed as individual human rights and public needs" (E. P. Odum, *Ecology and Our Endangered Life-Support Systems*, 2nd ed., 29).

14. Robert McIntosh pointed out that Henry David Thoreau coined the term *succession* to describe changes in the species composition of forests. According to McIntosh, early ecologists "strove to identify and classify communities in space, and the corollary was to examine change of a community in time, determine what stages it went through, and if, and when, it became stable or climax" (McIntosh, "The Succession of Succession: A Lexical Chronology," 256).

15. Eugene P. Odum, "The Strategy of Ecosystem Development," 266.

16. In her past-president's address for the Ecological Society of America, Meyer suggested that a prize be given by the ESA for "ecological research in the public interest" ("Beyond Gloom and Doom: Ecology for the Future").

17. Lucy Justus, "Eugene Odum: The Architect of Modern Ecology."

18. E. P. Odum, *Fundamentals*, 2nd ed., 494–496.

19. E. P. Odum, *Basic Ecology*, 518.

20. E. P. Odum, *Ecological Vignettes: Ecological Approaches to Dealing with Human Predicaments*, 58.

21. E. P. Odum, *Ecological Vignettes*, 58.

1. Chapel Hill

1. The others at the table were Merle Black, an Emory University scholar of politics and government; Lisa Howorth, from the University of Mississippi's Center for the Study of Southern Culture; Josephine Humphreys, a novelist from Charleston; Calvin Morris, dean of the Interdenominational Theological Center in Atlanta; John Shelton Reed, director of the University of North Carolina's Institute for Research in Social Science; David Satcher, director of the Centers for Disease Control and Prevention in Atlanta; and John Martin Taylor, a writer and culinary historian in Charleston.

2. Gene Odum's remarks were reported to me by John Shelton Reed, director of the University of North Carolina's Institute for Research in Social Science, which Howard Washington Odum, Gene's father, founded.

3. The entire list is as follows: John Cairns Jr., a researcher at Virginia Polytechnic Institute concerned with the restoration of damaged environments, sometimes called the "father of restoration ecology"; H. Ronald Pulliam, now director of the National Biological Service, who had chaired the governor's task force on environmental education; Howard T. Odum, an "innovative systems analyst, environmental engineer, and energy-economist" who believed that nonmarket goods and services and human-market goods and services should be given equal weight in economics; William H. Martin, a commissioner in the Department of Natural Resources in Kentucky, "one of the few persons in the S.E. who successfully interfaces academia and public service"; Judy Meyer, a recent president of the Ecological Society of America and an activist in public affairs; Whit Gibbons of the Savannah River Ecology Laboratory,

the author of a syndicated newspaper column on natural history; Lindsey Boring, director of the Jones Ecological Center, fostering cooperation between governmental and university efforts to preserve the natural environment; Norman L. Christensen, director of the School of the Environment at Duke University; John C. Avise of the Genetics Department of the University of Georgia, a pioneer in genetic engineering and author of "books readable by the layman"; Laurie Fowler, an attorney with the Georgia Environmental Policy Institute in Athens specializing in the land trust approach of turning private property into wildlife preserves; Camilla Herlevich, an attorney with the North Carolina Coastal Conservation Trust in Wilmington promoting land trusts; Dubos Porter, Georgia legislator and "friend of the environment"; and George W. Langdale, of the U.S. Department of Agriculture's Agricultural Research Station in Watkinsville, Georgia, who promoted conservation tillage as a means to reduce erosion and overuse of chemicals.

The *Olympic Atlanta* of 24 March 1996 selected Ron Pulliam as one of the "96 Southerners to Watch." It also included Governor George W. Bush of Texas. See Jim Auchmutey, "The New South: 96 Southerners to Watch."

4. See Wayne Douglas Brazil, *Howard W. Odum, The Building Years: 1884–1930*, 269–277, for a discussion of Howard W. Odum's understanding of society as a social system. According to Brazil, "[Odum's] belief in the interdependence of every part of the social organism dictated concern about these urban problems—he urged assaults on them not because of any deep affection for cities, but out of fear that they would contaminate neighboring rural areas" (275). Howard W. Odum wrote in 1914: "Progress in society is clearly the end in view, the attainment of which inevitably boosts progress in all divisions thereof" (Howard Washington Odum, "The Relation of the High School to Rural Life and Education," 139–147; quoted in Brazil, *Howard W. Odum*, 270–271).

5. The primary source of the biographical information about Howard Washington Odum is Rupert B. Vance and Katharine Jocher, "Howard W. Odum," 1–15. Other sources are Brazil, *Howard W. Odum*, which was originally a Harvard University Ph.D. dissertation; and Morton Sosna, *In Search of the Silent South: Southern Liberals and the Race Issue*, both of which draw on the Vance-Jocher article. Gene Odum supplied additional details of his father's career.

6. See Brazil, *Howard W. Odum*, 114–116, for an account of the reasons Howard Odum was drawn to social science. Brazil mentioned several influences: Howard's father, William's, commitment to agricultural reform as a means to improve eco-

nomic conditions in the rural South; his mother's awareness of the function of social classes; his family's Methodism, with its commitment to social service; and Bailey's belief in the use of social science for social service.

7. Vance and Jocher, "Howard W. Odum," 1–15; Sosna, *In Search of the Silent South,* 42–43. See Brazil, *Howard W. Odum,* 120–176, for a discussion of Odum's ideas about the races while under the influence of Bailey.

8. Sosna, *In Search of the Silent South,* 45.

9. Brazil, *Howard W. Odum,* 282–289. In an article published in 1916, Howard Odum wrote that every university should have a "department devoted to the promotion of better rural life and education, with opportunities to promote teacher training" (quoted in Brazil, 278).

10. Howard W. Odum, in *Social Forces* 1.2 (January 1923): 182.

11. Brazil, *Howard W. Odum,* 325.

12. Florence Gray Soltys, "Dr. Howard Washington Odum and the Founding of the School of Public Welfare at the University of North Carolina in Chapel Hill," 5.

13. Daniel Joseph Singal, *The War Within: From Victorian to Modernist Thought in the South, 1919–1945,* 121. Corrected by Eugene P. Odum, 18 April 2000.

14. Singal, *The War Within,* 121; Soltys, "Dr. Howard Washington Odum and the Founding of the School of Public Welfare," 8.

15. Howard W. Odum declared the purpose of the *Journal of Social Forces* in its first issue:

> *The Journal* will seek to contribute something in theory, something in application, toward making democracy effective in the unequal places—the supreme test of our democracy now. It will strive to touch the quickening social life about us. It will tend to emphasize movement, action, processes, forces. It will hope to add something to the efforts toward the increasing and utilizing of human adequacy. . . . It will strive to contribute something toward making our society well balanced as between business, agriculture and industry, town and country, trade and commerce, people and government, extremes and means. It will strive to develop human wealth. . . . More specifically, it will strive to provide an interstate medium of ideas, expression, and news, estimated to be of interest and benefit to all those who work for the public good. It will endeavor . . . to increase the reading and working power of its constituency. It will hope to contribute something to the growing standards of social work and public service. It will seek to discover and promote better methods of social work for rural areas. In each of

the several departments it will hope, from time to time, to make distinctive contributions of value. ("Editorial Notes" [January 1922], 56–57)

16. Singal, *The War Within*, 121.

17. H. W. Odum, "Editorial Notes" (November 1922), 56. Howard established *Social Forces* to advance his vision of a comprehensive democracy; by 1924 he had 1,700 subscribers, only half of whom lived in the South. In trenchant editorials and in investigative reports by contributors to the journal, *Social Forces* assaulted long-standing southern customs and values; social institutions, including the church; and the rising business class, whom Howard accused of "breeding a gross spirit of materialism." Odum was influenced by the organicist social theory of his teachers Bailey, Hall, and Giddings, in which society was understood metaphorically as an organism: Society, the constituent parts of which were interdependent, developed through progressive "differentiation" and "integration" of its various institutions until it became an integrated whole. See Singal, *The War Within*, 123–125, 133.

18. H. W. Odum, "Editorial Notes" (January 1923): 180.

19. In 1993, Gene Odum wrote the following in a letter to John Shelton Reed, who had just written a chapter titled "Howard Odum and Regional Sociology" for his book *Surveying the South: Studies in Regional Sociology:* "H. W. [Odum] was strongly motivated to develop the regional concept as an antidote for 'sectionalism' although he never made this clear in his writings. He was anxious for the south to quite [sic] trying to isolate itself, but instead to develop its culture and resources as a part of, not apart from, the nation. To me this is pretty important social science theory which unfortunately is not understood by people in central Europe where every little ethnic group is trying to segregate into little countries that can not possibly survive on their own" (letter in collection of Eugene P. Odum).

20. Howard W. Odum, "This Is Worth Our Best," 2–4.

21. Howard W. Odum, "Agenda for Integration" [1954], 73.

22. Fred Hobson, *Tell about the South*, 207–243.

23. See Singal, *The War Within*, 126–129, for an account of the religious fundamentalists' attack on *Social Forces* during the 1925 statewide battle over the teaching of evolution in the schools. Howard Odum had published in the January issue two articles offensive to fundamentalists: one by the book review editor Harry E. Barnes that mocked Christianity and Victorian ethics, and the other by the sociologist Luther L. Bernard that explored the psychological origins of religious belief. That January, a state legislator had introduced a bill to ban the teaching of Darwinian evolution, and he used Howard Odum's *Journal of Social Forces* as evidence that the

University of North Carolina employed atheists. Church organizations condemned the journal, some of them petitioning the governor to cut off its funding. Odum sent an open telegram to the church ministers taking full responsibility for the journal's contents but also accusing them of exaggeration for political purposes. In order to avoid such trouble in the future, Odum began to be more careful about publishing inflammatory material.

24. Singal, *The War Within*, 112–127.

25. Soltys, "Dr. Howard Washington Odum and the Founding of the School of Public Welfare," 10; Steve Levin, "unc's First Woman Teacher Honored on her 90th Birthday."

26. "Howard W. Odum, Sociologist, Dies," *New York Times*, 10 November 1954; Brooke Allan and Benjamin H. Trask, *Howard Washington Odum Papers Inventory*.

27. "Howard W. Odum, Sociologist, Dies."

28. "Howard Odum's Part in the State's Creative Life," *Chapel Hill News Leader*, 15 November 1954.

29. "Howard Odum and Human Welfare," 50.

30. Shelton Reed, *Surveying the South*, 3.

31. On 24 January 1944, Gene Odum received a letter from J. B. Bennett Jr., associate editor of the College Department of the Macmillan Company, that was a response to a letter Howard Odum had written a Mr. T. C. Morehouse about Gene's plans for a book on ecology. Howard had written Morehouse: "He [Gene] will be ready for a publisher in a year or two, and it occurred to me you might want the book" (letter from J. B. Bennett Jr. to Eugene P. Odum, 24 January 1944, in collection of Eugene P. Odum).

32. Letter from Howard W. Odum to Eugene and Martha Odum, 16 March 1947, in collection of Eugene P. Odum.

33. Anna Kranz Odum's master's thesis addressed the development of student honor systems and self-government. See Brazil, *Howard W. Odum*, 181.

34. Brazil, *Howard W. Odum*, 183–196.

35. William Covington Parker, "Fountain of Understanding: A Story of Howard Washington Odum," 13.

36. Letter from Anna Kranz Odum to Eugene Odum, 18 September 1953, in collection of Eugene P. Odum.

37. Account by Mary Frances Odum Schinhan.

38. Louis Graves, "Eugene Odum's Bird Magazine," 4.

39. Graves, "Eugene Odum's Bird Magazine," 4.

40. Eugene P. Odum and Coit M. Coker, "Bird Life in Chapel Hill," 6.

41. Interview with Martha Odum, 17 July 1987, audiotape in collection of Betty Jean Craige.

42. Louis Graves, "Motor-Camping Trip to California Costs Odum and Coker $33.44 Each."

43. Audiotaped interview with Martha Odum, 17 July 1987, in collection of Betty Jean Craige.

44. Audiotaped interview with Wyatt W. Anderson, 3 January 1996, in collection of Betty Jean Craige.

45. Interview with Betty Jean Craige, 20 July 1997.

46. Interview with Betty Jean Craige, 20 July 1997.

47. Interview with Betty Jean Craige, 20 July 1997.

48. Audiotaped interview with Wyatt W. Anderson, 3 January 1996, in collection of Betty Jean Craige.

49. Interview of Mary Frances Odum Schinhan by Betty Jean Craige, June 1996.

50. Interview of Mary Frances Odum Schinhan by Betty Jean Craige, June 1996.

51. Letter from Howard T. Odum to Eugene P. Odum, September 1940, in collection of Eugene P. Odum.

52. See Joel B. Hagen's *An Entangled Bank: The Origins of Ecosystem Ecology*, 122–123, for a discussion of the philosophical orientation of Howard Washington Odum, Eugene Pleasants Odum, and Howard Thomas Odum. Hagen said, "Undoubtedly, from his father Eugene inherited his commitment to organic holism."

53. Andrew Jamison, "A Tale of Two Brothers," 498.

54. Alston Chase, *In a Dark Wood: The Fight over Forests and the Rising Tyranny of Ecology*, 121.

2. The Ecologist's Early Years

1. The shift in ecologists' focus from structure to function propelled by Eugene Odum's ecosystem ecology was advocated earlier by Charles Christopher Adams, who called for increased attention to the processes of evolutionary change in the interactions of organisms and their environment; see Charles C. Adams, *Guide to the Study of Animal Ecology*; Sharon E. Kingsland, *Modeling Nature: Episodes in the History of Population Ecology*, 2nd ed.

2. The cardio-vibrometer that Odum created with the Brush Company's new aluminum pen was actually a modification of a more primitive instrument that an ear-

lier scientist at the Baldwin Bird Research Laboratory, Roscoe Franks, had built using Brush crystals. That instrument, Odum reported in his dissertation, was unsatisfactory for quantitative work because it was bulky, battery operated, and equipped with a photographic recorder. The aluminum pen proved more useful than the photographic recorder in making records that could be read immediately. See Eugene P. Odum, "Variations in the Heart Rate of Birds: A Study in Physiological Ecology," 1941, 302. Odum worked with C. H. Tower and Joseph J. Neff of the Bush Company's Engineering Department to construct the cardio-vibrometer. In his dissertation he credited them for designing the amplifier and building the apparatus. See Eugene P. Odum, "The Cardio-Vibrometer: A New Instrument for Measuring the Heart Rate and Other Body Activities of Animals," 106. Odum explained the piezoelectric principle in his dissertation and then in a 1940 article in *Ecology* as follows:

Certain crystalline substances, particularly Rochelle salt (sodium-potassium-tartrate), have the property of producing a difference of electrical potential between opposite sides of the crystal proportional to the pressure applied and, conversely, of producing motion proportional to the difference of electrical potential applied to opposite sides of the crystal. By the use of such crystals and an amplifier, a system may be constructed whereby very slight variations in pressure, as by the slight motions or "jars" of the body produced by each heart cycle, can be picked up, amplified, and recorded on moving paper and the frequency determined. Thus, the apparatus has been named the "cardio-vibrometer" or simply "vibrometer," literally, "an instrument recording vibrations." ("The Cardio-Vibrometer," 105)

3. E. P. Odum, "The Cardio-Vibrometer," 105–106.

4. The purposes of his dissertation Odum described as follows:

1. to determine the nature of the heart rate in small birds;

2. to determine the relation of the heart rate to other physiology-of-the-whole measurements, particularly rate of metabolism, rate of breathing, and muscular activity; and

3. to determine what the heart rate will reveal about the responses of birds to environmental conditions, particularly temperature. (E. P. Odum, "Variations," 301)

He studied mourning doves, English sparrows, song sparrows, house wrens, cardinals, towhees, black-capped chickadees, catbirds, cowbirds, brown thrashers, yellow warblers, northern yellowthroats, field sparrows, and ruby-throated hummingbirds. E. P. Odum, "Variations," 314.

5. E. P. Odum, "Variations," 305, 317–318.

6. E. P. Odum, "Variations," 301.

7. Frederic E. Clements and Victor E. Shelford, *Bio-Ecology*, 20–21. In 1916, Clements had presented his notion of the biome in the opening paper of the first meeting of the newly formed Ecological Society of America, of which Shelford was president. He defined a *biome* as a "biotic community . . . an organic unit comprising all the species of plants and animals at home in a particular habitat." Clements was not the first to propose a unified biotic concept, however.

8. Clements and Shelford, *Bio-Ecology*, 23; Jan Christiaan Smuts, *Holism and Evolution*, 122.

9. Robert A. Croker, *Pioneer Ecologist: The Life and Work of Victor Ernest Shelford, 1877–1968*, 74.

10. Croker quoted Odum's description of a Shelford field trip as follows:

We graduate students soon learned that to get the most out of a Shelford field trip one must keep within a few feet as he marched rather rapidly across the prairie or through the woods. All kinds of pearls of wisdom would drop out including appropriate sarcastic remarks about reductionist biologists, or that "Woods Hole establishment," which he viewed as anti-ecology. I think the reason he was not too well accepted by many of the more conventional biologists was that his holistic ideas were ahead of [the] time, but methods to deal with ecosystem level processes had not yet been developed. In other words, his concepts were great but field methods of the day were inadequate. (*Pioneer Ecologist*, 101)

11. Frederic E. Clements, *Plant Succession: An Analysis of the Development of Vegetation*, 6–7. In the introductory chapter in which he explained the concept of "succession," Clements wrote: "The student of succession must recognize clearly that developmental stages, like the climax, are only a record of what has already happened. Each stage is, temporarily at least, a stable structure, and the actual processes can be revealed only by following the development of one stage into the succeeding one. In short, succession can be studied properly only by tracing the rise and fall of each stage, and not by a floristic picture of the population at the crest of each invasion."

12. Clements and Shelford defined *habitat* as comprising "all the physical and chemical factors that operate upon the community," such as water, temperature, light, and oxygen. They described succession on land as follows:

In the plant matrix of the land biotic community, the causal sequence is a fairly simple cycle. The action of the habitat as expressed in stimuli gives rise to responses on the part of the plant or community. These in turn operate on the habitat, producing reactions that modify it, and then again in turn its action on plant life follows. Embraced within this primary cycle is a secondary one of inter-action or coaction between species and between individuals, both plant and ani-mal, well exemplified by plant parasites and saprophytes. The end results of these processes are still other reactions, especially on the soil. Animals too are acted upon directly by the habitat and then react upon it in some degree, but their en-ergy relations are primarily a matter of food supply. In consequence, coaction be-comes a response of paramount importance, and plants as middlemen between the supply of solar energy and animals may be regarded as constituting a group of secondary or intermediate causes. Plants likewise exert coactions upon animals, and in the case of lethal parasites these lead to soil reactions through the decom-position of organisms. Hence, the complete cycle of causes, and of effects that become causes in their turn, includes the action of the habitat followed by the responses thereto, which in turn become causes of further change.

On land, the plants as dominants and subdominants play the major role in re-action; in the large bodies of fresh water and in the sea the situation is more or less reversed. (*Bio-Ecology*, 26, 30–31)

13. Clements and Shelford, *Bio-Ecology*, 27.

14. Alfred George Tansley, "The Use and Abuse of Vegetational Concepts and Terms," 296–302. Tansley wrote: "This refusal [to accept the concept of the *biotic community*] is however far from meaning that I do not realise that various 'biomes,' the whole webs of life adjusted to particular complexes of environmental factors, are real 'wholes,' often highly integrated wholes, which are the living nuclei of *systems* in the sense of the physicist. Only I do not think they are properly described as 'or-ganisms' (except in the 'organicist' sense). I prefer to regard them, together with the whole of the effective physical factors involved, simply as 'systems'" (Tansley, "The Use and Abuse of Vegetational Concepts and Terms," 297).

15. Tansley, "The Use and Abuse of Vegetational Concepts and Terms," 291.

16. Tansley, "The Use and Abuse of Vegetational Concepts and Terms," 291, 303. For a discussion of the philosophical and long-term environmental implications of Tansley's argument, see Donald Worster, *Nature's Economy: A History of Ecological Ideas*, 2nd ed., 239–242. Worster pointed out that Clements's segregation of human activities from nonhuman nature allowed the measurement of the disturbance of

nonhuman nature by civilization, whereas Tansley's removal of any artificial dividing line led to an "environmental relativism" with "no exterior model against which the artificial environment could be evaluated scientifically."

17. Croker, *Pioneer Ecologist*, 102–104.

18. Audiotape of interview by Martha Odum, 17 July 1987, in collection of Betty Jean Craige; Croker, *Pioneer Ecologist*, 103–104.

19. Audiotape of interview by Betty Jean Craige, 15 October 1994, in collection of Betty Jean Craige.

20. Eugene P. Odum, "Annual Report for 1939–40," 1–2, 5. Gene prepared the report and submitted it in December 1940. Composing the Scientific Advisory Committee were W. J. Hamilton Jr., Cornell University, chairman; G. Kingsley Noble, American Museum of Natural History; John R. Greeley, New York State Museum; Thomas Ordway, Albany; Lewis A. Eldridge, New York; and William Vogt, New York.

21. E. P. Odum, "Annual Report," 3, 10–11.

22. The equipment on hand on 10 October 1939, according to Odum's "Annual Report," was as follows:

Bausch and Lomb dissecting Microscope No. 22054 1	Mole traps 3
	Small aquaria 2
Small Ohaus balance and set of weights 1	Preserving jars, ½ gallon 16
Sling hygrometer, Taylor 1	Preserving jars, pints 5
Mouse traps, snap back type 119	Preserving jars, ½ pints 4
Live mammal traps, small 17	Wire funnel fish traps 2
Live mammal traps, large 10	Small minnow seine 1

By September 1940 the equipment included:

Metal live traps, small 17	Hip boots 1
Metal live traps, large 10	Sieves 2
Mouse traps 15 approx.	Ladder 1
Small bird trap, tree type 3	5 cell flashlight 1
Large bird trap, ground type 1	Binocular dissecting micro-
Bird feeding station 2	scope B. & L. 1
Sling hygrometer 1	Small Ohaus balance and
Colman gas lantern 1	weights 1
Small bat gathering cage 1	Aquaria 2
Small bird gathering cage 1	½ gallon jars 9
Small seines 2	Small jars 24 plus
Buckets 3	Wire cages 2

Plant dryer and press 1
Watch glasses 4
Glass dishes 4
Metal trays 4
Small Taylor thermometer 1
Vials and corks 30 plus
Alcohol (about 3 gallons) and container 1
Lab stools 3
Misc.—wire, metal cans, boxes, screening,
    hardware cloth, paint.

Hammer 1
Saw 1
Brace and 3 bits
Chisels 3
Pliers 2
Small square 1
Screw driver 2
Coping saw 1

(28–30)

23. E. P. Odum, "Annual Report," 8–10.

24. Audiotaped interview of Gene Odum by Martha Odum, 17 July 1987, in collection of Betty Jean Craige.

25. Audiotaped interview of Gene Odum by Martha Odum, 17 July 1987, in collection of Betty Jean Craige; telephone interview of Gene Odum by Betty Jean Craige, 13 March 1996; E. P. Odum, "Annual Report," 34.

26. Odum spent most of the fall studying the composition, movements, and organization of the flocks of chickadees. During the winter and spring he banded 114 birds with colored bands to be able to identify them in the field, and then observed fifteen nesting territories and eleven nests. Audiotaped interview of Gene Odum by Martha Odum, 17 July 1987; E. P. Odum, "Annual Report" 19–23.

27. E. P. Odum, "Annual Report," 11.

28. See Kingsland, *Modeling Nature*, 23.

29. Telephone interview of Gene Odum by Betty Jean Craige, 11 March 1997.

30. Audiotaped interview of Gene Odum by Martha Odum, 17 July 1987, in collection of Betty Jean Craige.

31. James K. Reap, *Athens: A Pictorial History*, 159; Frances Taliaferro Thomas, *A Portrait of Historic Athens and Clarke County*, 184.

32. Audiotaped interview of Gene Odum by Martha Odum, 12 August 1987, in collection of Betty Jean Craige.

33. Quoted in Thomas G. Dyer, *The University of Georgia: A Bicentennial History, 1785–1985*, 229.

34. Dyer, *The University of Georgia*, 225–240; Thomas, *Portrait of Historic Athens*, 187. Dyer's book includes a detailed account of the series of events that led up to the disaccreditation by the Southern Association of Colleges and Schools. According to Dyer, Dean Walter Dewey Cocking of the College of Education, at the request

of the Board of Regents, had conducted a study of state-supported black institutions of higher education that disclosed the failure of the "separate but equal" doctrine, the inadequacy of financial support, and the low enrollment of blacks. Cocking's recommendation that the state increase its support for those institutions and improve their facilities aroused the suspicion that he favored "social equality" for blacks. Governor Talmadge, who packed the Board of Regents with his cronies after promising the removal of any person in the university system who stood for "communism or racial equality," managed to oust Cocking and several other faculty in the university system who supposedly showed sympathy for blacks. During the turmoil, Howard Odum, invited by the General Education Board to assess the situation, had advised Cocking to resign rather than force the governor to remove him, in order to avoid punitive action against the university system by the Southern Association of Colleges and Schools. Cocking did not resign, and the Board of Regents fired him and others on 14 July. On 4 December 1941, the four hundred delegates to the annual meeting of the Southern Association of Colleges and Schools voted unanimously to rescind accreditation from all the white institutions in the university system of Georgia effective fall 1942. Dyer, *The University of Georgia*, 225–240.

35. Odum was promoted to associate professor of zoology and elected a fellow of the American Ornithologists' Union in 1945. Audiotaped interview of Gene Odum by Martha Odum, 12 August 1987, in collection of Betty Jean Craige.

36. Telephone interview of Gene Odum with Betty Jean Craige, 9 March 1997.

37. Aldo Leopold, "The Land Ethic," in *A Sand County Almanac*, 216.

38. Raymond L. Lindeman, "The Trophic-Dynamic Aspect of Ecology." The paper was based on research he had conducted at Cedar Bog Lake, Minnesota.

39. Lindeman, "The Trophic-Dynamic Aspect of Ecology," 400.

40. See Frank B. Golley, *A History of the Ecosystem Concept in Ecology*, 58; Joel Hagen, *An Entangled Bank: The Origins of Ecosystem Ecology*, 125–126; Alfred J. Lotka, *Elements of Mathematical Biology*.

41. Telephone conversation with Betty Jean Craige, 12 March 1997.

42. Telephone conversation with Betty Jean Craige, 18 March 1997.

43. Letter from J. B. Bennett Jr., associate editor of the the Macmillan Company's College Department, to Eugene P. Odum, 24 January 1944; letter from Howard W. Odum to Eugene P. Odum, 26 January 1944, both in collection of E. P. Odum.

44. Telephone conversation with Betty Jean Craige, 19 March 1997.

45. Letter from Eugene P. Odum to J. B. Bennett Jr., 7 February 1944, in collection of Eugene P. Odum.

46. Letter from E. P. Odum to J. B. Bennett Jr., 7 February 1944, in collection of E. P. Odum.

47. Dyer, *The University of Georgia*, 255.

48. Audiotaped interviews of Gene Odum by Martha Odum, 12 August 1987, September 1987, in collection of Betty Jean Craige.

49. Eugene P. Odum, "The Emergence of Ecology as a New Integrative Discipline," 1289.

50. Audiotaped interview of Gene Odum by Martha Odum, September 1987, in collection of Betty Jean Craige.

51. Letters from Howard T. Odum to Eugene P. Odum, in collection of E. P. Odum.

52. Letter from Howard T. Odum to Eugene P. Odum, in collection of E. P. Odum.

53. Eugene P. Odum, *Fundamentals of Ecology*, 1st ed.

54. Odum frequently attributed the importance of *Fundamentals* to its "top-down, ecosystem first" approach to the study of nature.

55. E. P. Odum, "The Emergence of Ecology," 1290.

56. See E. P. Odum, *Fundamentals*, 1st ed., ix–xii.

57. E. P. Odum, *Fundamentals*, 1st ed., vi.

58. E. P. Odum, *Fundamentals*, 1st ed., vii. Howard T. Odum contributed to the following chapters: "Principles and Concepts Pertaining to Energy in Ecological Systems," "Introduction to Population and Community Ecology," "Principles and Concepts Pertaining to Organization at the Species Population Level," and "Principles and Concepts Pertaining to Organization at the Interspecies Population Level."

59. Interview of Howard T. Odum by Betty Jean Craige, 9 February 1997, at the opening of an exposition of Martha Odum's watercolors in the Georgia Museum of Art.

60. E. P. Odum, *Fundamentals*, 1st ed., 9.

61. E. P. Odum, *Fundamentals*, 1st ed., 187–189, 198. Early in the book Odum stated: "The second law of thermodynamics deals with the transfer of energy and is related to what is known as the stability principle. According to this concept any natural enclosed system, whether the earth itself or a smaller unit, such as a lake, tends to change until a stable state, with self-regulating mechanisms, is developed. Self-regulating mechanisms are mechanisms which bring about a return to constancy if a system is caused to change from the stable state by a momentary outside influence" (E. P. Odum, *Fundamentals*, 67).

62. E. P. Odum, *Fundamentals*, 1st ed., 196.

63. E. P. Odum, *Fundamentals*, 1st ed., 188.

64. E. P. Odum, *Fundamentals*, 1st ed., 165, 178. Odum described the types of possible interaction between two species as follows:

(1) *neutralism*, in which neither population is affected by association with the other; (2) *competition*, in which each population adversely affects the other in the struggle for food, nutrients, living space, or other common need; (3) *mutualism*, in which growth and survival of both populations is benefited and neither can survive under natural conditions without the other; (4) *protocooperation*, in which both populations benefit by the association but relations are not obligatory; (5) *commensalism*, in which one population is benefited but the other is not affected; (6) *amensalism*, in which one population is inhibited and the other not affected; (7) *parasitism* and (8) *predation*, in which one population adversely affects the other by direct attack but is dependent on the other. (165)

65. E. P. Odum, *Fundamentals*, 1st ed., 178.

66. E. P. Odum, *Fundamentals*, 1st ed., 88.

67. Smuts, *Holism and Evolution*, 123.

68. E. P. Odum, *Fundamentals*, 1st ed., 181, 7, 88.

69. E. P. Odum, *Fundamentals*, 1st ed., 182.

70. E. P. Odum, *Fundamentals*, 1st ed., 187–188.

71. E. P. Odum, *Fundamentals*, 1st ed., 317.

72. E. P. Odum, *Fundamentals*, 1st ed., 12.

73. E. P. Odum, *Fundamentals*, 1st ed., 343.

74. E. P. Odum, *Fundamentals*, 1st ed., 345.

75. Worster, *Nature's Economy*, 363.

76. Leopold, "The Land Ethic," 201–204.

77. Observation of ecologist Judy Meyer, colleague at the University of Georgia; telephone interview with Betty Jean Craige, 19 July 1997.

3. The Atomic Age

1. Information on book sales provided by Eugene P. Odum. The first edition of *Fundamentals of Ecology* (1953) sold 9,000 copies; the second edition (1959), 103,000; and the third edition (1971), 170,500. Sales for the second and third editions together peaked in 1971, when 41,800 copies were sold. See "Ecology: The New Jeremiahs," 38, 40; "The Length and the Breadth and the Sweep of the Marshes

of Glynn," 88–92; and "Dawn for the Age of Ecology," 35–40. All three articles carried photographs of Eugene Odum.

2. Eugene P. Odum's textbooks — *Fundamentals of Ecology* and *Basic Ecology*, which was actually the fourth edition of *Fundamentals* — were translated into Chinese, Czech, French, German, Japanese, Korean, Malaysian, Polish, Portuguese, Russian, Spanish, Swedish, and Indonesian.

3. Eugene P. Odum, in collaboration with Howard T. Odum, *Fundamentals of Ecology*, 2nd ed., v.

4. E. P. Odum and H. T. Odum, *Fundamentals*, 2nd ed., v.

5. Anne R. Gibbons, "The Savannah River Ecology Laboratory," 468. The Savannah River Plant Reservation occupies three hundred square miles along the Savannah River southeast of Augusta, Georgia, in Aiken, Barnwell, and Allendale Counties of South Carolina. The main contractor for the facility was E. I. du Pont de Nemours and Company. Eugene P. Odum, "Early University of Georgia Research, 1952–62," 43.

6. Eugene P. Odum, "Early University of Georgia Research," 60–61.

7. E. P. Odum, "Early University of Georgia Research," 43–44. This first proposal, which was not funded, described a study that would be conducted by six teams of scientists — five from the University of Georgia and one from Emory — in two phases: (1) a "preoperational phase," in which the scientists would produce a complete ecological type map of the area, determining land use history and successional relations; detailed lists of plants and animals in the major habitats, with an evaluation of ecologically important species and indicator species; and quantitative data for streams, ponds, and other habitats in the immediate vicinity of the installations; and (2) a "postoperational phase" in which scientists would record their observations after the reactors and other installations had started operating. In the proposal Odum listed six "study divisions": (1) limnology and fisheries biology, (2) aquatic plant ecology, (3) terrestrial plant ecology, (4) terrestrial animal ecology, (5) physical ecology, and (6) ecological geography. The administrative director was to be George H. Boyd, dean of the Graduate School, director of research, and professor of zoology at the University of Georgia; and the field director was to be Eugene Odum. The other scientists named in the proposal were James Jenkins, W. J. Hauck, George Mc-Cammon, Robert L. Humphries, Molton Hopkins, and Terry A. McGowan, all from the University of Georgia; and R. B. Platt, from Emory University. The total budget requested from the Atomic Energy Commission was $150,089. Eugene P. Odum, "Early University of Georgia Research," 60–72.

8. E. P. Odum, "Early University of Georgia Research," 44–45.

9. E. P. Odum, "Early University of Georgia Research," 45.

10. E. P. Odum, "Early University of Georgia Research," 45–46, 74–77; Gibbons, "The Savannah River Ecology Laboratory," 470.

11. E. P. Odum, "Early University of Georgia Research," 46.

12. Letter from Howard T. Odum to Eugene P. Odum, summer 1951, in collection of Eugene P. Odum.

13. Frank B. Golley, "Establishing the Network," unpublished.

14. E. P. Odum, "Early University of Georgia Research," 46–47. Cross, Kuenzler, and Davenport each completed a Ph.D. at the University of Georgia.

15. E. P. Odum, "Early University of Georgia Research," 47–48; Gibbons, "The Savannah River Ecology Laboratory," 468–470. According to Odum, the AEC-SRP office provided some vehicles and services in 1952 to allow his team to add a fourth graduate research assistant, Robert Pearson, an ornithologist who was completing his master's degree at the University of Illinois under Charles Kendeigh. Pearson arrived in March 1952.

16. E. P. Odum, "Early University of Georgia Research," 47–48; Gibbons, "The Savannah River Ecology Laboratory," 468–470.

17. E. P. Odum, "Early University of Georgia Research," 50–51. Karl Herde came to the Savannah River Plant from a position at the Hanford Laboratory in Washington State. Odum described him as "our most enthusiastic helper."

18. See Eugene P. Odum and Frank B. Golley, "Radioactive Tracers as an Aid to the Measurement of Energy Flow at the Population Level in Nature," 403. Joel Hagen pointed out that radioactive tracers were used before World War II to study the metabolism of individual plants and animals, and the method was discussed during that period in scientific journals. G. Evelyn Hutchinson experimented with a radioactive tracer on Linsley Pond in 1941, but he was unsuccessful because the Yale cyclotron produced only half the amount he needed. Nuclear reactors changed the situation because they produced a plentiful amount. See Joel B. Hagen, *An Entangled Bank: The Origins of Ecosystem Ecology*, 113–115.

19. Hagen, *An Entangled Bank*, 114.

20. Eugene P. Odum, "Relationships between Structure and Function in the Ecosystem," 115–116.

21. E. P. Odum, "Early University of Georgia Research," 51; Eugene P. Odum, "The Emergence of Ecology as a New Integrative Discipline," 1289.

22. In that article Odum defined "the new ecology" as "a new integrative disci-

pline that deals with the supra-individual levels of organization," hailing it as "a response to the need for greater attention to holism in science and technology" (E. P. Odum, "The Emergence of Ecology," 1289, 1291).

23. Audiotaped interview of Gene Odum by Martha Odum, September 1987, in collection of Betty Jean Craige.

24. E. P. Odum, "Early University of Georgia Research," 56; Gibbons, "The Savannah River Ecology Laboratory," 471; Golley, "Establishing the Network."

25. Eugene P. Odum, telephone conversation with Betty Jean Craige, 18 March 1997.

26. Eugene P. Odum, "Sapelo Chronology (The First Decade as Documented by Eugene Odum)," manuscript in collection of Eugene P. Odum, 1; James H. Jenkins, "The Occurrence of the Chachalaca on Sapelo Island, Georgia," 11–12; audiotaped interview of Gene Odum by Martha Odum, September 1987, in collection of Betty Jean Craige; telephone interview of Gene Odum by Betty Jean Craige, 21 March 1997.

27. Lawrence R. Pomeroy and Donald C. Scott, "The University of Georgia Marine Institute: The First Decade," manuscript in collection of Eugene P. Odum; audiotaped interview of Gene Odum by Martha Odum, September 1987, in collection of Betty Jean Craige.

28. Audiotaped interview of Gene Odum by Martha Odum, September 1987, in collection of Betty Jean Craige; telephone interview of Gene Odum by Betty Jean Craige, 21 March 1997.

29. Besides Aderhold and Odum, the delegation included Administrative Associate George King, Dean C. C. Murray of Agriculture, and Dean J. D. Weddell of Forestry. See Pomeroy and Scott, "The University of Georgia Marine Institute," 2–3; and E. P. Odum, "Sapelo Chronology," for a detailed discussion of the negotiations.

30. E. P. Odum, "Sapelo Chronology," 2; telephone interview of Gene Odum by Betty Jean Craige, 5 July 1997.

31. E. P. Odum, "Sapelo Chronology," 2; audiotaped interview of Gene Odum by Martha Odum, September 1987, in collection of Betty Jean Craige.

32. Theodore J. Starr, a microbiologist, was the first scientist recruited to the Sapelo project after Ragotzkie, but he left in September 1955. Ragotzkie, Pomeroy, and Teal worked as a team until 1960, when Ragotzkie left for the University of Wisconsin and Teal for Halifax, Nova Scotia. Pomeroy moved to the university's campus in Athens, where he continued to work on marine projects until his retirement

as Alumni Foundation Distinguished Professor. Audiotaped interview of Gene Odum by Martha Odum, September 1987, in collection of Betty Jean Craige; Pomeroy and Scott, "The University of Georgia Marine Institute," 4–6, 14.

33. According to Odum, Boyd removed him from the Sapelo project, perhaps because he would not have been a good long-term administrator of the laboratory. Odum had many other demands on his time: the publication of *Fundamentals of Ecology* in 1953, the collaboration with H. T. on the coral reefs of the Eniwetok Atoll during the summer of 1954, and the continuing work on the Savannah River project with the Atomic Energy Commission. In 1959, when the University of Georgia Marine Biological Laboratory became the University of Georgia Marine Institute, Reynolds's Sapelo Island Agriculture and Forestry Foundation became the Sapelo Island Research Foundation, and then later the Sapelo Island Foundation. One of Martha Odum's watercolors was used for the cover of *Ecology: A Bridge between Science and Society* (1997). Pomeroy and Scott, "The University of Georgia Marine Institute," 7, 14.

34. Eugene P. Odum, "Living Marsh," 19–20.

35. E. P. Odum and H. T. Odum, *Fundamentals*, 2nd ed., 358.

36. The study of the coral reef, supported by a grant from the U.S. Atomic Energy Commission through a contract between the AEC and the University of Georgia, is reported in Howard T. Odum and Eugene P. Odum, "Trophic Structure and Productivity of a Windward Coral Reef Community on Eniwetok Atoll."

37. Howard T. Odum published the results of his four-year study of a warm mineral springs in Florida in "Trophic Structure and Productivity of Silver Springs, Florida." After the summer in Eniwetok, he moved from the University of Florida to Duke University as assistant professor of zoology.

38. In their paper the Odums described their approach as follows: "Many varied sampling procedures were combined to estimate the standing crop of the major component groups of the reef biota. Then chemical methods were used upstream and downstream to estimate the primary production and total respiratory metabolism of the reef. From these standing crop and productivity estimates, the turnover was obtained. Productivity data were combined with calculated light intensities to obtain an estimate of energetic efficiency" (H. T. Odum and E. P. Odum, "Trophic Structure and Productivity of a Windward Coral Reef Community on Eniwetok Atoll," 293, 301–302). See also Hagen, *An Entangled Bank*, 101–106; Eugene P. Odum, *Ecological Vignettes: Ecological Approaches to Dealing with Human Predicaments*, 93–96; and E. P. Odum, "The Emergence of Ecology as a New Integrative Discipline," 1290.

39. E. P. Odum, *Fundamentals*, 1st ed., 165.

40. Eugene P. Odum, *Ecology: A Bridge between Science and Society*, 258.

41. In their article, the Odums described the method that H. T. had developed for his Silver Springs study (on the basis of a flow-rate technique developed in 1949 by M. C. Sargent and T. S. Austin and described in "Organic Productivity of an Atoll," 245–249) as follows:

> The oxygen content of the water upstream and downstream is measured simultaneously. The oxygen increase between stations during the day is the net photosynthetic production of the community. The oxygen decrease between stations during the night is the total respiration of the community. By taking a series of measurements over the daily cycle, one obtains the course of production during the day. Measurement of the current transport permits calculation of total reef metabolism. The respiration at night plus the net production during the day gives the total production. By comparing the area of the graph between the day curve and the zero line with areas of the graph under the zero line at night one can obtain an indication of what part of the excess production during the day is used up by respiration during the night. (H. T. Odum and E. P. Odum, "Trophic Structure and Productivity of a Windward Coral Reef Community on Eniwetok Atoll," 314)

42. The Odums wrote: "The gains and losses are only 4% apart. In view of the rough nature of some of the estimates it is not certain whether this is a significant difference or whether the community is in a perfect steady state with losses matching gains. . . . We may tentatively conclude, at least, that the Japtan Reef is a true climax community, in the ecological sense, under present ocean level conditions, since there is little if any net increase in living bio-mass" (H. T. Odum and E. P. Odum, "Trophic Structure and Productivity of a Windward Coral Reef Community on Eniwetok Atoll," 317–318). They cited S. J. Holmes, "The Principle of Stability as a Cause of Evolution," 324–333.

43. Hagen, *An Entangled Bank*, 103.

44. Eugene P. Odum, "Ecosystem Management: A New Venture for Humankind," 119.

45. Hagen, *An Entangled Bank*, 105–106.

46. J. Baird Callicott, in "The Metaphysical Implications of Ecology," published in *In Defense of the Land Ethic* (104), characterized the West's traditional model of nature as follows:

> The terrestrial natural environment consists of a collection of bodies composed of molecular aggregates of atoms. A living natural body is in principle a

very elaborate machine. That is, its generation, gestation, development, decay, and death can be exhaustively explained reductively and mechanically. Some of these natural machines are mysteriously inhabited by a conscious monad, a "ghost in the machine." Living natural bodies come in a wide variety of types or species, which are determined by a logico-conceptual order, and have, otherwise, no essential connection to one another. They are, as it were, loosed upon the landscape, each outfitted with its (literally God-given) Platonic-Aristotelian essence, to interact catch-as-catch can.

47. Callicott, "The Metaphysical Implications of Ecology," 109.

48. Callicott, "The Metaphysical Implications of Ecology," 110–111.

49. E. P. Odum, "The Emergence of Ecology as a New Integrative Discipline," 1290.

50. Eugene P. Odum, *Basic Ecology*, 5–6.

51. In 1973 William Drury and Ian Nisbet challenged the notion, promulgated by Clements and Odum, that succession leads directly to a "climax state," or equilibrium. Their study of northeastern American forests appeared to show that change in nature is undirectional and that "stability" does not exist. See William H. Drury and Ian C. T. Nisbet, "Succession," 331–368. See also Donald Worster, *The Wealth of Nature: Environmental History and the Ecological Imagination*, 162–163.

52. Daniel Botkin, *Discordant Harmonies: A New Ecology for the Twenty-first Century*, 8.

53. E. P. Odum, *Ecological Vignettes*, 27.

54. E. P. Odum, *Ecological Vignettes*, 96.

55. See Eugene P. Odum, "Ecology and the Atomic Age," 27; Eugene P. Odum, "Ecological Aspects of Waste Disposal," 95; and E. P. Odum and H. T. Odum, *Fundamentals*, 2nd ed., v.

56. E. P. Odum, *Ecological Vignettes*, 232.

57. E. P. Odum, "Consideration of the Total Environment in Power Reactor Waste Disposal."

58. E. P. Odum, "Consideration of the Total Environment in Power Reactor Waste Disposal."

59. E. P. Odum, "Ecological Aspects of Waste Disposal," 96, 102.

60. Frank B. Golley, *A History of the Ecosystem Concept in Ecology: More Than the Sum of the Parts*, 73. According to Golley:

The initial studies described the accumulation of radioactive material in organisms collected at different distances from the source of contamination and at different times after the detonation. Soon it became clear that these scientists were dealing with two different types of problems. First, they were concerned with the physical-chemical problems of radioactive decay and the deposition, absorption, and accumulation of radioactive materials. Second, they were concerned with food chain dynamics and the problems of metabolic turnover, the efficiency of trophic transfer, biological uptake, release, and other problems faced in ecosystem studies. Thus, there was a juxtaposition between the development of ecosystem studies as a part of basic ecology and the practical need to understand the transfer of radioactive materials among ecosystem compartments.

61. Golley, *A History of the Ecosystem Concept in Ecology*, 105.

62. Letter of 8 October 1957, from Eugene P. Odum to "Georgians" (colleagues at the University of Georgia, the Marine Institute on Sapelo Island, and the Savannah River Site), in collection of Betty Jean Craige.

63. Audiotaped interview of Gene Odum by Martha Odum, 1987. See also E. P. Odum and H. T. Odum, *Fundamentals*, 2nd ed., 475–477.

64. E. P. Odum and H. T. Odum, *Fundamentals*, 2nd ed., 467.

65. Donald Worster, *Nature's Economy*, 299.

66. See Eugene P. Odum, R. P. Martin, and B. C. Loughman, "Scanning Systems for the Rapid Determination of Radioactivity in Ecological Materials," 171–173.

67. E. P. Odum, "Early University of Georgia Research," 56.

68. E. P. Odum and H. T. Odum, *Fundamentals*, 2nd ed., 465.

69. Eugene P. Odum, "Ecology Course at Woods Hole."

70. Golley, *A History of the Ecosystem Concept in Ecology*, 105; Golley, "Establishing the Network."

71. E. P. Odum and F. B. Golley, "Radioactive Tracers as an Aid to the Measurement of Energy Flow at the Population Level in Nature."

72. For information about the development of the Institute of Ecology at the University of Georgia I am indebted to Frank B. Golley, who was among its founders and is among its historians. See Golley's essay "Establishing the Network."

73. E. P. Odum, "Early University of Georgia Research," 57.

74. Golley, "Establishing the Network."

75. Golley, "Establishing the Network."

76. Frank B. Golley, in "Establishing the Network," wrote about university funding during the first decade of the institute's establishment: "Over all departments and intervals (except botany in 1969–1979), the growth rate of funding ecologists was less than for funding nonecologists. The consequence was a shift in faculty expertise

away from ecology toward other disciplines. If the administrative decisions behind these statistics was to bring other parts of biology up to the level of ecology, it was highly successful."

77. Golley, "Establishing the Network."

78. P. F. Hendrix, E. P. Odum, D. A. Crossley Jr., and D. C. Coleman, "Horseshoe Bend Research: Old-Field Studies, 1966–1975; Agroecosystem Studies, 1976 to date." According to Odum, Barrett's research, which demonstrated that herbivorous insects recover more quickly than parasitic wasps and bees from Sevin and documented the long-term side effects of the insecticide on the mammal population, plant-herbivore relationships, and litter decomposition, was supported by an unsolicited $5,000 grant from the Fleishman Yeast Company.

79. Golley, "Establishing the Network."

4. The Age of Ecology

1. Sales figures were provided by Eugene Odum.

2. Donald Worster, *Nature's Economy: A History of Ecological Ideas*, 2nd ed., 346–347.

3. Worster, *Nature's Economy*, 354–355.

4. "Ecology: The New Jeremiahs," 38.

5. "The Ravaged Environment," 31; "Dawn for the Age of Ecology," 35.

6. "Ecology: The New Jeremiahs," 38, 40. *Time* quoted Vice Admiral Hyman G. Rickover as saying that ecology was "the key science for correctly assessing the negative aspects of technology." *Time* featured G. Evelyn Hutchinson of Yale, who was described as a "quietist"; Kenneth E. P. Watt, a systems analyst, ecologist, and environmental activist at the University of California at Davis; Crawford S. Holling, an ecologist and environmental activist at the University of British Columbia; Barry Commoner, a plant physiologist and environmental activist at Washington University in St. Louis; and Eugene Odum, who was then engaged in a political campaign to save Georgia's wetlands.

7. "Dawn for the Age of Ecology," 35.

8. "Needed: A Rebirth of Community," 47.

9. "Ecology: The New Jeremiahs," 38.

10. The address was published the following August under the same title.

11. E. P. Odum, "Relationships between Structure and Function in the Ecosystem," 108–118. Odum defined *structure* and *function* as follows:

By structure we mean: (1) The composition of the biological community including species, numbers, biomass, life history and distribution in space of populations; (2) the quantity and distribution of the abiotic (non-living) materials such as nutrients, water, etc.; (3) the range, or gradient, of conditions of existence such as temperature, light, etc. . . .

By function we mean: (1) The rate of biological energy flow through the eco-system, that is, the rates of production and the rates of respiration of the popula-tions and the community; (2) the rate of material or nutrient cycling, that is, the biogeochemical cycles; (3) biological or ecological regulation including both regulation of organisms by environment (as, for example, in photoperiodism) and regulation of environment by organisms (as, for example, in nitrogen fixation by micro-organisms).

12. Eugene P. Odum, in collaboration with Howard T. Odum, *Fundamentals of Ecology*, 2nd ed., 43.

13. Odum explained the relation between productivity and cost of maintenance in "The Strategy of Ecosystem Development" as follows:

In the early stages of ecological succession, or in "young nature," so to speak, the rate of primary production or total (gross) photosynthesis (P) exceeds the rate of community respiration (R), so that the P/R ratio is greater than 1. In the spe-cial case of organic pollution, the P/R ratio is typically less than 1. In both cases, however, the theory is that P/R approaches 1 as succession occurs. In other words, energy fixed tends to be balanced by the energy cost of maintenance (that is, total community respiration) in the mature or "climax" ecosystem. The P/R ratio, therefore, should be an excellent functional index of the relative maturity of the system. (262–270)

14. E. P. Odum, "Relationships between Structure and Function in the Ecosys-tem," 114–115.

15. E. P. Odum, "Relationships between Structure and Function in the Ecosys-tem," 111.

16. Odum began using the word *homeostasis* in the late 1950s and explained its applicability to ecosystems in the second edition of *Fundamentals of Ecology*, 25–27.

17. See "Homeostasis," in *The American Heritage Dictionary of Science*, 291. The dictionary definition applies to organisms and cells.

18. According to Robert McIntosh, for Clements, *development* was synonymous with *succession*, which was nonhaphazard because a system's plant composition was

like a "complex organism." See Robert P. McIntosh, *The Background of Ecology: Concept and Theory*, 80–81.

19. Eugene P. Odum, "The New Ecology," 14–16.

20. Odum defined *ecological succession* in terms of three "parameters":

1. It is an orderly process of community development that is reasonably directional and, therefore, predictable.

2. It results from modification of the physical environment by the community; that is, succession is community-controlled even though the physical environment determines the pattern, the rate of change, and often sets limits as to how far development can go.

3. It culminates in a stabilized ecosystem in which maximum biomass (or high information content) and symbiotic function between organisms are maintained per unit of available energy flow. (E. P. Odum, "The Strategy of Ecosystem Development," 262)

21. E. P. Odum, "The Strategy of Ecosystem Development," 262.

22. Eugene Odum pointed out that Howard T. Odum and R. C. Pinkerton were building on the "law of maximum energy in biological systems" discovered by Alfred Lotka. See H. T. Odum and R. C. Pinkerton, "Times Speed Regulator, the Optimum Efficiency for Maximum Output in Physical and Biological Systems," 331; E. P. Odum, "The Strategy of Ecosystem Development," 263.

23. E. P. Odum, "The Strategy of Ecosystem Development," 262.

24. Odum wrote, citing *Theory of Island Biogeography*, by R. H. MacArthur and E. O. Wilson:

Species with high rates of reproduction and growth . . . are more likely to survive in the early uncrowded stages of island colonization. In contrast, selection pressure favors species with lower growth potential but better capabilities for competitive survival under the equilibrium density of late stages. Using the terminology of growth equations, where r is the intrinsic rate of increase and K is the upper asymptote or equilibrium population size, we may say that "r selection" predominates in early colonization, with "K selection" prevailing as more and more species and individuals attempt to colonize. . . .

. . . [Q]uantity production characterizes the young ecosystem while quality production and feedback control are the trademarks of the mature system. (E. P. Odum, "The Strategy of Ecosystem Development," 266)

25. E. P. Odum, "The Strategy of Ecosystem Development," 266.

26. E. P. Odum, "The Strategy of Ecosystem Development," 266.

27. E. P. Odum, "The Strategy of Ecosystem Development," 269.

28. E. P. Odum, "The Strategy of Ecosystem Development," 269.

29. E. P. Odum, "The Strategy of Ecosystem Development," 268. Odum said that more emphasis needs to be placed on compartmentalization, so that growth-type, steady-state, and intermediate-type ecosystems can be linked with urban and industrial areas for mutual benefit. Knowing the transfer coefficients that define the flow of energy and the movement of materials and organisms (including man) between compartments, it should be possible to determine, through analog computer manipulation, rational limits for the size and capacity of each compartment. We might start, for example, with a simplified model . . . consisting of four compartments of equal area, partitioned according to the basic biotic-function criterion — that is, according to whether the area is (i) productive, (ii) protective, (iii) a compromise between (i) and (ii), or (iv) urban-industrial.

30. E. P. Odum, "The Strategy of Ecosystem Development," 268–269.

31. E. P. Odum, "The Strategy of Ecosystem Development," 262.

32. Henry A. Gleason, "The Individualistic Concept of the Plant Association," 16, 23. See Donald Worster's account of Gleason's relationship to Drury and Nisbet, and the relationship of their model to ecosystem ecology, in *The Wealth of Nature: Environmental History and the Ecological Imagination*, 162–164.

33. Gleason, "The Individualistic Concept of the Plant Association," 26, 117.

34. Worster, *The Wealth of Nature*, 163.

35. William H. Drury and Ian C. T. Nisbet, "Succession," 334. See E. P. Odum, "The Strategy of Ecosystem Development," 262; and Robert H. Whittaker, *Communities and Ecosystems*.

36. Drury and Nisbet, "Succession," 338.

37. Drury and Nisbet, "Succession," 362–262.

38. Joseph H. Connell and Ralph O. Slatyer, "Mechanisms of Succession in Natural Communities and Their Role in Community Stability and Organization," 1135–1137.

39. J. Engelberg and L. L. Boyarsky, "The Noncybernetic Nature of Ecosystems," 317–324.

40. Bernard C. Patten and Eugene P. Odum, "The Cybernetic Nature of Ecosystems," 888–889.

41. Andrew Carnegie, *The Gospel of Wealth and Other Timely Essays*, 16. See also Betty Jean Craige, *Laying the Ladder Down: The Emergence of Cultural Holism*, 18–19.

42. Petr Kropotkin, *Mutual Aid: A Factor of Evolution*, 228. See also Craige, *Laying the Ladder Down*, 20–21.

43. Joel Hagen, "Research Perspectives and the Anomalous Status of Modern Ecology," 4, 434, 439; G. Evelyn Hutchinson, *An Introduction to Population Ecology*, 214–215.

44. Eugene P. Odum, *Basic Ecology*, 23.

45. Eugene P. Odum, *Fundamentals of Ecology*, 3rd ed., 273, 274.

46. Aldo Leopold, *A Sand County Almanac, and Sketches Here and There*, 202.

47. Worster, *The Wealth of Nature*, 165.

48. Daniel Botkin, *Discordant Harmonies: A New Ecology for the Twenty-first Century*, 193.

49. Alfred C. Redfield, "The Biological Control of Chemical Factors in the Environment," 205–221. In his 1971 edition of *Fundamentals* Odum wrote in a brief section devoted to Redfield's theory: "Individual organisms not only adapt to the physical environment, but by their concerted action in ecosystems they also adapt the geochemical environment to their biological needs" (*Fundamentals*, 3rd ed., 23).

50. See also J. E. Lovelock, *Gaia: A New Look at Natural History*; Lynn Margulis and J. E. Lovelock, "Biological Modulation of the Earth's Atmosphere"; and Lynn Margulis and J. E. Lovelock, "The Atmosphere as Circulatory System of the Biosphere — The Gaia Hypothesis."

51. Lynn Margulis, *Symbiotic Planet (A New View of Evolution)*, 119, 33.

52. E. P. Odum, *Basic Ecology*, 24, 26.

53. R. Harré, *The Philosophies of Science*.

54. George Salt, "A Comment on the Use of the Term *Emergent Properties*," 145.

55. E. P. Odum, *Basic Ecology*, 6.

56. Salt, "A Comment on the Use of the Term *Emergent Properties*," 146.

57. Hagen, "Research Perspectives and the Anomalous Status of Modern Ecology," 4, 434.

58. Frank B. Golley, *A History of the Ecosystem Concept in Ecology: More Than the Sum of the Parts*, 203.

59. Golley, *History of the Ecosystem Concept in Ecology*, 195–198. Golley cited studies by paleoecologists Margaret Davis (1981) and Hazel Delcourt and Paul Delcourt (1988).

60. Larry Pomeroy, then affiliated with the Marine Institute on Sapelo Island and later appointed to the faculty of the University of Georgia on campus, had been studying phosphorus levels in the marshlands. Edward Kuenzler had examined the

function of the common horse mussel in the phosphorus cycle for his Ph.D. dissertation. And Ed Smalley had studied *Spartina* marsh grass on Sapelo for his dissertation. Eugene P. Odum, "The Role of Tidal Marshes in Estuarine Production," 13–14.

61. E. P. Odum, "The Role of Tidal Marshes in Estuarine Production," 35.

62. E. P. Odum, "The Role of Tidal Marshes in Estuarine Production," 12–13. Odum wrote: "We now estimate that our Sapelo marshes and estuaries taken together have an estimated gross primary production of somewhere around 2,500 grams of dry matter per square meter per year. We think about 500 of these grams are used by the plants in their own respiration leaving about 2,000 grams net production average for each square meter of the system."

63. E. P. Odum, "The Role of Tidal Marshes in Estuarine Production," 12–15, 35.

64. Eugene P. Odum, "A Research Challenge: Evaluating the Productivity of Coastal and Estuarine Water," 63.

65. See "The Length and the Breadth and the Sweep of the Marshes of Glynn," 93.

66. "The Length and the Breadth and the Sweep of the Marshes of Glynn," 92–93.

67. "The Length and the Breadth and the Sweep of the Marshes of Glynn," 93.

68. See "Filling in the Bay."

69. Eugene P. Odum, "Turning Points in the History of the Institute of Ecology."

70. Mary Lacy, "Environment Saving Pinpointed," 29.

71. William E. Odum accepted a postdoctoral position at the University of British Columbia in Vancouver to work on an International Biological Program site studying heterotrophy in a lake in the area.

72. When the Environmental Biology, Evolution, and Ecology section of the National Academy opened a few years later, Odum and other ecologists joined it.

5. Ecosystem Environmentalism

1. "The Dawning of Earth Day," 46.

2. Eugene P. Odum, "Production, Maintenance and Environmental Law," 113–114.

3. Howard T. Odum, "Energy, Ecology, and Economics," in *Ecological Vignettes*, by E. P. Odum, 207.

4. Eugene P. Odum and Howard T. Odum, "Natural Areas as Necessary Components of Man's Total Environment," in *Ecological Vignettes: Ecological Approaches to Dealing with Human Predicaments*.

5. E. P. Odum and H. T. Odum, "Natural Areas as Necessary Components of Man's Total Environment," 133–135.

6. E. P. Odum and H. T. Odum, "Natural Areas as Necessary Components of Man's Total Environment," 135–136.

7. E. P. Odum and H. T. Odum, "Natural Areas as Necessary Components of Man's Total Environment," 134. The Odums explained the relationship as follows:

> For example, it is well known that the cost of maintenance (C) of a network of services increases roughly as the square of the number of units (N) in the network, as shown in the following equation:
>
> $$C = \frac{N(N - 1)}{2}, \text{ or, approximately, } C = \frac{N^2}{2}$$
>
> Thus, if a city doubles from 10 to 20 million units, the cost goes up 4 times.
>
> Later, when the power function was shown to be variable, and sometimes less than 2, the Odums refrained from specifying the equation.

8. Eugene P. Odum, *Basic Ecology*, 157. The scientist was C. E. Shannon.

9. Eugene P. Odum, *Ecological Vignettes*, 45–46.

10. Eugene P. Odum, "Ecology: The Common-Sense Approach," in *Ecological Vignettes*, 242–243.

11. Lucy Justus, "Eugene Odum: The Architect of Modern Ecology," 4–5, 8.

12. Eugene P. Odum, Earth Day Talk outline, 22 April 1980, in collection of Eugene P. Odum.

13. Eugene P. Odum, "The Attitude Lag," 403.

14. Eugene P. Odum, "Production, Maintenance and Environmental Law," 113–114.

15. Eugene P. Odum, "Diversity and the Survival of the Ecosystem," 187–191.

16. E. P. Odum, "The Attitude Lag," 403.

17. Eugene P. Odum, "Harmony between Man and Nature: An Ecological View," in *Ecological Vignettes*, 63.

18. E. P. Odum, "Harmony between Man and Nature," 67.

19. E. P. Odum, "Harmony between Man and Nature," 61–71.

20. Eugene P. Odum, "The Strategy of Ecosystem Development," 266–267.

21. E. P. Odum, "Harmony between Man and Nature," 63–64.

22. E. P. Odum, "Production, Maintenance and Environmental Law," 114.

23. E. P. Odum, "The Strategy of Ecosystem Development," 262.

24. Eugene P. Odum, *Fundamentals of Ecology*, 3rd ed., 510.

25. Aldo Leopold, "The Land Ethic," 201–204.

26. Eugene P. Odum and H. T. Odum, *Fundamentals of Ecology*, 2nd ed., 26.

27. H. T. Odum, "Energy, Ecology, and Economics," 205.

28. Eugene P. Odum, "Prerequisites for Sustainability," in *Ecological Vignettes,* 219.

29. Eugene P. Odum, "The Emergence of Ecology as a New Integrative Discipline," 1292.

30. E. P. Odum, "The Emergence of Ecology as a New Integrative Discipline," 1289.

31. Odum's acceptance speech for the 1975 Prix de l'Institut de la Vie was published as E. P. Odum, "The Emergence of Ecology as a New Integrative Discipline."

32. E. P. Odum, "The Emergence of Ecology as a New Integrative Discipline," 1289.

33. E. P. Odum, "The Emergence of Ecology as a New Integrative Discipline," 1292.

34. Lucy Justus, "Odum: He Wrote the Book on Ecology," 4.

35. H. T. Odum, "Energy, Ecology, and Economics," 199.

36. William E. Odum, "Environmental Degradation and the Tyranny of Small Decisions," in *Ecological Vignettes,* by E. P. Odum, 221–224.

37. Eugene P. Odum, "Ecosystem Management: A New Venture for Humankind," in *Ecological Vignettes,* 116.

38. Eugene P. Odum, "The Mesocosm," 559.

39. E. P. Odum, "Ecosystem Management: A New Venture for Humankind," 118.

40. E. P. Odum, *Ecological Vignettes,* 28.

41. Eugene P. Odum, "Introductory Review: Perspective of Ecosystem Theory and Application," 6–7.

> It is very important to recognize that the cybernetics of ecosystems is rather fundamentally different from the cybernetics of organisms and Man-made engineering systems. . . . In both engineering (servo-mechanism) and organisms, a distinct mechanical or anatomical "controller" has a specified "set point." In a familiar household heating-system, the thermostat controls the furnace. In a warm-blooded animal, a specific brain-center controls the temperature. In contrast, it is the interplay of material cycles and energy-flow along with subsystem feedbacks that control large ecosystems. Ecosystems thus have self-correcting homeostasis *via* feedback from subsystems, but no outside controls or goals. Ecosystems are not goal-oriented but are self-organizing and controlled.

See B. C. Patten and E. P. Odum, "The Cybernetic Nature of Ecosystems."

42. See Eugene P. Odum, "How Universities Should Grow," in *Ecological Vignettes,* 101–104.

43. Ervin Laszlo and H. Margenau, "The Emergence of Integrating Concepts in Contemporary Science," 252–259; E. P. Odum, *Basic Ecology*, 7.

44. "Metabolism," in *American Heritage Dictionary of Science*, 395; see also "Metabolism," in *Shorter Oxford English Dictionary*, 1754. The OED defines *metabolism* as "the sum of the chemical processes, in a cell or organism, by which complex substances are synthesized and broken down, and growth and energy production sustained; anabolism and catabolism considered together; the overall rate at which these processes occur; the sum of the chemical changes undergone in the body by any particular substance."

45. "Homeostasis," in *New Shorter Oxford English Dictionary*, 1251.

46. E. P. Odum, "The Strategy of Ecosystem Development," 262.

47. Quoted in E. P. Odum, "Harmony between Man and Nature," 62. Kenneth Boulding's essay appears in *Energy, Economic Growth, and the Environment*, ed. Sam H. Schurr (Baltimore: Johns Hopkins University Press, 1972).

48. Conversation with Betty Jean Craige, 14 July 1999. In the 1953 edition of *Fundamentals of Ecology* Odum wrote about succession in the climax community: "The community sere is analogous to the life history of the organism, the seral stages are suggestive of the life history stages, and the clmax represents the 'adult community.'"

49. Eugene P. Odum, *Fundamentals of Ecology*, 1st ed., 187–188.

50. E. P. Odum, "Harmony between Man and Nature," 62.

51. See Petr Kropotkin, *Mutual Aid: A Factor of Evolution*; Frederic E. Clements, *Plant Succession: An Analysis of the Development of Vegetation*; W. C. Allee et al., *Principles of Animal Ecology*; and Aldo Leopold, *A Sand County Almanac*.

52. Eugene P. Odum, "The Ecosystem Approach in the Teaching of Ecology Illustrated with Sample Class Data," 532.

53. Interview with Joe H. K. Pechmann, 22 July 1995, in the Humanities Center of the University of Georgia.

54. *Georgia Bell Notes* 8.11 (1970): 1.

55. Lucy Justus, "Odum: He Wrote the Book on Ecology," 2.

56. Martha Odum's Christmas letter, 1971.

6. The Big Picture

1. Eugene Odum, "The Environment in 2010," 16.

2. E. Odum, "The Environment in 2010," 16.

3. The entire issue of the *Journal of the Estuarine Research Foundation*, which included papers by all of Bill Odum's former Ph.D. students, was devoted to the symposium. The symposium was supported by the William E. Odum Memorial Fund.

4. Eugene P. Odum, *Ecology and Our Endangered Life-Support Systems*, ix. The second edition appeared in 1993, and the third edition, retitled *Ecology: A Bridge between Science and Society*, appeared in 1997, echoing the title of his 1975 *Ecology: The Link between the Natural and the Social Sciences*.

5. Eugene P. Odum, *Ecological Vignettes: Ecological Approaches to Dealing with Human Predicaments*, 53–54.

6. Eugene P. Odum, "Great Ideas in Ecology for the 1990s," 542–545.

7. S. J. Gould, "Darwinism and the Expansion of Evolutionary Theory; R. Axelrod, *Evolution of Cooperation*; R. Axelrod and W. D. Hamilton, "The Evolution of Cooperation"; D. S. Wilson, "Evolution on the Level of Communities"; D. S. Wilson, *The Natural Selection of Populations and Communities*.

8. Eugene P. Odum, "The Transition from Youth to Maturity in Nature and Society," 61.

9. Eugene P. Odum, "When to Confront and When to Cooperate," 4.

10. Donald Worster, *The Wealth of Nature: Environmental History and the Ecological Imagination*, 169.

11. Daniel Botkin, *Discordant Harmonies: A New Ecology for the Twenty-first Century*, 193.

12. William U. Eiland, "Acknowledgments," 2.

13. Jennifer DePrima, *Martha Odum: Watercolors*.

14. Eugene P. Odum, introduction to *Martha Odum: Watercolors*, 4–5.

15. Betty Jean Craige, "Biography," 14–15.

16. *Eugene Odum: An Ecologist's Life*, written and directed by Philip Lee Williams, may be purchased from the Georgia Center for Continuing Education, University of Georgia, Athens, GA 30602. It won a Finalist's Award from the New York Film and Video Festival.

Works Cited

Adams, Charles C. *Guide to the Study of Animal Ecology.* New York: Macmillan, 1913.

Allaby, Michael. *A Dictionary of the Environment.* 2nd ed. New York: New York University Press, 1983.

Allan, Brooke, and Benjamin H. Trask. *Howard Washington Odum Papers Inventory.* Chapel Hill: Manuscripts Department, Library of the University of North Carolina at Chapel Hill, Southern Historical Collection.

Allee, W. C., Alfred E. Emerson, Orlando Park, Thomas Park, and Karl P. Schmidt. *Principles of Animal Ecology.* Philadelphia: W. B. Saunders, 1949.

Alling, Abigail, and Mark Nelson. *Life under Glass: The Inside Story of Biosphere 2.* Oracle, Ariz.: Biosphere Press, 1993.

Auchmutey, Jim. "The New South: 96 Southerners to Watch." *Atlanta Journal/Atlanta Constitution,* 24 March 1996.

Axelrod, R. *Evolution of Cooperation.* New York: Basic Books, 1984.

Axelrod, R., and W. D. Hamilton. "The Evolution of Cooperation." *Science* 211 (1981): 1390–1396.

Botkin, Daniel. *Discordant Harmonies: A New Ecology for the Twenty-first Century.* New York: Oxford University Press, 1990.

Brazil, Wayne Douglas. *Howard W. Odum, the Building Years: 1884–1930.* New York: Garland, 1988.

Callicott, J. Baird. *In Defense of the Land Ethic.* Albany: State University of New York Press, 1989.

Cannon, Walter B. *The Wisdom of the Body.* New York: W. W. Norton, 1932.

Carnegie, Andrew. *The Gospel of Wealth and Other Timely Essays.* Ed. Edward C. Kirkland. Cambridge: Harvard University Press, 1962.

Carson, Rachel. *Silent Spring.* New York: Houghton Mifflin, 1962.

Chase, Alston. *In a Dark Wood: The Fight over Forests and the Rising Tyranny of Ecology.* Boston: Houghton Mifflin, 1995.

Cittadino, Eugene. "Ecology and the Professionalization of Botany in America, 1890–1905." *Studies in History of Biology* 4 (1980): 171–198.

Clements, Frederic E. *Dynamics of Vegetation: Selections from the Writings of Frederic E. Clements, Ph.D.* Comp. and ed. B. W. Allred and Edith S. Clements. New York: H. W. Wilson, 1949.

———. *Plant Succession: An Analysis of the Development of Vegetation.* Washington, D.C.: Carnegie Institution of Washington, 1916.

Clements, Frederic E., and Victor E. Shelford. *Bio-Ecology.* New York: John Wiley and Sons, 1939.

Connell, Joseph H., and Ralph O. Slatyer. "Mechanisms of Succession in Natural Communities and Their Role in Community Stability and Organization." *American Naturalist* 111 (1977): 1119–1144.

Corey, John C., ed. *The Savannah River and Its Environs: Proceedings of a Symposium in Honor of Ruth Patrick for 35 Years of Studies at the Savannah River.* Aiken: Savannah River Ecology Laboratory, 1987.

Craige, Betty Jean. "Biography." In *Martha Odum: Watercolors,* ed. Jennifer De-Prima, 10–15. Athens: Georgia Museum of Art, 1997.

———. *Laying the Ladder Down: The Emergence of Cultural Holism.* Amherst: University of Massachusetts Press, 1992.

Croker, Robert A. *Pioneer Ecologist: The Life and Work of Victor Ernest Shelford, 1877–1968.* Washington, D.C.: Smithsonian Institution Press, 1991.

Darwin, Charles. *On the Origin of Species*. Facsimile of 1st ed. Ed. Ernst Mayr. Cambridge: Harvard University Press, 1964.

"Dawn for the Age of Ecology." *Newsweek* 75.4 (26 January 1970): 35–36.

"The Dawning of Earth Day." *Time* (27 April 1970): 46.

DePrima, Jennifer. *Martha Odum: Watercolors*. Acknowledgments by William U. Eiland. Preface by Edward Lambert. Biography by Betty Jean Craige. Catalog entries by Jennifer DePrima. Athens: Georgia Museum of Art, 1997.

Descartes, René. *Discourse on Method*. In *The Philosophical Works of Descartes*. Vol. 1. Trans. Elizabeth S. Haldane and G. R. T. Ross. Cambridge: Cambridge University Press, 1978.

Drury, William H., and Ian C. T. Nisbet. "Succession." *Journal of the Arnold Arboretum* 54.3 (1973): 331–368.

Dyer, Thomas G. *The University of Georgia: A Bicentennial History, 1785–1985*. Athens: University of Georgia Press, 1985.

"Ecology." In *The New Shorter Oxford English Dictionary on Historical Principles*, ed. Leslie Brown. Oxford: Clarendon, 1993.

"Ecology: The New Jeremiahs." *Time* 94.7 (15 August 1969): 38–39.

"Ecotage." In *The New Shorter Oxford English Dictionary*, ed. Leslie Brown. Oxford: Clarendon, 1993.

Eiland, William U. "Acknowledgments." In *Martha Odum: Water Colors*, ed. Jennifer DePrima, 2–3. Athens: Georgia Museum of Art, 1997.

Engelberg, J., and L. L. Boyarsky. "The Noncybernetic Nature of Ecosystems." *American Naturalist* 114 (1979): 317–324.

"Filling in the Bay." *Atlanta Constitution*, 30 January 1970, 4-A.

Gibbons, Anne R. "The Savannah River Ecology Laboratory." In *Encyclopaedia Britannica 1994 Yearbook of Science and the Future*, 468–488.

Gleason, Henry A. "The Individualistic Concept of the Plant Association." *Bulletin of the Torrey Botanical Club* 53 (1926): 7–26. (Reprinted in *Foundations of Ecology: Classic Papers with Commentaries*, ed. Leslie A. Real and James H. Brown, 98–117. Chicago: University of Chicago Press, 1991.)

Gleick, James. *Chaos: Making a New Science*. New York: Viking, 1987.

Golley, Frank Benjamin. "Establishing the Network." Manuscript.

———. *A History of the Ecosystem Concept in Ecology: More Than the Sum of the Parts*. New Haven: Yale University Press, 1993.

Gould, Stephen Jay. "Darwinism and the Expansion of Evolutionary Theory." *Science* 216 (1982): 380–387.

———. "Kropotkin Was No Crackpot." *Natural History* 97.7 (1988): 12+.

Graves, Louis. "Eugene Odum's Bird Magazine." *Chapel Hill Weekly,* 2 August 1929.

———. "Motor-Camping Trip to California Costs Odum and Coker $33.44 Each." *Chapel Hill Weekly,* 27 July 1934.

Hagen, Joel P. *An Entangled Bank: The Origins of Ecosystem Ecology.* New Brunswick: Rutgers University Press, 1992.

———. "Research Perspectives and the Anomalous Status of Modern Ecology." *Biology and Philosophy* 4 (1989): 433–455.

Harré, R. *The Philosophies of Science.* London: Oxford University Press, 1972.

Hendrix, P. F., E. P. Odum, D. A. Crossley Jr., and D. C. Coleman. "Horseshoe Bend Research: Old-Field Studies, 1966–1975; Agroecosystem Studies, 1976 to date." Manuscript.

Hewlett, Richard G., and Francis Duncan. *Atoms for Peace and War, 1953–1961: Eisenhower and the Atomic Energy Commission.* Berkeley: University of California Press, 1989.

Hines, Neal O. *Proving Ground: An Account of the Radiobiological Studies in the Pacific.* Seattle: University of Washington Press, 1962.

Hobson, Fred. *Tell about the South.* Baton Rouge: Louisiana State University Press, 1983.

Holmes, S. J. "The Principle of Stability as a Cause of Evolution." *Quarterly Review of Biology* 23 (1948): 324–333.

"Homeostasis." In *The American Heritage Dictionary of Science,* ed. Robert K. Barnhart, 291. Boston: Houghton Mifflin, 1986.

"Homeostasis." In *The New Shorter Oxford English Dictionary,* ed. Leslie Brown, 1251. Oxford: Clarendon Press, 1993.

"Howard Odum and Human Welfare." *Emory Alumnus* 29.6 (1953): 4+.

"Howard Odum's Part in the State's Creative Life." *Chapel Hill News Leader,* 15 November 1954.

"Howard W. Odum, Sociologist, Dies." *New York Times,* 10 November 1954.

Hutchinson, G. Evelyn. *An Introduction to Population Ecology.* New Haven: Yale University Press, 1978.

Jamison, Andrew. "A Tale of Two Brothers." *Science* 261 (23 July 1993): 497–498.

Jenkins, James H. "The Occurrence of the Chachalaca on Sapelo Island, Georgia." *Oriole* 14.1–2 (1949): 11–12.

Jones, Richard. "Howard T. Odum." *Florida Engineer* (winter 1993): 33–34.

Justus, Lucy. "Eugene Odum: The Architect of Modern Ecology." *Outdoors in Georgia* (May 1979): 3–9.

———. "Odum: He Wrote the Book on Ecology." *Georgia Alumni Record* (April 1975): 2–5.

Kingsland, Sharon E. *Modeling Nature: Episodes in the History of Population Ecology.* 2nd ed. Chicago: University of Chicago Press, 1995.

Kropotkin, Petr. *Mutual Aid: A Factor of Evolution.* Boston: Porter Sargent Publishers, 1904.

Lacy, Mary. "Environment Saving Pinpointed." *Richmond News Leader,* 19 November 1970, 29.

Laszlo, Ervin, and H. Margenau. "The Emergence of Integrating Concepts in Contemporary Science." *Philosophy of Science* 39 (1972): 252–259.

"The Length and the Breadth and the Sweep of the Marshes of Glynn." *Life* (14 November 1969): 88–93.

Leopold, Aldo. *A Sand County Almanac, and Sketches Here and There.* Intro. Robert Finch. New York: Oxford University Press, 1987.

Levin, Steve. "UNC's First Woman Teacher Honored on her 90th Birthday." *Chapel Hill Newspaper,* 24 September 1978.

Lindeman, Raymond L. "The Trophic-Dynamic Aspect of Ecology." *Ecology* 23.4 (1942): 399–418.

Lotka, Alfred J. *Elements of Mathematical Biology* [formerly published under the title *Elements of Physical Biology*]. New York: Dover, 1956.

———. *Elements of Physical Biology.* Baltimore: Williams and Wilkins, 1925.

Lovelock, J. E. *Gaia: A New Look at Life on Earth.* New York: Oxford University Press, 1987.

———. *Gaia: A New Look at Natural History.* New York: Oxford University Press, 1979.

Lovelock, J. E., and Lynn Margulis. "Atmospheric Homeostasis by and for the Biosphere: The Gaia Hypothesis." *Tellus* 26 (1973): 1–10.

MacArthur, Robert H., and Edward O. Wilson. *Theory of Island Biogeography.* Princeton: Princeton University Press, 1967.

McIntosh, Robert P. *The Background of Ecology: Concept and Theory.* Cambridge: Cambridge University Press, 1985.

———. "The Succession of Succession: A Lexical Chronology." *Bulletin of the Ecological Society of America* 80.4 (1999): 256–265.

Margulis, Lynn. *Symbiotic Planet (A New View of Evolution)*. New York: Basic Books, 1998.

Margulis, Lynn, and J. E. Lovelock. "The Atmosphere as Circulatory System of the Biosphere—The Gaia Hypothesis." *Coevolution Quarterly* (summer 1975).

———. "Biological Modulation of the Earth's Atmosphere." *Icarus* 21 (1974): 471–489.

"Metabolism." In *The American Heritage Dictionary of Science*, ed. Robert K. Barnhart, 395. Boston: Houghton Mifflin, 1986.

"Metabolism." In *The New Shorter Oxford English Dictionary*, ed. Leslie Brown. Oxford: Clarendon Press, 1993.

Meyer, Judy L. "Beyond Gloom and Doom: Ecology for the Future." Past-president's address for the Ecological Society of America, 1996. *Bulletin of the Ecological Society of America* 77 (1996): 199–205.

"Needed: A Rebirth of Community." *Newsweek* 75.4 (26 January 1970): 47.

Odum, Anna Kranz. "Some Negro Folk-Songs from Tennessee." *Journal of American Folk-Lore* 27.105 (1914): 255–265.

Odum, Eugene P. "Annual Report for 1939–40." Biological Research Division, Edmund Niles Huyck Preserve, Rensselaerville, N.Y. Pp. 1–68.

———. "The Attitude Lag." *BioScience* 19.5 (1969): 403.

———. *Basic Ecology*. Philadelphia: Saunders College Publishing, 1983.

———. "Consideration of the Total Environment in Power Reactor Waste Disposal." Including work by Eugene P. Odum and Howard T. Odum. Paper presented at the International Conference on the Peaceful Uses of Atomic Energy, Geneva, 12 July 1955.

———. "Diversity and the Survival of the Ecosystem." In *American Tissue Culture*. Paper presented at the Fiftieth Anniversary Symposium of the Society for Microbiology, 1976. (Reprinted in *Ecological Vignettes: Ecological Approaches to Dealing with Human Predicaments*, 187–191. Amsterdam: Harwood Academic Publishers, 1998.)

———. "Early University of Georgia Research, 1952–1962." In *The Savannah River and Its Environs: Proceedings of a Symposium in Honor of Dr. Ruth Patrick*, ed. John C. Corey, 43–83. DP-1745, E. I. du Pont de Nemours and Co. Aiken, S.C.: Savannah River Laboratory, 1987. Report available from National Technical Information Service, U.S. Department of Commerce, Springfield, VA 22161.

———. "Ecological Aspects of Waste Disposal." In *A Conference on Radioactive Isotopes in Agriculture*, 95–102. Proceedings of the Conference on Radioactive Isotopes in Agriculture at East Lansing, Michigan, 12–14 January 1956. aec Report tid-7512. Washington, D.C.: U.S. Government Printing Office, 1956.

———. *Ecological Vignettes: Ecological Approaches to Dealing with Human Predicaments*. Amsterdam: Harwood Academic Publishers, 1998.

———. *Ecology: A Bridge between Science and Society*. Sunderland, Mass.: Sinauer Associates, 1997.

———. *Ecology and Our Endangered Life Support Systems*. Sunderland, Mass.: Sinauer Associates, 1989. 2nd ed., 1993.

———. "Ecology and the Atomic Age." *asb Bulletin* 4.2 (1957): 27–29.

———. "Ecology Course at Woods Hole." *aibs Bulletin* (January 1958): 427.

———. "The Ecosystem Approach in the Teaching of Ecology Illustrated with Sample Class Data." *Ecology* 38.3 (July 1957): 532.

———. "Ecosystem Management: A New Venture for Humankind." In *Perspectives on Ecosystem Theory and Application*, ed. Nicholas Palunin. New York: John Wiley and Sons, 1986. (Reprinted in *Ecological Vignettes: Ecological Approaches to Dealing with Human Predicaments*, 115–125. Amsterdam: Harwood Academic Publishers, 1998.)

———. "The Emergence of Ecology as a New Integrative Discipline." *Science* 195 (25 March 1977): 1289–1292.

———. "The Environment in 2010." In *Vision 2010: A Dozen Short Glimpses of the Possible*, 16. Athens: University of Georgia Office of Strategic Planning, 1999.

———. *Fundamentals of Ecology*. 1st ed. Philadelphia: W. B. Saunders, 1953. 2nd ed., in collaboration with Howard T. Odum, 1959. 3rd ed., 1971.

———. "Great Ideas in Ecology for the 1990s." *BioScience* 42.7 (1992): 542–545.

———. "Harmony between Man and Nature: An Ecological View." In *Beyond Growth: Essays on Alternative Futures*, 43–55. Yale University School of Forestry Bulletin 88, 1975. (Reprinted in *Ecological Vignettes: Ecological Approaches to Dealing with Human Predicaments*, 61–71. Amsterdam: Harwood Academic Publishers, 1998.)

———. Introduction to *Martha Odum: Watercolors*, ed. Jennifer DePrima, 4–5. Athens: Georgia Museum of Art, 1997.

———. "Introductory Review: Perspective of Ecosystem Theory and Application." In *Ecosystem Theory and Application*, ed. Nicholas Polunin for Environmental Monographs and Symposia. New York: John Wiley and Sons, 1986.

———. "Living Marsh." Introduction to *Guale: The Golden Coast of Georgia*, by Robert Hanie, 19–28. San Francisco: Friends of the Earth, 1974.

———. "The Mesocosm." *BioScience* 34.9 (1984): 558–562.

———. "The New Ecology." *BioScience* 14.7 (1964): 14–16.

———. "Notes on the History of the Germ Cells in the Toadfish (*Opsanus tau*)." *Journal of the Elisha Mitchell Scientific Society* 52.2 (1936): 235–246.

———. "Production, Maintenance and Environmental Law." Foreword to *Environmental Law Review*, ed. H. Floyd Sherrod. New York: Clark Boardman Company, 1970. (Reprinted in *Ecological Vignettes: Ecological Approaches to Dealing with Human Predicaments*, 113–114. Amsterdam: Harwood Academic Publishers, 1998.)

———. "Relationships between Structure and Function in the Ecosystem." *Japanese Journal of Ecology* 12.3 (1962): 108–118. [The actual pages give the publication date as June 1962.]

———. "A Research Challenge: Evaluating the Productivity of Coastal and Estuarine Water." In *Proceedings from Second Sea-Grant Conference*, 63–64. Newport: University of Rhode Island Graduate School of Oceanography, 1968.

———. "The Role of Tidal Marshes in Estuarine Production." *The Conservationist* (New York State), ser. 3 (1964): 88–96.

———. "Sapelo Chronology (The First Decade as Documented by Eugene Odum)." Manuscript in collection of Eugene P. Odum.

———. "The Strategy of Ecosystem Development." *Science* 164 (18 April 1969): 262–270.

———. "The Transition from Youth to Maturity in Nature and Society." *Bridges* 2.1–2 (1990): 57–61.

———. "Turning Points in the History of the Institute of Ecology." Manuscript.

———. "Variations in the Heart Rate of Birds: A Study in Physiological Ecology." *Ecological Monographs* 11.3 (1941): 301–326.

———. "When to Confront and When to Cooperate." In *The Georgia Landscape*, 4. Athens: University of Georgia School of Environmental Design, 1992.

Odum, Eugene P., and Coit M. Coker. "Bird Life in Chapel Hill." No. 4. *Chapel Hill Weekly*, 3 April 1931, 6.

Odum, Eugene P., and Frank B. Golley. "Radioactive Tracers as an Aid to the Measurement of Energy Flow at the Population Level in Nature." In *Radioecology*, ed. V. Schultz and A. W. Klement Jr. Proceedings of the First National Symposium on Radioecology held at Colorado State University, Fort Collins, Colorado, 10–15 September 1961. New York: Reinhold, 1963.

Odum, Eugene P., R. P. Martin, and B. C. Loughman. "Scanning Systems for the Rapid Determination of Radioactivity in Ecological Materials." *Ecology* 43.1 (1962): 171–173.

Odum, Eugene P., and Howard T. Odum. "Natural Areas as Necessary Components of Man's Total Environment." In *Transactions of the Thirty-seventh North American Wildlife and Natural Resources Conference*, 12–15 March 1972. (Reprinted in *Ecological Vignettes: Ecological Approaches to Dealing with Human Predicaments*. Amsterdam: Harwood Academic Publishers, 1998.)

Odum, Eugene P., Howard T. Odum, and William E. Odum. "Nature's Pulsing Paradigm." *Journal of the Estuarine Research Federation* 4.18 (1985): 547–555.

Odum, Howard T. "Energy, Ecology, and Economics." In *Ambio*. Stockholm: Royal Swedish Academy of Sciences, 1972. (Reprinted in *Ecological Vignettes: Ecological Approaches to Dealing with Human Predicaments*, by E. P. Odum, 207. Amsterdam: Harwood Academic Publishers, 1998.)

———. *Environment, Power and Society.* New York: John Wiley and Sons, 1971.

———. "Trophic Structure and Productivity of Silver Springs, Florida." *Ecological Monographs* 27 (1957): 55–112.

Odum, Howard T., and Eugene P. Odum. "Trophic Structure and Productivity of a Windward Coral Reef Community on Eniwetok Atoll." *Ecological Monographs* 25.3 (1955): 291–320.

Odum, Howard T., and R. C. Pinkerton. "Times Speed Regulator, the Optimum Efficiency for Maximum Output in Physical and Biological Systems." *American Science* 43 (1955): 331–343.

Odum, Howard Washington. "Agenda for Integration [1954]." In *Folk, Region, and Society: Selected Papers of Howard W. Odum.* Ed. Katharine Jocher, Guy B. Johnson, George L. Simpson, and Rupert B. Vance. Chapel Hill: University of North Carolina Press, 1964. (Reprinted from "An Approach to Diagnosis and Direction of the Problem of Negro Segregation in the Public Schools of the South," by Howard W. Odum. *Journal of Public Law* 3 [1954]: 8–37.)

———. "Editorial Notes." *Journal of Social Forces* 1.1 (1922): 56–61.

———. "Editorial Notes." *Journal of Social Forces* 1.2 (1923): 178–183.

———. "Fundamental Principles Underlying Inter-racial Co-operation." *Journal of Social Forces* 1.3 (1923): 282–285.

———. "The Glory That Was, and the Southern Grandeur That Was Not." *Saturday Review of Literature* 26.4 (23 January 1943): 9–10+.

———. "The Relation of the High School to Rural Life and Education." *High School Quarterly* 2 (April 1914): 139–147.

————. *Southern Regions of the United States*. Chapel Hill: University of North Carolina Press, 1936.

————. "This Is Worth Our Best." *Southern Packet* 5.1 (1949): 2–4.

Odum, William E. "Environmental Degradation and the Tyranny of Small Decisions." *Bioscience* 32 (1982): 728–729. (Reprinted in *Ecological Vignettes: Ecological Approaches to Dealing with Human Predicaments*, by Eugene P. Odum, 221–224. Amsterdam: Harwood Academic Publishers, 1998.)

Parker, William Covington. "Fountainhead of Understanding: A Story of Howard Washington Odum." Manuscript in collection of E. P. Odum.

Patten, Bernard C., and Eugene P. Odum. "The Cybernetic Nature of Ecosystems." *American Naturalist* 118 (1981): 886–895.

Pomeroy, Lawrence R., and Donald C. Scott. "The University of Georgia Marine Institute: The First Decade." Manuscript.

"The Ravaged Environment." *Newsweek* 75.4 (26 January 1970): 30–47.

Reap, James K. *Athens: A Pictorial History*. Norfolk: Donning Company, 1985.

Redfield, Alfred C. "The Biological Control of Chemical Factors in the Environment." *American Scientist* 46 (1958): 205–221.

Reed, John Shelton. *Surveying the South: Studies in Regional Sociology*. Columbia: University of Missouri Press, 1993.

Salt, George. "A Comment on the Use of the Term *Emergent Properties*." *American Naturalist* 113.1 (1979): 145–148.

Sanders, Jane M., and J. Whitfield Gibbons. *40 Years and Beyond*. Aiken, S.C.: Savannah River Ecology Laboratory, 1992.

Sargent, M. C., and T. S. Austin. "Organic Productivity of an Atoll." *American Geophysical Union Transactions* 30.2 (1949): 245–249.

Schlesinger, Arthur Meier Jr. *The Cycles of American History*. Boston: Houghton Mifflin, 1986.

Singal, Daniel Joseph. *The War Within: From Victorian to Modernist Thought in the South, 1919–1945*. Chapel Hill: University of North Carolina Press, 1982.

Smuts, Jan Christiaan. *Holism and Evolution*. New York: Macmillan, 1926.

Soltys, Florence Gray. "Dr. Howard Washington Odum and the Founding of the School of Public Welfare at the University of North Carolina in Chapel Hill." Manuscript dated 1982, in collection of E. P. Odum.

Sosna, Morton. *In Search of the Silent South: Southern Liberals and the Race Issue*. New York: Columbia University Press, 1977.

Tansley, Alfred George. "The Use and Abuse of Vegetational Concepts and Terms." *Ecology* 16.3 (1935): 284–307.

Taylor, Peter J. "Technocratic Optimism, H T Odum and the Partial Transformation of Ecological Metaphor after World War II." *Journal of the History of Biology* 21 (1988): 212–244.

Teal, Mildred, and John Teal. *Portrait of an Island.* New York: Atheneum, 1964.

Thomas, Frances Taliaferro. *A Portrait of Historic Athens and Clarke County.* Athens: University of Georgia Press, 1992.

Vance, Rupert B., and Katharine Jocher. "Howard W. Odum." *Social Forces* 33.3 (1955): 1–15.

White, Lynn Jr. "The Historical Roots of Our Ecologic Crisis." *Science* 155 (10 March 1967): 1203–1207. (Reprinted in *The Ecocriticism Reader: Landmarks in Literary Ecology,* ed. Cheryll Glotfelty and Harold Fromm, 3–14. Athens: University of Georgia Press, 1996.)

Whitehead, Alfred North. *Science and the Modern World: Lowell Lectures, 1925.* New York: Macmillan, 1928.

Robert H. Whittaker. *Communities and Ecosystems.* London: Macmillan, 1970.

Wilson, D. S. "Evolution on the Level of Communities." *Science* 192 (1976): 1358–1360.

———. *The Natural Selection of Populations and Communities.* Menlo Park, Calif.: Benjamin Cummings, 1980.

Worster, Donald. *Nature's Economy: A History of Ecological Ideas.* 2nd ed. Cambridge: Cambridge University Press, 1994.

———. *The Wealth of Nature: Environmental History and the Ecological Imagination.* New York: Oxford University Press, 1993.

Index

interdependence: within developed systems, 92, 110–115, 122–123, 136; within natural systems, 42–43, 59–66, 92, 122–123, 190 (n. 64)

Japan, Odum in, 81–84
Japtan Reef. *See* Eniwetok Atoll

Kahn, Alfred E., 118
Kerr-McGee Corporation, 100
Kropotkin, Petr, 92

Laboratory of Radiation Ecology. *See* Savannah River Ecology Laboratory
land ethic, 107–110, 114. *See also* ethics, environmental; Leopold, Aldo
Leopold, Aldo, 22, 34, 45, 62, 94, 114
Lindeman, Raymond, 34–35, 62
Lotka, Alfred, 35
Lovelock, James, 95

Margulis, Lynn, 95
Marine Biology Laboratory (Woods Hole, Mass.), 74–75
Mercury, Nevada (Nevada Proving Grounds), 68–71
metaphors, Odum's use of, 120–126
Mutual Aid: A Factor of Evolution (Kropotkin), 92

Nevada Proving Grounds, 68–71
Nisbet, Ian, 88–90
"Noncybernetic Nature of Ecosystems, The" (Engelberg and Boyarsky), 91

nuclear energy. *See* environmentalism, and atomic energy

Odum, Anna Louise Kranz (mother), 4, 10–12
Odum, Bill. *See* Odum, William Eugene
Odum, Daniel Thomas (Tommy; son), 9, 37, 134
Odum, Eugene Pleasants, 18–19, 128–130; at atomic energy conference, 66–68; early years, 12–15; endowments by, 142; at Eniwetok Atoll, 58–66, 83–84; and environmental ethics, xix–xxii, 65–66, 110–115, 132–139; as futurist, 132–133, 137–139; graduate work of, 16–17, 21–27; at Hanford Atomic Energy Plant, 71; honors bestowed on, xxi–xxii, 73, 102–103, 116, 126–128, 141–142, 171–174; at the Huyck Preserve, 27–32; and the Institute of Ecology, 75–78, 102–103, 127, 131–132; in Japan, 81–84; at Nevada Proving Grounds, 68–71; in 1940s (at University of Georgia), 32–37, 39; at Oxford University, 71–73; retirement of, 131–134, 142–144; on Sapelo Island, 54–58, 194 (n.33); and Savannah River Ecology Laboratory, 48–54; students' reactions to, 123–126; at Woods Hole, 74–75. *See also* ecosystem ecology; holism; publications, Eugene Odum's
Odum, H. T. (brother), xvi, 2, 34–35, 66, 134, 194 (n. 37); early years, 17–

radioecology, studies on, 75; at Oxford, 72; at Savannah River Ecology Laboratory, 52–54; at UCLA, 68

Raney, Edward C., 28–29

reductionism. *See* atomism (dualism); holism, *versus* reductionism

Reynolds, Richard J., Jr., 55–56

Salt, George, 96–97

Sapelo Island (Georgia), 54–58, 194 (n. 33)

Savannah River Ecology Laboratory (SREL): establishment of, 48–52; radioecology studies at, 52–54

Savannah River Plant (SRP). *See* Savannah River Ecology Laboratory

Save Our Marshes Committee, 101

Shelford, Victor, 21, 24–27, 184 (n. 10)

Silent Spring (Carson), 80, 104–105

Slatyer, Ralph O., 91

Smuts, Jan Christiaan, xvi, 24, 43

Social and Mental Traits of the Negro: Research into the Conditions of the Negro Race in Southern Towns (Howard Odum), 4

Southern Regions of the United States (Howard Odum), 6

Spencer, Herbert, 92

"Strategy of Ecosystem Development, The" (Odum), xix–xx, 85–88, 110; criticism of, 88–91, 121

structure, *versus* function, 72–73, 81–84. *See also* ecosystem ecology; energetics

succession: defined, 25, 176 (n. 14), 184–185 (n. 12); Odum's view of, xix, 42–43, 82–84, 200 (n. 20); studies of, 28, 30–31, 48–53. *See also* ecosystem development

superorganism, 24–25, 83, 89, 121

symbiosis. *See* interdependence

Talmadge, Eugene, 33

Tansley, Sir Arthur. *See* ecosystem, defined by Tansley

Thomas, Carolyn Lee, 125

University of Georgia, 119; in 1940s, 32–37, 39. *See also* Institute of Ecology; Sapelo Island; Savannah River Ecology Laboratory

University of South Carolina, at Savannah River Ecology Laboratory, 48–49

Untitled Film, The: A Search for Ecological Balance (West and West), 101

West, Clifford, 101

West, Sandy, 101

wetlands, 54–58, 118; economic importance of, 98–102, 107

White, Lynn, 105

Whittaker, Robert, 90

Woods Hole, Mass., 74–75

Worster, Donald, 138